ANCIENT
CIVILIZATIONS

Guided Reading Workbook

Contents

How to Use this Book

The *Guided Reading Workbook* was developed to help you get the most from your reading. Using this book will help you master world history content while developing your reading and vocabulary skills. Reviewing the next few pages before getting started will make you aware of the many useful features in this book.

Lesson summary pages allow you to interact with the content and key terms and people from each lesson of a module. The summaries explain each lesson of your textbook in a way that is easy to understand.

The Main Idea statements help focus your attention as you read the summaries.

Definitions for the Key Terms and People from your textbook are given.

Headings under each lesson summary match those in your textbook. This will help you find the material you need.

Lesson numbers make it easy to find your place in the workbook.

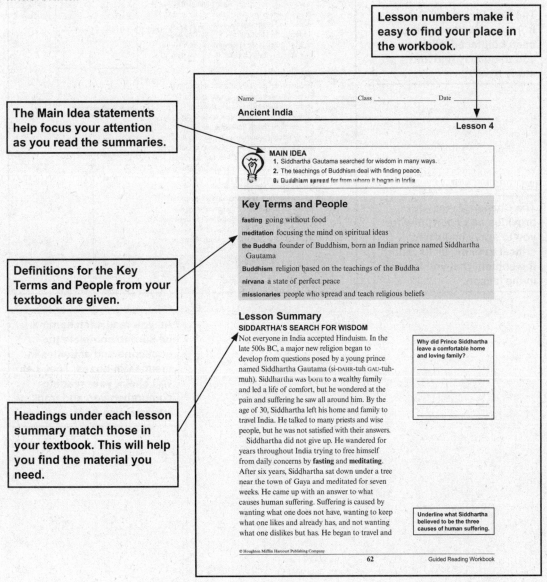

Name _____ Class _____ Date _____

Ancient India

Lesson 4

MAIN IDEA
1. Siddhartha Gautama searched for wisdom in many ways.
2. The teachings of Buddhism deal with finding peace.
3. Buddhism spread far from where it began in India.

Key Terms and People

fasting going without food

meditation focusing the mind on spiritual ideas

the Buddha founder of Buddhism, born an Indian prince named Siddhartha Gautama

Buddhism religion based on the teachings of the Buddha

nirvana a state of perfect peace

missionaries people who spread and teach religious beliefs

Lesson Summary
SIDDHARTHA'S SEARCH FOR WISDOM
Not everyone in India accepted Hinduism. In the late 500s BC, a major new religion began to develop from questions posed by a young prince named Siddhartha Gautama (si-DAHR-tuh GAU-tuh-muh). Siddhartha was born to a wealthy family and led a life of comfort, but he wondered at the pain and suffering he saw all around him. By the age of 30, Siddhartha left his home and family to travel India. He talked to many priests and wise people, but he was not satisfied with their answers.

Siddhartha did not give up. He wandered for years throughout India trying to free himself from daily concerns by **fasting** and **meditating**. After six years, Siddhartha sat down under a tree near the town of Gaya and meditated for seven weeks. He came up with an answer to what causes human suffering. Suffering is caused by wanting what one does not have, wanting to keep what one likes and already has, and not wanting what one dislikes but has. He began to travel and

Why did Prince Siddhartha leave a comfortable home and loving family?

_____
_____
_____
_____

Underline what Siddhartha believed to be the three causes of human suffering.

© Houghton Mifflin Harcourt Publishing Company

62

Guided Reading Workbook

teach his ideas, and was soon called **the Buddha**, or "Enlightened One." From his teachings sprang the religion **Buddhism**.

TEACHINGS OF BUDDHISM

Buddhism is intent on relieving human suffering. It is based upon the Four Noble Truths. These truths are: suffering and unhappiness are a part of life; suffering stems from our desire for pleasure and material goods; people can overcome their desires and reach **nirvana**, a state of perfect peace, which ends the cycle of reincarnation; and people can overcome desire and ignorance by following an eightfold path to nirvana.

These teachings were similar to some Hindu concepts but went against some traditional Hindu ideas. Buddhism questioned the need for animal sacrifice and challenged the authority of the Brahmins, the Hindu priests. The Buddha said that each individual could reach salvation on his or her own. Buddhism also opposed the caste system.

BUDDHISM SPREADS

Buddhism spread quickly throughout India to eventually become a major global religion. With the help of Indian king Asoka, Buddhist **missionaries** were sent to other countries to teach their religious beliefs. Buddhism quickly took hold in neighboring countries like Nepal, Sri Lanka, and China. Buddhism soon became very influential in Japan and Korea. Over time, two branches of Buddhism developed—Theravada and Mahayana.

CHALLENGE ACTIVITY

Critical Thinking: Make Inferences Could you leave your family, home, and everything you know to preach what you believe to be a spiritual truth? What do you think inspired the Buddha to do so? Write a short essay in which you explain his choice.

Underline the name of the central teachings of Buddhism.

What is one difference between Buddhism and Hinduism?
_____
_____
_____
_____
_____
_____

Name three countries to which Buddhism spread.
_____
_____
_____

63   Guided Reading Workbook

The Key Terms and People from your textbook have been boldfaced, allowing you to quickly find and study them.

The Challenge Activity provides an opportunity for you to apply important critical thinking skills using the content that you learned in the lesson.

As you read each summary, be sure to complete the questions and activities in the margin boxes. They help you check your reading comprehension and track important content.

Each lesson has at least one vocabulary activity that will help you demonstrate your understanding of the key terms and people introduced in the lesson.

Some activities have a word bank. You can use it to help find answers or complete writing activities.

Various types of activities help you check your knowledge of key terms and people.

Writing activities require you to include Key Terms and People in what you write. Remember to check to make sure that you are using the terms and names correctly.

Name _____ Class _____ Date _____

Lesson 5, *continued*

| Asoka | Chandra Gupta II | Chandragupta Maurya |
| establish | Gupta Dynasty | Huns |

DIRECTIONS Read each sentence and fill in the blank with the word in the word pair that best completes the sentence.

1. Under Emperor _____, Indian civilization reached a high point. The empire's economy strengthened and people prospered. **(Chandra Gupta II/Chandragupta Maurya)**

2. _____ was the strongest ruler of the Mauryan dynasty. Later, he converted to Buddhism and worked toward improving the lives of his people. **(Asoka/Huns)**

3. The Mauryan Empire was founded by _____, who ruled with a complex government that included a network of spies and a huge army. **(Chandra Gupta II/Chandragupta Maurya)**

4. When the _____ from Central Asia invaded India, it led to the end of the Gupta Dynasty. **(Asoka/Huns)**

5. Under the _____, Hinduism became popular again, but the rulers also supported Buddhism and Jainism. **(Gupta Dynasty/Huns)**

DIRECTIONS Use the vocabulary terms from the word bank to write a summary of the Mauryan Empire and the Gupta Dynasty.

_____

_____

_____

_____

_____

_____

_____

_____

_____

_____

© Houghton Mifflin Harcourt Publishing Company

67   Guided Reading Workbook

Uncovering the Past

Lesson 1

MAIN IDEAS
1. History is the study of the past.
2. We can improve our understanding of people's actions and beliefs through the study of history.
3. Historians use clues from various sources to learn about the past.

Key Terms and People

history the study of the past

culture the knowledge, beliefs, customs, and values of a group of people

archaeology the study of the past based on what people left behind

fossil a part or imprint of something that was once alive

artifacts objects created by and used by humans

primary source an account of an event created by someone who took part in or witnessed the event

secondary source information gathered by someone who did not take part in or witness an event

Lesson Summary
THE STUDY OF THE PAST

History is the study of the past. Historians are people who study history. Historians want to know how people lived and why they did the things they did. They try to learn about the problems people faced and how they found solutions. They are interested in how people lived their daily lives. They study the past to understand people's culture. **Culture** is the knowledge, beliefs, customs, and values of a group of people.

The study of the past based on what people left behind is called **archaeology** (ahr-kee-AH-luh-jee). Archaeologists explore places where people once lived, worked, or fought. They examine the things that people left in these places to learn about how these people lived.

> What do we call people who study how people lived in the past?
>
> _____
> _____
> _____

> Underline the sentence that tells why archaeologists examine the things that people left behind.

UNDERSTANDING THROUGH HISTORY

Understanding the past helps you understand the world today. History can even teach you about yourself. What if you did not know about your own past? You would not know what makes you proud about yourself. You would not know what mistakes you should not repeat.

History is just as important for groups. What would happen if countries had no record of their past? People would not remember their nation's great triumphs or tragedies. History shapes our identity and teaches us the values that we share.

History also teaches about cultures that are unlike your own. Learning other people's stories can help you respect and understand different opinions. You also learn to understand how today's events are shaped by events of the past. History encourages you to ask important questions.

> How can studying history teach you about yourself?
> _____
> _____
> _____
> _____

> Underline the sentence that explains why history helps you relate more easily to people of different backgrounds.

USING CLUES

We learn about history from a variety of sources. **Fossils**, such as bones or footprints preserved in rock, give us clues to life very long ago. **Artifacts**, such as tools, coins, or pottery, also give us information. People invented writing about 5,000 years ago. Since then, laws, poems, speeches, letters, and other things have been written. People have learned from these written sources. Writing can be a **primary source**, which was written by someone who took part in or witnessed an event. Writing can also be a **secondary source**, which is information gathered by someone who did not take part in or witness an event.

> What sources give us clues to life very long ago?
> _____
> _____

CHALLENGE ACTIVITY

Critical Thinking: Make Inferences Imagine a tribe or group of people that might have lived a long time ago. Write a short essay about its culture.

archaeology	artifacts	culture	fossil
history	primary source	secondary source	

DIRECTIONS Use the seven vocabulary terms from the lesson to write a summary of what you learned in the lesson.

DIRECTIONS On the line provided before each statement, write **T** if a statement is true and **F** if a statement is false. If the statement is false, write the correct term on the line after each sentence that makes the sentence a true statement.

_____ 1. A <u>fossil</u> is a part or imprint of something that was once alive.

_____

_____ 2. A <u>primary source</u> is information gathered by someone who did not take part in or witness an event.

_____

_____ 3. <u>Artifacts</u> are objects that were created and used by humans.

_____

_____ 4. A <u>secondary source</u> is an account of an event created by someone who took part in or witnessed the event.

_____

_____ 5. The study of the past is called <u>history</u>.

_____

_____ 6. The study of the past based on what people left behind is called <u>history</u>.

_____

Uncovering the Past

| **MAIN IDEAS** |
| 1. Geography is the study of places and people. |
| 2. Studying location is important to both physical and human geography. |
| 3. Geography and history are closely connected. |

Key Terms and People

geography the study of the earth's physical and cultural features

environment all the living and nonliving things that affect life in an area

landforms the natural features of the land's surface

climate the pattern of weather conditions in a certain area over a long period of time

region area with one or more features that makes it different from surrounding areas

resources materials found in the earth that people need and value

Lesson Summary
STUDYING PLACES AND PEOPLE

Historians study geography to understand where events took place and who was there. **Geography** is the earth's physical and cultural features. It includes mountains, rivers, people, cities, and countries.

| What subject helps historians understand where events took place? |
| _____ |

Geography has two main areas of study. Physical geography is the study of the earth's land and features. Human geography is the study of people and the places where they live. Physical geographers study the **environment**, which includes all the living and nonliving things that affect life in an area. The environment is shaped by the physical processes of weathering, erosion, and pollution. The most important features for physical geographers are **landforms**, the natural features of the land's surface. Physical geographers also study **climate**, the pattern of weather conditions in a certain area over a long period of time.

| What are the two main areas of study in geography? |
| _____ |
| _____ |

| Underline the sentence that explains what climate is. |

Guided Reading Workbook

Lesson 2, *continued*

Specialists in human geography study many interesting questions about how people and the environment affect each other.

STUDYING LOCATION

No two places are exactly alike. That is why geographers try to understand how different locations can affect human populations, or groups of people. Geographers use maps to study and compare locations. A map is a drawing of an area. Some maps show physical features, such as mountains, forests, and rivers. Other maps show cities and the boundaries of states or countries. Studying location is often helped by learning about **regions,** or areas with one or more features that make them different from surrounding areas.

What are maps used for?
_____
_____

GEOGRAPHY AND HISTORY

Geography gives us clues about the people and places that came before us. We can piece together information about past cultures by knowing where people lived and what the area was like.

Early people settled in places that were rich in resources. **Resources** are materials that are found in the earth that people need and value. They include water, animals, fertile land, stone for tools, and metals. Resources influence the development of cultures and the growth of civilizations and societies. For example, early societies formed along rivers. The relationship between geography and people is not one sided. People have influenced their environments positively by planting trees. They have influenced the environment negatively by creating wastelands where forests once existed.

Underline the sentence that explains how geography gives us clues about the past.

Why might early societies have formed along rivers?
_____
_____
_____

CHALLENGE ACTIVITY

Critical Thinking: Design Draw a map of an imaginary country or region. Include features such as mountains, rivers, and cities.

climate	environment	geography
landforms	region	resources

DIRECTIONS Look up the vocabulary terms in the word bank in a dictionary. Write the dictionary definition of the word that is closest to the definition used in your textbook.

1. climate _____

   _____

   _____

2. environment _____

   _____

   _____

3. geography _____

   _____

   _____

4. landforms _____

   _____

   _____

5. region _____

   _____

   _____

6. resources _____

   _____

   _____

   _____

Uncovering the Past

MAIN IDEAS
1. The main problem in economics is scarcity.
2. Businesses and countries have to make decisions about economic resources.
3. Businesses and other organizations help people meet their needs and wants.
4. Money is used as a medium of exchange, a store of value, and a unit of account.
5. Economics helps explain events in world history.

Key Terms and People

economy a system of producing, selling, and buying goods and services

scarcity not enough resources to meet people's wants

profit the money an individual or business has left after paying expenses

entrepreneur a person who organizes, manages, and assumes the risk of a business

mixed economy economy in which businesses are free to operate but they must obey a government's laws and rules

trade the activity of buying, selling, or exchanging goods and services

wealth the value of all possessions that a person or country has

Lesson Summary
ECONOMIC FUNDAMENTALS

An **economy** is a system of producing, selling, and buying goods and services. A main economic problem is **scarcity**, or not enough resources to meet people's wants. It forces them to make choices about what they want. The laws of supply and demand determine the price of a good or service.

   Profit is money left over after expenses have been paid. Profit and saving money are incentives for people to buy and sell goods and services.

SYSTEMS TO ORGANIZE RESOURCES

Businesses have to make choices about factors of production. These factors are: natural resources, capital, labor, and **entrepreneurs**, people who organize, manage, and assume business risk.

> Why is scarcity a main economic problem?
> _____
> _____
> _____
> _____

> Underline the phrase that explains what entrepreneurs do.

Guided Reading Workbook

Countries make production choices, too. Their economic system addresses how they distribute economic resources. Types of economies are traditional, command, and market. Today, many countries follow a **mixed economy**. Businesses are basically free to operate as they wish, but they must follow government laws and rules.

> **What is an advantage of following a mixed economy?**
> _____
> _____

NEEDS AND WANTS

Today, large businesses aid the economy. They have the resources and tools to produce goods people need and want. The government and nonprofit organizations also help meet people's needs and wants.

MONEY AND TRADE

Trade is buying, selling, or exchanging goods and services. Early trade was called the barter system. Over time, trade routes formed, such as the Silk Road. Trade led to the exchange of languages, religions, tools, and inventions. With more trading, it became harder to agree on the value of products. So countries began to use money as a medium of exchange. Money is a form of wealth. **Wealth** is the value of all possessions that a person or country has.

> **Why did money become a medium of exchange?**
> _____
> _____
> _____
> _____

THE IMPORTANCE OF ECONOMICS

Studying economics can help people make everyday decisions about money. It can also help people interpret the past, explain the present, and predict future consequences of economic decisions. Economic growth has been affected by the discovery of new resources and expansion, which increased trade. It also has been helped by technology and education, which increased productivity.

> **Underline the factors that have helped economic growth.**

CHALLENGE ACTIVITY

Critical Thinking: Identify Cause and Effect

What is the effect of scarcity? Write a
short essay about why scarcity is likely to
continue to exist.

DIRECTIONS Write a word that has a similar meaning, or synonym,
for the term given.

1. entrepreneur _____

2. profit _____

3. scarcity_____

4. trade_____

DIRECTIONS Read each sentence and fill in the blank with the word
in the word pair that best completes the sentence.

5. The value of all possessions that a person or country has is called
   _____. **(money/wealth)**

6. In a _____ economy, businesses are basically free to operate as they
   please but must obey laws and government rules. **(mixed/traditional)**

7. The activity of buying, selling, or exchanging goods and services is known as
   _____. **(scarcity/trade)**

8. The _____ is a system of producing, selling, and buying goods and
   services. **(profit/economy)**

9. _____ occurs when there are not enough resources to meet people's
   wants. **(wealth/scarcity)**

10. When a business or individual has money left after expenses have been paid,
    that person or business has made a _____. **(profit/trade)**

Uncovering the Past

MAIN IDEAS
1. A country's government affects the lives of its people
2. There have been many different forms of government throughout history.
3. Governments have a role to play in the economy, including providing services and collecting taxes.

Key Terms and People

civics the study of citizenship and government

government the organizations and individuals who have the right to rule over a group of people

constitution a written plan of government

democracy the people either rule directly or they elect officials who act on their behalf

republic a system of government in which people elect representatives to carry on the work of government

tax a charge people pay to a government

Lesson Summary
NEED FOR GOVERNMENTS

Civics is the study of citizenship and government. A person who is a citizen is legally recognized by his or her country. The **government** is the organizations and individuals who have the right to rule over the people. Government provides a way for people to unite, solve problems, and cooperate. Government makes people's lives safer and easier.

Government provides services such as establishing schools and providing police and fire departments. It creates highways between its borders and establishes a system of money.

Government provides laws for society. Many countries are ruled by a written plan of government, or a **constitution**. It describes the government's purpose and how it will be organized. Laws cannot go against it, and they

What makes a person a citizen of a country?
_____
_____
_____

List three ways governments affect people.
_____
_____
_____
_____

Guided Reading Workbook

must be recorded so people know about them.
Many laws guarantee freedoms, such as freedom
of speech, press, and religion.

Underline the sentence that describes what laws may guarantee.

FORMS OF GOVERNMENT

Some governments are nondemocratic, so
citizens do not have the power to rule. Other
governments are democratic. In a **democracy**, the
people either rule directly or elect officials who
act for them.

Democracy began in Athens in ancient Greece.
Then, for a time, Rome had a republic. In a
republic, the people agree to be ruled by their
elected leaders. The United States is a republic. In
European countries, governments were monarchies
ruled by a king or queen. Then in 1215, Britain's
King John was forced to sign the Magna Carta. It
protected the rights of English citizens. In the 17th
and 18th centuries, John Locke and others said
people were born equal with natural rights. These
ideas inspired Americans to fight for independence
from Great Britain.

Why might it be better to live in a democracy instead of a nondemocratic government?

_____
_____
_____
_____
_____
_____
_____

Underline the sentences that tells the ideas that inspired America to seek its independence from Great Britain.

THE ROLE OF GOVERNMENT IN THE ECONOMY

Governments influence economics, because they
determine how goods and services are produced
and distributed. Many democracies have market
or mixed economies.

To be able to provide services and protection,
governments collect taxes. A **tax** is a charge
people pay to a government. Governments may
also participate in economies by making trade
laws. They do this to protect jobs and industries
from foreign competition. Even still, most
governments support international trade.

What is the government's role in the economy?

_____
_____
_____
_____
_____

CHALLENGE ACTIVITY

Critical Thinking: Develop Imagine a country
that has just become independent. Draft a
constitution to protect its citizens.

Lesson 4, *continued*

| civics | constitution | democracy |
| government | republic | tax |

DIRECTIONS Match the terms on the left to their definitions on the right. Write the correct letter on the line before each term.

_____ 1. civics

a. the people either rule directly or they elect officials who act for them

_____ 2. tax

b. a written plan of government

_____ 3. government

c. the study of citizenship and government

_____ 4. democracy

d. system of government in which people elect representatives to carry on the work of government for them

_____ 5. republic

e. the organizations and individuals who have the right to rule over a group of people

_____ 6. constitution

f. a charge people pay to a government

DIRECTIONS On the line provided before each statement, write **T** if a statement is true and **F** if a statement is false. If the statement is false, write the correct term on the line after each sentence that makes the sentence a true statement.

_____ 7. A republic is a written plan of government.

_____

_____ 8. A tax is a charge people pay to a government.

_____

_____ 9. Democracy is the study of citizenship and government.

_____

Lesson 2, *continued*

Humans began to migrate around 100,000 years ago. They moved from East Africa to southern Africa and Asia. Most scholars believe the first people used a land bridge to cross from Asia to North America. They also went to Australia, but scientists are not sure how they were able to get there. Early humans often migrated because the climate changed, and they needed to find new food sources.

> **Why did early humans often migrate?**
> _____
> _____
> _____

PEOPLE ADAPT TO NEW ENVIRONMENTS

Early people had to learn to adapt to new environments. The places to which they migrated were often much colder than the places they left and often had new plants and animals.

To keep warm, they learned to sew animal skins together to make clothing. At first they took shelter in caves. When they moved to areas with no caves, they built their own shelters. At first these shelters were pits in the ground with roofs of branches and leaves. Later, people learned to build more permanent structures with wood, stone, clay, or other materials, even bones from large animals such as mammoths.

People also began to make new types of tools. These tools were smaller and more complex than tools from the Paleolithic Era. They defined the **Mesolithic** (me-zuh-LI-thik) **Era,** which began more than 10,000 years ago and lasted to about 5,000 years ago in some places. These new tools included hooks and spears for fishing, and bows and arrows for hunting.

> **What materials did early humans use to build more permanent structures?**
> _____
> _____
> _____

People in the Mesolithic Era also developed new technologies to improve their lives. For example, they learned how to make pots from clay and how to hollow out logs to make canoes.

> **How did early humans make canoes?**
> _____
> _____

CHALLENGE ACTIVITY

Critical Thinking: Design Draw a building plan with written instructions for a Mesolithic dwelling.

| ice ages | land bridge | Mesolithic Era | migrate |

DIRECTIONS Read each sentence and fill in the blank with the word
from the word bank that best completes the sentence.

1. During the _____, people made tools that were smaller
   and more complex than those made during the Old Stone Age.

2. During the _____, huge sheets of ice were formed from
   ocean water, so ocean levels were lower than they are now.

3. A _____ is a strip of land that connects two continents.

4. In response to the Earth's changing climate and geography, people began to
   _____.

DIRECTIONS Write three adjectives or descriptive phrases that
describe the term.

5. land bridge _____

   _____

6. migrate _____

   _____

The Stone Ages and Early Cultures

Lesson 3

MAIN IDEAS
1. The first farmers learned to grow plants and raise animals in the New Stone Age.
2. Farming changed societies and the way people lived.

Key Terms and People

Neolithic Era the New Stone Age, which began about 10,000 years ago in Southwest Asia and much later in other places

domestication the process of changing plants or animals to make them more useful to humans

agriculture the development of farming from the domestication of plants

megaliths huge stones used as monuments or sites for religious gatherings

Lesson Summary
THE FIRST FARMERS

A warming trend brought an end to the ice ages, and new plants began to grow in some areas. Throughout Southwest Asia, people came to depend on wild barley and wheat for food. People soon learned that they could plant seeds to grow their own crops. This shift from food gathering to food producing defined the **Neolithic** (nee-uh-LI-thik) **Era.**

This **domestication** of plants led to the development of **agriculture,** or farming. The first farmers also learned to domesticate animals. Instead of following wild herds, they could now keep sheep and goats for milk, food, and wool. People could also use large animals like cattle to carry loads or to pull large tools used in farming. Domestication greatly improved people's chances of surviving.

FARMING CHANGES SOCIETIES

With survival more certain, people could focus on activities other than finding food. People began to make clothing from plant fibers, wool,

> **What change defined a shift during the Neolithic Era?**
> _____
> _____
> _____

> **What were three tasks for which early people used domesticated animals?**
> _____
> _____
> _____

Lesson 3, *continued*

and animal skins. As early farmers learned to control their own food production and to make better shelters and clothing, populations grew. People began to build permanent settlements. In some areas, farming communities developed into towns.

Neolithic communities like Çatal Hüyük and Jericho had traditional economies. People made decisions based on customs and beliefs passed down from generation to generation. They decided things like which crops to plant and how to distribute them.

Farmers stored food in large pits because they began to have an extra amount of it. This surplus made barter possible. People would barter when they would trade goods and services for other goods and services.

Some groups gathered to perform religious ceremonies around huge stone monuments called **megaliths.** These people probably believed in gods and goddesses associated with air, water, fire, earth, and animals. Scholars also believe that some prehistoric people prayed to their ancestors or buried their bones in the floors of homes.

Archaeologists have found clues about prehistoric governments. Çatal Hüyük did not appear to have a leader, but men and women seemed to have been treated equally. Jericho had a wall around it. This likely means the city had a government. A person or group probably had to give directions for the wall.

What materials were first used by Neolithic people to make clothing?
_____
_____
_____

What would people do during barter?
_____
_____
_____

What clues have given archaeologists information about the governments of Çatal Hüyük and Jericho?
_____
_____
_____
_____

CHALLENGE ACTIVITY

Critical Thinking: Evaluate Use the Internet or a library to research theories about how the megaliths at Stonehenge in England were built. Then write your own theory.

Guided Reading Workbook

The Fertile Crescent, Mesopotamia, and the Persian Empire

Lesson 2

MAIN IDEAS
1. The Sumerians created the world's first advanced society.
2. Religion played a major role in Sumerian society.
3. The Sumerians invented the world's first writing system.
4. Technical advances and inventions changed Sumerian lives.
5. Many types of art developed in Sumer.

Key Terms and People

rural having to do with the countryside

urban having to do with the city

city-state a political unit consisting of a city and the surrounding countryside

Gilgamesh a Uruk king who became a legend in Sumerian literature

Sargon Akkadian emperor who defeated Sumer and built the world's first empire

empire land with different territories and peoples under a single rule

polytheism the worship of many gods

priests people who performed religious ceremonies

social hierarchy a division of society by rank or class

cuneiform world's first system of writing

pictographs picture symbols

scribe writer and record keeper

epics long poems that tell the stories of heroes

architecture the science of building

ziggurat a pyramid-shaped temple tower

Lesson Summary
AN ADVANCED SOCIETY

In southern Mesopotamia in about 3000 BC, people known as the Sumerians (soo-MER-ee-unz) created an advanced society. Most people in Sumer (soo-muhr) lived in **rural** areas, but they were governed from **urban,** or city, areas. The size of these **city-states** depended on its military strength. Stronger city-states controlled larger

> Why do you think governments are usually located in cities?
>
> _____
> _____
> _____
> _____

areas. Individual city-states gained and lost power over time. For 1,000 years, the city-states of Uruk and Ur fought for power. One Uruk king, **Gilgamesh**, became a legend in Sumerian literature.

Around 2300 BC, **Sargon** was the leader of the Akkadians (uh-KAY-dee-uhns), a people who lived to the north of Sumer. Sargon built a large army and defeated all the city-states of Sumer as well as all of northern Mesopotamia. He established the world's first **empire.** It stretched from the Persian Gulf to the Mediterranean Sea and lasted about 150 years.

RELIGION SHAPES SOCIETY

Religion played an important role in nearly every aspect of Sumerian public and private life. Sumerians practiced **polytheism,** the worship of many gods. They believed that their gods had enormous powers bringing either illness or good health and wealth. Every area of life depended on pleasing the gods. Each city-state had one god as its special protector. People relied on **priests** to help them gain the gods' favor. Priests interpreted the wishes of the gods and made offerings to them.

A **social hierarchy** developed in Sumerian city-states. Kings were at the top, followed by priests and nobles. The middle ranks included skilled craftspeople, merchants, and traders. Traders had a great impact as they traded grain for precious metals and lumber. Farmers and laborers made up the large working class. Slaves were at the bottom of the social order. Most women were limited to the home and raising children; some upper-class women were educated and even became priestesses.

> **What type of religion did the Sumerians practice?**
> _____
> _____

> **In Sumerian religious practice, what did priests do to try to please the gods?**
> _____
> _____
> _____

> **Which two groups formed the Sumerian upper classes?**
> _____
> _____
> _____

Lesson 2, *continued*

THE INVENTION OF WRITING

The Sumerians developed **cuneiform** (kyoo-NEE-uh-fohrm), the world's first system of writing. They used sharp tools to make symbols on clay tablets. Earlier writing was **pictographs**, or picture symbols. In cuneiform, symbols could also be syllables or basic parts of words. At first, Sumerian **scribes** used cuneiform for business records. Later, they wrote works on history, law, math, and even literature. Some were **epics**, long poems about heroes

> **How was cuneiform different from pictographs?**
> _____
> _____
> _____
> _____

ADVANCES AND INVENTIONS

The Sumerians invented many important tools. They were the first to build wheeled vehicles like carts and wagons. They invented the ox-drawn plow and greatly improved farm production. They built sewers under city streets and learned to use bronze to make strong tools. They also excelled in math and science, developing the clock and calendar we use today.

> **List three items the Sumerians invented.**
> _____
> _____
> _____
> _____
> _____

THE ARTS OF SUMER

Sumerian remains reveal great skills in the fields of art, metalwork, and **architecture**. Artists and craftspeople created statues in clay as well as jewelry made from imported gold, silver and gems. A special art form, the cylinder seal, was a stone engraved with designs for rolling over wet clay to decorate objects or to "sign" documents. A pyramid-shaped **ziggurat** rose above each city. Most people lived in one-story houses with rooms arranged around a small courtyard.

> **Which Sumerian skill or invention do you think was most important to Sumerian society?**
> _____
> _____
> _____

CHALLENGE ACTIVITY

Critical Thinking: Compare Consider the invention of writing and of the wheel. As you go through a normal day, keep a list of the things you do that rely on one of these two inventions.

Guided Reading Workbook

Lesson 2, *continued*

architecture	city-state	cuneiform	empire
epics	Gilgamesh	impact	pictographs
polytheism	priests	rural	Sargon
scribe	social hierarchy	urban	ziggurat

DIRECTIONS Read each sentence and fill in the blank with a word from the word bank that best completes the sentence.

1. Land with different territories and peoples under a single rule is called an

   _____.

2. _____ is a division of society by rank or class.

3. Countryside areas are considered to be _____.

4. _____ are people who perform religious ceremonies.

5. A _____ consists of a city, which is the political center, and the surrounding countryside.

6. The practice of worshipping many gods is called _____.

7. The temple's _____ was taller than all of the other buildings in the city.

8. Trade had a positive _____ on Sumerian society, allowing artists to be more creative.

9. Scribes wrote on clay tablets using _____ in order to keep business records.

The Fertile Crescent, Mesopotamia, and the Persian Empire

Lesson 3

MAIN IDEAS
1. The Babylonians conquered Mesopotamia and created a code of law.
2. Invasions of Mesopotamia changed the region's culture.

Key Terms and People

monarch a ruler of a kingdom or empire

Hammurabi the city of Babylon's greatest monarch

Hammurabi's Code the earliest known written collection of laws, comprising 282 laws that dealt with almost every part of daily life

chariot a wheeled, horse-drawn battle cart

Nebuchadnezzar the Chaldean king who rebuilt Babylon

Lesson Summary
THE BABYLONIANS CONQUER MESOPOTAMIA

By 1800 BC, a powerful government had arisen in Babylon, an old Sumerian city on the Euphrates. Babylon's greatest **monarch** (MAH-nark), **Hammurabi**, had conquered all of Mesopotamia.

Hammurabi was not just a brilliant war leader. During his 42-year reign, Hammurabi oversaw many building and irrigation projects, improved the tax collection system, and brought prosperity through increased trade. He is most famous, however, for **Hammurabi's Code**, the earliest known written collection of laws. It contained laws on everything from trade, loans, and theft to injury, marriage, and murder. Some of its ideas are still found in laws today. The code was important not only for how thorough it was, but also because it was written down for all to see.

> On what river was the city of Babylon located?
>
> _____

> Why do you think it is important for laws to be written down?
>
> _____
> _____
> _____
> _____
> _____

Guided Reading Workbook

Lesson 3, *continued*

INVASIONS OF MESOPOTAMIA

Several other civilizations developed in and around the Fertile Crescent. As their armies battled one another for Mesopotamia's fertile land, control of the region passed from one empire to another. The Hittites of Asia Minor captured Babylon in 1595 BC with strong well-made iron weapons and the skillful use of the **chariot** on the battlefield. Soon the Hittite king was killed, and the Kassites captured Babylon and ruled for almost 400 years.

In the 1200s BC, the Assyrians briefly took over Babylon but were overrun by invaders. It took 300 years, but by around 900 BC they were the next group to conquer all of the Fertile Crescent and parts of Asia Minor and Egypt. The key to their success was their strong, fierce army. They also used iron weapons and chariots. They were well organized. Every soldier knew his role.

The Assyrians ruled from Nineveh (NI-nuh-vuh), a city in the north. They collected taxes, enforced laws, and raised troops through local leaders. The Assyrians also built roads to link distant parts of the empire. One Assyrian king built a royal library with tens of thousands of cuneiform tablets.

A series of wars started in 652 BC. In 612, BC the Chaldeans, a group from the Syrian Desert, conquered the Assyrians and set up a new empire of their own.

Nebuchadnezzar (neb-uh-kuhd-NEZ-uhr), the most famous Chaldean king, rebuilt Babylon into a beautiful city. According to legend, his grand palace featured the famous Hanging Gardens. The Chaldeans revived Sumerian culture and made notable advances in astronomy and mathematics.

> **Name four groups that conquered all of Mesopotamia after the Babylonians.**
>
> _____
>
> _____
>
> _____

> **Which older Mesopotamian civilization did the Chaldeans admire and study?**
>
> _____
>
> _____

Guided Reading Workbook

CHALLENGE ACTIVITY

Critical Thinking: Sequence Make a timeline with
approximate dates showing the various empires
and invasions that characterized the history of
Mesopotamia up to the time of the Chaldeans.

chariot	Hammurabi	Hammurabi's Code
monarch	Nebuchadnezzar	

DIRECTIONS Read each sentence and fill in the blank with the word
in the word pair that best completes the sentence.

1. _____ was the most famous Chaldean king who rebuilt
   Babylon into a beautiful city and whose palace was famous for the Hanging
   Gardens. **(Hammurabi/Nebuchadnezzar)**

2. A powerful ruler of a kingdom or empire is known as a
   _____ . **(monarch/chariot)**

3. _____ was a brilliant military leader who brought all of
   Mesopotamia into the Babylonian Empire. **(Nebuchadnezzar/Hammurabi)**

4. The Hittites skillfully used the _____ , a wheeled, horse-
   drawn battle cart, to move quickly around the battlefield and fire arrows at
   their enemy. **(chariot/monarch)**

5. _____ was famous for his code of laws, which dealt
   with almost every part of daily life and was written down for all to see.
   (Nebuchadnezzar/Hammurabi)

DIRECTIONS On the line provided before each statement, write **T** if
a statement is true and **F** if a statement is false. If the statement is
false, write the correct term on the line after each sentence that
makes the sentence a true statement.

_____ 6. The Hittite soldiers used the <u>monarch</u> in their battles to capture
   Babylon.

   _____

_____ 7. Under the laws of <u>Nebuchadnezzar</u>, injuring a rich man brought a
   greater penalty than injuring a poor man.

   _____

The Fertile Crescent, Mesopotamia, and the Persian Empire

Lesson 4

> **MAIN IDEAS**
> 1. The Phoenicians built a trading society in the eastern Mediterranean region.
> 2. Phoenicians developed one of the world's first alphabets.

Key Terms and People

alphabet a set of letters than can be combined to form written words

Lesson Summary
PHOENICIA

A land known as Phoenicia, at the western end of the Fertile Crescent along the Mediterranean Sea, created a wealthy trading society. Major Phoenician city-states, including Byblos, Sidon, and Tyre, began as early as 3000 BC. At times controlled by Egyptians and Hittites, by 1200 BC the Phoenician cities formed a loose association of city-states, each ruled by its own king. Phoenicia was conquered by the Persian Empire in 538 BC.

Phoenicia had few resources other than cedar trees to trade. But its location was valuable. Its city-states connected Mediterranean Sea routes with land routes into the Fertile Crescent. Phoenician leaders looked to the sea to trade and expand their economy.

> On what body of water were most Phoenician city-states located?
>
> _____
>
> _____

PHOENICIAN TRADE AND CULTURE

Fleets of fast Phoenician trading ships sailed all around the Mediterranean Sea and even into the Atlantic Ocean through the Strait of Gibraltar. The Phoenicians built trade networks and founded new cities. Many became expert sailors, and they built ships with both sails and oars. They founded colonies along their trade routes. Carthage (KAHR-thij), on the northern coast of Africa, was the most famous and powerful city on the Mediterranean.

Guided Reading Workbook

Phoenicia grew wealthy from its trade. They traded silverwork, ivory carvings, and slaves. After the invention of glassblowing, beautiful glass objects were traded. Phoenicians made a purple dye from a type of shellfish and traded cloth dyed with this purple color. Phoenicians used their goods to trade for resources that were not local to them, such as ivory, gold, copper, tin, and iron.

> **Underline the sentence that explains what Phoenicians did with their resources.**

The Phoenicians made several important contributions to early civilization. They created trade and communication routes throughout the Mediterranean area. Different cultures came to know one another better as they exchanged goods. To navigate the Mediterranean Sea they learned to use Polaris, the North Star, to make sure they were moving in the right direction.

The Phoenicians' most important achievement, however, was the development of one of the world's first alphabets. The Phoenician **alphabet** was a set of 22 letters that could be combined to form words. Instead of pictographs or cunieform to communicate ideas, the alphabet made it easier to use writing to communicate big ideas. Later civilizations, including our own, have benefited from this development. The English alphabet is based on the Phoenician alphabet.

> **Circle the three forms of writing used by early civilizations.**

CHALLENGE ACTIVITY

Critical Thinking: Evaluate Consider this statement: The invention of the alphabet was the Phoenicians' most important achievement. Write a paragraph explaining why you agree or disagree.

| alphabet | Carthage | cuneiform |
| fleet | navigate | Polaris |

DIRECTIONS Read each sentence and fill in the blank with the word
in the word pair that best completes the sentence.

1. Sailors safely arrived at ports because they learned to track the location of
   the star named _____. **(Carthage/Polaris)**

2. A set of letters that can be combined together to form words is known as an
   _____, which was developed by the Phoenician traders.
   (alphabet/cuneiform)

3. Phoenicians could successfully _____ their ships to many
   ports on the Mediterranean Sea. **(navigate/fleet)**

4. The Phoenicians had a large _____ of ships to trade goods
   all along the Mediterranean Sea. **(navigate/fleet)**

DIRECTIONS On the line provided before each statement, write **T** if
a statement is true and **F** if a statement is false. If the statement is
false, write the correct term on the line after each sentence that
makes the sentence a true statement.

_____ 5. The Phoenicians wrote using <u>cuneiform</u> to record their trades.

_____

_____ 6. The port of <u>Polaris</u> on the north coast of Africa was a famous
          Phoenician center of trade on the Mediterranean.

_____

_____ 7. The <u>alphabet</u> developed by the Phoenicians is similar to the one we use
          today.

_____

The Fertile Crescent, Mesopotamia, and the Persian Empire

Lesson 5

MAIN IDEAS
1. Persia became an empire under Cyrus the Great.
2. The Persian Empire grew stronger under Darius I.
3. The Persians fought Greece twice in the Persian Wars.

Key Terms and People

cavalry a unit of soldiers mounted on horses

Cyrus the Great founder of the Persian Empire

Darius I Persian emperor who organized and expanded the empire

Persian Wars a series of wars between Persia and Greece beginning in 490 BC

Xerxes I Persian emperor who led the second invasion of Greece in 480 BC

Lesson Summary

PERSIA BECOMES AN EMPIRE

Early in their history, the Persians often fought other peoples of Southwest Asia. In 550 BC, the Persian leader Cyrus II won independence from a people called the Medes (MEEDZ). He went on to conquer almost all of Southwest Asia. His well-organized and loyal army included a powerful **cavalry** that charged the enemy and used arrows. Cyrus II let the people he conquered keep their own customs. As a result, few people rebelled and the empire remained strong. By the time he died around 529 BC, Cyrus ruled the largest empire the world had ever seen. He became known in history as **Cyrus the Great.**

> Underline the sentence that explains strategies Cyrus II used to make his army strong.

> Why do you think Cyrus II became known as Cyrus "the Great"?
>
> _____
> _____
> _____
> _____
> _____

THE PERSIAN EMPIRE GROWS STRONGER

Darius I seized power when the death of Cyrus's son left Persia without a clear leader. Darius organized the empire by dividing it into 20 provinces. Then he chose governors called satraps (SAY-traps) to rule the provinces for him. Darius expanded the Persian Empire eastward to the Indus Valley and westward into Southeastern

Lesson 5, *continued*

Europe. He called himself king of kings to remind other rulers of his power.

During his rule, Persia made advances in art and architecture. Darius's improvements to Persian society included roads that messengers used to travel quickly throughout Persia. Darius built a new capital called Persepolis that he filled with artwork, including carvings and statues made with gold, silver, and jewels.

During his reign, a popular new religion called Zoroastrianism (zawr-uh-WAS-tree-uh-nih-zuhm) arose in Persia. This religion taught that the forces of good and evil were fighting for control of the universe.

> **What new religion arose during the reign of Darius?**
> _____

THE PERSIANS FIGHT GREECE

In 499 BC, several Greek cities in Asia Minor (in what is now Turkey) rebelled against Persian rule. They were joined by a few city-states from mainland Greece. The Persians put down the revolt, but nine years later Darius invaded Greece and began the **Persian Wars.** The Greeks won the first battle at Marathon because they had better weapons and armor.

> **Underline the sentence that explains why the Greeks defeated the Persians at the Battle of Marathon.**

Ten years later, Darius's son, **Xerxes I** (ZUHRK-seez), sent another army into Greece. The city-states of Athens and Sparta joined forces to defend Greece. Despite a brave stand by the Spartans at Thermopylae (thuhr-MAH-puh-lee), the Persians succeeded in attacking and burning Athens. However, in the subsequent battles of Salamis (SAH-luh-muhs) and Plataea (pluh-TEE-uh), the Greeks overcame the Persians and brought an end to the wars. The Greeks had defeated a powerful foe and defended their homeland.

> **Who won the Persian Wars?**
> _____

Guided Reading Workbook

CHALLENGE ACTIVITY

Critical Thinking: Make Inferences Draw a simple
map of a location where three armed soldiers
could prevent an entire army of foot-soldiers
from moving forward.

DIRECTIONS Read each sentence and fill in the blank with a choice
from the word pair that best completes each sentence.

1. _____ let conquered people keep their own customs in
   the hope that this would make them less likely to rebel. **(Cyrus the Great/
   Darius I)**

2. A unit of soldiers mounted on horseback is called a _____.
   (cavalry/satrap)

3. After Cyrus the Great's son died, _____ claimed the Persian
   throne and killed all of his rivals, after which he restored order in Persia.
   (Darius I/Xerxes I)

4. Greece fought off two major Persian invasions in the _____.
   (Battle of Salamis/Persian Wars)

5. Darius I organized the Persian Empire by dividing it into 20 provinces ruled
   over by governors called _____. **(cavalry/satraps)**

DIRECTIONS Write three adjectives or a descriptive phrase to
describe the term or person.

6. cavalry _____

7. Cyrus the Great _____

8. Darius I _____

9. Persian Wars _____

10. Xerxes I _____

Kingdoms of the Nile

MAIN IDEAS
1. Egypt was called "the gift of the Nile" because the Nile River was so important.
2. Civilization developed after people began farming along the Nile.
3. Strong kings unified all of Egypt.

Key Terms and People

cataracts steep river rapids, almost impossible to sail by boat

delta triangle-shaped area of land made of soil deposited by a river

Menes Egyptian leader who united both Upper and Lower Egypt into one kingdom

pharaoh ruler of unified Egypt, literally means "great house"

dynasty series of rulers from the same family

Lesson Summary
THE GIFT OF THE NILE

The existence of Egypt was based solely around the Nile, the world's longest river. The Nile carries water from central Africa through a vast stretch of desert land. The river was so important that the Greek writer Herodotus called Egypt "the gift of the Nile."

Ancient Egypt developed along a 750-mile stretch of the Nile and was originally organized into two kingdoms—Upper Egypt and Lower Egypt. The Nile flowed through the desert of Upper Egypt. This kingdom was located upriver in relation to the Nile's flow. Lower Egypt was the northern region and was located down river.

Cataracts, or steep rapids, marked the southern border of Upper Egypt. Lower Egypt was centered in the river **delta,** a triangle-shaped area of land made of soil deposited by the river. In midsummer, the Nile would flood Upper Egypt, and in the fall the river would flood Lower Egypt. This made sure that the farmland would stay moist and fertile from rich silt. Because the

> **Why is a river a "gift" to a desert land?**
> _____
> _____

> **Why were the Nile's floods so important in Ancient Egypt?**
> _____
> _____
> _____
> _____
> _____

land surrounding the Nile Valley was arid desert, this watered area made farming possible in Egypt.

CIVILIZATION DEVELOPS IN EGYPT

With dry desert all around, it is no wonder that ancient settlers were attracted to this abundant and protected area of fertile farmland. Hunter-gatherers first moved to the area around 12,000 years ago and found plenty of wild animals, plants, and fish to hunt and eat. By 4500 BC, farmers were living in villages and growing wheat and barley. They also raised cattle and sheep, while hunters trapped wild geese and ducks along the banks of the Nile.

Egypt had natural barriers, so it was a hard place to invade. Egyptian villages grew and became organized into two kingdoms. The capital of Lower Egypt was located in the northwest Nile Delta at a town called Pe. The capital city of Upper Egypt was called Nekhen. It was located on the west bank of the Nile.

> What did hunter-gatherers find when they moved to the Nile Valley?
>
> _____
>
> _____
>
> _____

KINGS UNIFY EGYPT

Around 3100 BC, **Menes** (MEE-neez), the king of Upper Egypt, invaded Lower Egypt. He married a princess there in order to unite the two kingdoms under his rule. Menes was the first **pharaoh**, which literally means ruler of a "great house." He also started the first Egyptian **dynasty**, or series of rulers from the same family. He built a new capital city, Memphis, which became a popular cultural center. His dynasty ruled for nearly 200 years.

> Why do you think Menes united Egypt's two kingdoms?
>
> _____
>
> _____
>
> _____
>
> _____

CHALLENGE ACTIVITY

Critical Thinking: Elaborate Powerful leaders like Menes unite territories and people under one organization. Imagine that you are an ancient Egyptian interested in becoming a leader. Write a speech explaining what would make you a powerful person fit for ruling a large village.

DIRECTIONS On the line provided before each statement, write **T** if a statement is true and **F** if a statement is false. If the statement is false, write the correct term on the line after each sentence that makes the sentence a true statement.

_____ 1. <u>Cataracts</u> are triangle-shaped areas of land made of soil that is deposited by a river.

_____

_____ 2. <u>Deltas</u> are steep rapids that made sailing portions of rivers such as the Nile very difficult.

_____

_____ 3. <u>Menes</u> was a leader who united Upper and Lower Egypt into one kingdom.

_____

_____ 4. Menes founded Egypt's first <u>pharaoh</u>, a series of rulers from the same family.

_____

_____ 5. Historians consider Menes to be Egypt's first <u>dynasty</u>, the title used by the rulers of Egypt.

_____

Kingdoms of the Nile

MAIN IDEAS
1. Life in the Old Kingdom was influenced by pharaohs, roles in society, and trade.
2. Religion shaped Egyptian life.
3. The pyramids were built as huge tombs for Egyptian pharaohs.

Key Terms and People

Old Kingdom the third Egyptian dynasty, which lasted nearly 500 years

theocracy a government where religious leaders have power to make, approve, or enforce laws

Khufu the most famous pharaoh of the Old Kingdom

nobles people from rich and powerful families

afterlife life after death, a widely held ancient Egyptian belief

mummies dead bodies preserved by wrapping them in cloth

elite people of wealth and power

pyramids huge stone tombs with four triangle-shaped walls that meet at a top point

engineering application of scientific knowledge for practical purposes

Lesson Summary
LIFE IN THE OLD KINGDOM

Around 2700 BC, the Third Dynasty, or the **Old Kingdom**, came to power in Egypt. During the next 500 years, the Egyptians developed a **theocracy**. Religious leaders had power to make, approve, or enforce laws in this government. Egyptians believed the pharaoh was both a king and a god. The most famous pharaoh of the Old Kingdom was **Khufu**. Many monuments were built to him.

Egyptians believed that a well-ordered society would keep their kingdom strong. Social classes developed. The pharaoh was at the top and **nobles** from rich and powerful families made up

> Why was there no distinction between religion and politics in Egypt's Old Kingdom?
>
> _____
> _____
> _____
> _____

the upper class. The middle class included lesser government officials, scribes, and rich craftspeople. Most people, including farmers, belonged to the lower class. Lower-class people were often used by the pharaoh as laborers.

Trade also developed during the Old Kingdom. Traders sailed on the Mediterranean and south on the Nile and the Red Sea to acquire gold, copper, ivory, slaves, wood, and stone.

> **Of the upper, middle, and lower classes, which was the largest in ancient Egypt?**
>
> _____
>
> _____

RELIGION AND EGYPTIAN LIFE

Officials in the Old Kingdom expected everyone to worship the same gods. Over time certain cities built temples and were associated with particular gods. The Egyptians had gods for nearly everything.

There was also much focus on the **afterlife**. Each person's *ka* (KAH), or life force, existed after death but remained linked to the body. To keep the *ka* from suffering, the Egyptians developed a method called embalming to preserve bodies. Royalty and other members of the **elite** had their bodies preserved as **mummies**, specially treated bodies wrapped in cloth.

> **What is the *ka*?**
>
> _____
>
> _____

THE PYRAMIDS

Pyramids, spectacular stone monuments, were built to house dead rulers. Many pyramids are still standing today, amazing reminders of Egyptian **engineering**.

> **Why do you think the Egyptians believed that royal burial sites were so important?**
>
> _____
>
> _____
>
> _____
>
> _____
>
> _____

CHALLENGE ACTIVITY

Critical Thinking: Make Judgments Write a one-page essay considering whether a god-king pharaoh ruling today would be loved or hated by his people.

Guided Reading Workbook

DIRECTIONS Write two adjectives or descriptive phrases that describe the term.

1. afterlife _____

2. elite _____

3. engineering _____

   _____

4. Khufu _____

5. mummies _____

   _____

6. nobles _____

7. Old Kingdom _____

8. pyramids _____

   _____

9. theocracy _____

Kingdoms of the Nile

MAIN IDEAS
1. The Middle Kingdom was a period of stable government between periods of disorder.
2. The New Kingdom was the peak of Egyptian trade and military power, but its greatness did not last.
3. Work and daily life were different among Egypt's social classes.

Key Terms and People

Middle Kingdom period of stability and order in ancient Egypt between about 2050 and 1750 BC

New Kingdom the height of Egypt's power and glory, between 1550 and 1050 BC

trade routes paths followed by traders

Queen Hatshepsut New Kingdom ruler renowned for expanding Egyptian trade

Ramses the Great important New Kingdom pharaoh who defended Egypt from invaders and strengthened defenses

Lesson Summary
THE MIDDLE KINGDOM

The Old Kingdom ended with the pharaohs in debt. Ambitious nobles serving in government positions managed to take power from the pharaohs and rule for nearly 160 years. Egypt had no central ruler during this time. Finally, a powerful pharaoh regained control around 2050 BC and started a peaceful period of rule. This era was called the **Middle Kingdom** and lasted until Southwest Asian invaders conquered Lower Egypt around 1750 BC.

> Who ruled Egypt before the Middle Kingdom began?
>
> _____
> _____
> _____

THE NEW KINGDOM

When an Egyptian named Ahmose (AHM-ohs) drove away the invaders and declared himself king of Egypt in 1550 BC, he began Egypt's eighteenth dynasty and the start of the **New Kingdom**. Responding to invasions, Egypt took control of possible invasion routes and quickly became the leading military power in the region, with an empire extending from the Euphrates River in the northeast to Nubia in the south. These conquests also made Egypt rich, through gifts and vastly expanded **trade routes**. One particular ruler, **Queen Hatshepsut**, was active in establishing new paths for traders.

Despite the strong leadership of **Ramses the Great**, a tide of invasions from the west and Southwest Asia eventually reduced Egypt to violence and disorder.

Why did Egypt become the leading military power in the region?
_____
_____

WORK AND DAILY LIFE

During the Middle and New Kingdoms daily life in Egypt did not change very much. The population continued to grow and become more complex. Professional and skilled workers like scribes, artisans, artists, and architects were honored. These roles in society were usually passed on in families, with young boys learning a trade from their fathers.

What sort of workers were respected in ancient Egyptian society?
_____
_____

Farmers and peasants made up the vast majority of the population. In addition to hard work on the land, they were required to pay taxes and were subject to special labor duty at any time. Only slaves were beneath them in social status.

Most Egyptian families lived in their own homes. Boys were expected to marry young and start their own families. Women focused on the home, but many also had other jobs. Egyptian women had the legal rights to own property, make contracts, and divorce their husbands.

What was daily life like in Egypt for farmers and peasants?
_____
_____
_____
_____

CHALLENGE ACTIVITY

Critical Thinking: Design Design an ancient Egyptian "job want ad," and then write a letter to a potential employer explaining why you should be hired.

Name _____ Class _____ Date _____

Middle Kingdom	Queen Hatshepsut	trade routes
New Kingdom	Ramses the Great	

DIRECTIONS Read each sentence and choose the correct term from the word bank to replace the underlined phrase. Write the term in the space provided and then define the term in your own words.

1. <u>Queen Hatshepsut</u> could not stop invasions from the west and Southwest Asia.

   _____

   Your definition: _____

   _____

2. Ahmose's dynasty began the <u>Middle Kingdom</u>. _____

   Your definition: _____

   _____

3. One ruler who worked to increase Egyptian trade was <u>Ramses the Great</u>.

   _____

   Your definition: _____

   _____

4. Paths followed by traders are <u>New Kingdoms</u>. _____

   Your definition: _____

   _____

5. The period during which Egypt had a peaceful period of rule is called the <u>trade routes</u>. _____

   Your definition: _____

   _____

Kingdoms of the Nile

MAIN IDEAS
1. Egyptian writing used hieroglyphics.
2. Egypt's great temples were lavishly decorated.
3. Egyptian art filled tombs.

Key Terms and People

hieroglyphics Egyptian writing system, one of the world's first, which used symbols

papyrus long-lasting, paperlike substance made from reeds

Rosetta Stone a stone slab discovered in 1799 that was inscribed with hieroglyphics and their Greek meanings

sphinxes huge ancient Egyptian statues of imaginary creatures with the heads of people or animals and bodies of lions

obelisk a tall, four-sided pillar that is pointed on top

King Tutankhamen a pharaoh whose tomb was untouched by raiders, leaving much information about Egyptian art and burial practices

Lesson Summary
EGYPTIAN WRITING

Egyptians invented one of the world's first writing systems, using a series of more than 600 images, symbols, and pictures called **hieroglyphics** (hy-ruh-GLIH-fiks). Each symbol represented one or more sounds in the Egyptian language.

At first, hieroglyphics were carved in stone. Later they were written with brushes and ink on **papyrus** (puh-PY-ruhs). It was made by pressing layers of reeds together and pounding them into sheets.

Because papyrus didn't decay, many ancient Egyptian texts still survive, including government records, science texts, and literary works, such as *The Book of the Dead*. The discovery of the **Rosetta Stone** in 1799 provided the key to reading Egyptian writing because its text was inscribed both in hieroglyphics and Greek.

> **How was papyrus made?**
> _____
> _____
> _____

> **What language helped scholars to understand the meaning of hieroglyphics on the Rosetta Stone?**
> _____

Lesson 4, *continued*

The Egyptians created two 12-month calendars. One was based on the moon and the other on the sun. The solar calendar was more accurate.

EGYPT'S GREAT TEMPLES

Egyptian architects are known for designing magnificent temples. These structures were the homes of the gods. Temples were lavishly decorated with numerous statues and beautifully painted walls and pillars. **Sphinxes** and **obelisks** were usually found near the entrances to the temples.

EGYPTIAN ART

Many great works are found in either the temples or the tombs of the pharaohs. Most Egyptians, however, never saw these paintings, because only kings, priests, or other important people could enter these places.

Egyptian paintings depict a variety of subjects, like royal events, religious rituals, and daily life. The paintings also have a particular style. People are drawn as if they were twisting as they walked. They are shown in different sizes depending upon their stature in society. In contrast, animals appear more realistically. The Egyptians were also skilled stone and metal workers, creating beautiful statues and jewelry.

Much of what we know about Egyptian art and burial practices comes from the tomb of **King Tutankhamen**. It was one of the few Egyptian tombs that was left untouched by raiders looking for valuables. The tomb was discovered in 1922.

Why did only some people get to see ancient Egyptian sculptures and paintings?

_____

_____

_____

_____

_____

_____

What determined a person's size in an Egyptian painting?

_____

_____

Why is King Tutankhamen's tomb so important for the study of Egyptian history?

_____

_____

_____

_____

CHALLENGE ACTIVITY

Critical Thinking: Analyze Using the library or an online resource, find a key to translate Egyptian hieroglyphics into English. Write a message using hieroglyphics and trade off with another student to see if you can read each other's messages. Provide a copy of your message and the translation to your teacher.

hieroglyphics	obelisk	Rosetta Stone
King Tutankhamen	papyrus	sphinxes

DIRECTIONS Read each sentence and fill in the blank with the word in the word pair that best completes the sentence.

1. _____ is a long-lasting, paperlike substance made from reeds. **(Sphinxes/Papyrus)**

2. The Egyptian writing system is known as _____. **(obelisk/hieroglyphics)**

3. The tomb of _____ was one of the few Egyptian tombs left untouched by raiders. **(King Tutankhamen/Rosetta Stone)**

4. The _____ had hieroglyphics inscribed on it and became the key to deciphering Egyptian writing. **(obelisk/Rosetta Stone)**

5. _____ were imaginary creatures with the bodies of lions and the heads of people. **(Sphinxes/Papyruses)**

6. A(n) _____ is a tall, four-sided pillar that is pointed on top. **(obelisk/sphinx)**

Kingdoms of the Nile

MAIN IDEAS
1. The geography of early Nubia helped civilization develop there.
2. Kush and Egypt traded, but they also fought.
3. Later Kush became a trading power with a unique culture.
4. Both internal and external conflicts led to the decline of Kush and Aksum.

Key Terms and People

Piankhi Kushite king who conquered all of Egypt

trade network a system of people in different lands who trade goods back and forth

merchants traders

exports items sent for sale in other countries or regions

imports goods brought in from other countries or regions

Queen Shanakhdakheto the first woman to rule Kush

Aksum an ancient kingdom located near the Red Sea in northeast Africa

King Ezana Aksumite king who destroyed Meroë and took over the kingdom of Kush

Lesson Summary
THE GEOGRAPHY OF EARLY NUBIA

The kingdom of Kush developed in Nubia, south of Egypt. Just as in Egypt, yearly Nile floods provided fertile soil and farming thrived. The area was also rich in gold, copper, and stone. Kerma (KAR-muh), the capital city on the Nile, was protected by a cataract, or stretch of shallow rapids.

> **How was Kush like Egypt?**
>
> _____
> _____
> _____

KUSH AND EGYPT

Kush and Egypt were trading partners. The Kushites sent Egypt gold, copper, ebony, ivory, and slaves. At times, Kush and Egypt were at war. By around 850 BC, Kush had freed itself from Egypt and was a power again. During the 700s under the king Kashta, the Kushites began to invade Egypt. Kashta's son, **Piankhi** (PYANG-kee), conquered all of Egypt by the time he died.

Guided Reading Workbook

Lesson 5, *continued*

Piankhi's brother became pharaoh of the Kushite dynasty. Egyptian culture thrived. But by 670 BC, Assyrians invaded Egypt. Their iron weapons were better than Kush's bronze weapons. Kush lost control of Egypt.

LATER KUSH

Meroë (MER-oh-wee) became the center of a **trade network**. Africa's first iron industry developed here because iron ore and wood for fuel were available. Egyptian and Greek **merchants** shipped goods from Kush and sent them to the Mediterranean and beyond. Kush's **exports** included gold, pottery, iron tools, ivory, and slaves. **Imports** included luxury items from Egypt, Asia, and the Mediterranean.

The Kushites worshipped their own gods and developed their own writing. Women were active in society, and some rose to positions of authority. **Queen Shanakhdakheto** (shah-nahk-dah-KEE-toh) was the first of many women who ruled Kush.

THE DECLINE OF KUSH

By the AD 300s, another trading center, **Aksum** (AHK-soom), located in what is now Eritrea, began competing with Kush for trade. The Aksum leader **King Ezana** (AY-zah-nah) invaded, and Kush fell.

Aksum became a major trading power. Traders also brought new beliefs, such as Christianity. In the late 300s, King Ezana made Christianity the official religion. Aksum was never conquered, but it became cut off from its allies. The people of Aksum then retreated to Ethiopia.

CHALLENGE ACTIVITY

Critical Thinking: Summarize Pretend you are a Kushite leader in 850 BC. Write a short essay summarizing the details of a plan to defeat Egypt.

> **What made Assyrian weapons better than Kushite weapons?**
> _____
> _____
> _____

> **What items did Kush export?**
> _____
> _____

> **What was the role of women in Kushite society?**
> _____
> _____
> _____
> _____

> **Circle the name and kingdom of the ruler who eventually defeated Kush.**

Guided Reading Workbook

DIRECTIONS Look at each set of four vocabulary terms. On the line provided, write the letter of the term that does not relate to the others.

_____ 1. a. Piankhi
  b. an Egyptian
  c. son of Kashta
  d. a Kushite

_____ 2. a. Piankhi
  b. trade network
  c. Meroë
  d. a system of people in different lands who trade goods

_____ 3. a. merchants
  b. traders
  c. Egyptian and Greek
  d. King Ezana

_____ 4. a. imports
  b. exports
  c. goods brought in
  d. fine jewelry and luxury items

_____ 5. a. imports
  b. exports
  c. items sent out
  d. gold and slaves

_____ 6. a. King Ezana
  b. first woman to rule Kush
  c. 170 BC to 150 BC
  d. Queen Shanakhdakheto

_____ 7. a. King Ezana
  b. Queen Shanakhdakheto
  c. King of Aksum
  d. destroyed Meroë

_____ 8. a. in northeast Africa
  b. near the Red Sea
  c. ruled by women
  d. an ancient kingdom

Guided Reading Workbook

MAIN IDEA
1. The geography of India includes high mountains, great rivers and heavy seasonal rain.
2. Harappan civilization developed along the Indus River.

Key Terms and People

subcontinent a large landmass smaller than a continent

monsoons seasonal wind patterns that cause wet and dry seasons

seal a stamped image with images of humans and animals

Lesson Summary
GEOGRAPHY OF INDIA

India is home to one of the world's earliest civilizations. India is so huge it's called a **subcontinent**, which is a large landmass that is smaller than a continent. A subcontinent is usually separated from a continent by physical features, such as mountains. The world's highest mountains, the Himalayas, are in India. India also has a vast desert, many fertile plains, and rugged plateaus. The Indus River, which flows from the Himalayas and is located mainly in present-day Pakistan, is one cradle of ancient Indian civilization. Early cities also developed on the nearby Sarasvati River, which has since disappeared. As in Egypt and Mesopotamia, flooding created fertile plains where people first settled. The Ganges River is shorter than the Indus, but it flows through a fertile and populated area. It has been used for irrigation since early times. The Ganges has long been used for transportation, and today it is an important source of hydroelectric power. India's hot and humid climate is heavily influenced by **monsoons**, wind patterns that cause wet and dry seasons.

> Underline India's geographic features.

> Circle the name of the world's highest mountains.

> What effect do monsoons have on India's climate?
>
> _____
> _____

HARAPPAN CIVILIZATION

India's first-known civilization is called the Harappan (huh-RA-puhn) civilization. It is named after the modern city of Harappa, Pakistan. Archaeologists believe Harappans thrived between 2600 and 1700 BC. Most of what historians know about the Harappans comes from studying the ruins of their cities, including Harappa and Mohenjo-Daro on the Indus River and Kalibangan, which was on the Sarasvati. Each city was well planned with a large fortress nearby that could easily oversee the city streets. The buildings were built of brick made from mud left by the river flooding. The cities had public wells. Harappan farmers used irrigation to help produce a surplus of food.

> **Why was it an advantage for the streets of early Harappan cities to be viewed from a fortress?**
>
> _____
> _____
> _____
> _____

The cities were very advanced. Most houses had indoor plumbing. The Harappans developed beautiful artisan crafts and a system of weights and measures. They made elaborate **seals**, stamped images with figures of humans and animals. The Harappans also developed India's first writing system, but scholars have not yet learned to read it.

Little is known about Harappan society. We do know that they traded with other regions, because Harappan seals have been found in Mesopotamia. The Persian Gulf may have been a sea trade route. It's also unclear why the Harappan civilization ended by the early 1700s BC.

> **Why do we know so little about the Harappans?**
>
> _____
> _____
> _____
> _____
> _____
> _____

CHALLENGE ACTIVITY

Critical Thinking: Make Inferences Write a short essay explaining what you think might have happened to the Harappan civilization.

DIRECTIONS Write a word or phrase that has the same meaning as the term given.

1. monsoons _____

_____

2. seals _____

_____

3. subcontinent _____

_____

DIRECTIONS Read each sentence and fill in the blank with the word in the word pair that best completes the sentence.

4. The _____ civilization was India's first civilization. **(Mesopotamian/ Harappan)**

5. The _____, which are located in northern India, are the highest mountains in the world. **(Ganges/Himalayas)**

6. The _____ River flows out of the Himalaya mountain range in what is now Pakistan. **(Ganges/Indus)**

7. A _____ is usually separated from the rest of the continent by physical features, such as mountains. **(monsoon/subcontinent)**

8. In the summertime, _____ blow into India from the ocean, bringing heavy rains that can cause terrible floods. **(monsoons/seals)**

9. Today the _____ River is an important source of _____ power. **(Ganges/Indus)**; **(human/hydroelectric)**

10. Harappan _____ have been found in Mesopotamian cities, showing that the people traded goods with other civilizations. **(monsoons/seals)**

11. Little is known about the _____ civilization because scholars have not yet learned to read their writing system. **(Himalayan/Harappan)**

Ancient India

> **MAIN IDEA**
> **1.** A new civilization developed in India during the Vedic period.
> **2.** The Aryans practiced a religion known as Brahmanism.
> **3.** Indian society divided into distinct groups under the Aryans.

Key Terms and People

Sanskrit ancient India's most important language, on which the Hindi language is based

caste system a division of Indian society into groups based on a person's birth, wealth, or occupation

Lesson Summary
THE ROOTS OF VEDIC SOCIETY

Following the Harappan civilization, a new civilization developed in India. It was created by the Aryans. Historians debate whether the Aryans migrated to India from another region or were native to the subcontinent. Unlike the Harappans, they did not build big cities but lived in small communities based on family ties, each run by a local leader, or raja.

The Aryans spoke **Sanskrit** and developed a rich tradition of poems and hymns, but they did not have a writing system. Instead, their works survived from generation to generation by word of mouth. Aryans eventually figured out how to write Sanskrit to keep records. The lasting influence of these early written works made Sanskrit the most important language of ancient India. Much of what we know about the early Aryans comes to us through Sanskrit works. Sanskrit is not widely spoken today. However, it is the root of many modern South Asian languages, including Hindi.

> The early Aryans had a rich and expressive language, but they did not write. How did they preserve their poems and their history without writing?
>
> _____
>
> _____
>
> _____

EARLY HINDUISM AND VEDIC RELIGION

The religion practiced by the Aryan priests became known as Brahmanism. It was based on the Vedas, first passed down orally and then written down. The Vedas contained sacred hymns and poems. Over time, the Aryans wrote their thoughts about the Vedas, which were compiled into Vedic texts. The texts described rituals, explained how to perform sacrifices, and offered reflections from religious scholars.

In the later Vedic period between 800 BC and 500 BC, some rajas became the rulers of powerful kingdoms. Priests and the upper class grew more wealthy, leading to a division within society.

> **Underline what the Vedic texts contained.**

INDIAN SOCIAL STRUCTURE

Aryan society was divided into social classes. There were four main groups called *varnas*. The Brahmins (BRAH-muhns) were priests, teachers, and scholars. The Kshatriyas (KSHA-tree-uhs) were rulers and warriors. The Vaisyas (VYSH-yuhs) were farmers, craftspeople, and traders. The Sudras (SOO-drahs) were laborers and servants..

Over several centuries, the *varnas* were divided into thousands of smaller groups called *jatis* or castes. Indian society developed a **caste system** based on a person's birth, wealth, or occupation. Generally, caste came to determine a person's place in society.

In time, communities created rules about what jobs members of castes could hold and whom they could marry. One group, the Dalits or "untouchables," emerged around AD 500. They lived outside the caste system and could only hold certain jobs.

> **How did the caste system in India change over time?**
> _____
> _____
> _____
> _____

Guided Reading Workbook

CHALLENGE ACTIVITY

Critical Thinking: Interpret The caste system in
Indian society became more complex over time.
Why did this happen? Write a letter to a friend
explaining why you believe this may have
happened.

DIRECTIONS On the line provided before each statement, write **T** if
a statement is true and **F** if a statement is false. If the statement is
false, write the correct term on the line after each sentence that
makes the sentence a true statement.

_____ 1. Ancient writings known as the <u>Sanskrit</u> include poems, hymns, myths,
and rituals.

_____

_____ 2. The leader of each village was given the title of <u>raja</u>.

_____

_____ 3. Sanskrit was the language of the <u>Harappan civilization</u>.

_____

_____ 4. Today <u>Sanskrit</u> is no longer widely spoken, but the modern Hindi
language is based on it.

_____

_____ 5. Aryan society was divided into four social classes called <u>Sudras</u>.

_____

_____ 6. Brahmanism was practiced by the <u>Harappans</u>, who based their religion
on the Vedas.

_____

_____ 7. The <u>caste system</u> came to divide Indian society into groups based on
birth, wealth, or occupation.

_____

Ancient India

Lesson 3

MAIN IDEA

1. Hinduism developed out of Brahmanism and influences from other cultures.
2. A few groups reacted to Hinduism by breaking away to form their own religions.

Key Terms and People

Hinduism the most widespread religion in India today

reincarnation the belief that the soul, once a person dies, is reborn in another person

karma the effects that good or bad actions have on a person's soul

samskaras rites of passage to prepare a person for an event or next stage in life

Jainism a nonviolent religion based on the teachings of Mahavira

Mahavira founder of Jainism who taught four basic nonviolent principles to follow

nonviolence the avoidance of violent actions

Sikhism monotheistic religion founded in India in the 1400s

Guru Nanak teacher whose ideas became the basis of the religion called Sikhism

Lesson Summary
HINDUISM DEVELOPS

Hinduism is India's largest religion today. It developed from Brahmanism and ideas from other cultures. Hindus believe that there are many deities but all of them are part of a universal spirit called Brahman. Hindus believe everyone has a soul, or *atman*. Many Hindus believe that a person's ultimate goal should be to reunite that with Brahman. This joining will happen when the soul recognizes that the world we live in is an illusion. Hindus believe this recognition can take several lifetimes, so **reincarnation**, or rebirth, is necessary. The form a person takes when he or she is reborn depends upon his or her **karma**, the effect one's actions in

> Underline the Hindu name for the soul.

life have on one's soul. Those who build good karma through good actions see benefits in future births. Those who create bad karma through evil actions are reborn into lower castes or life forms. Hinduism teaches that each person has a *dharma*, a set of spiritual duties to fulfill in each life. *Dharma* is Hinduism's guidelines for living a moral life and includes nonviolence, self-restraint, and honesty.

> **What is karma?**
> _____
> _____
> _____
> _____

Hindu religious practices vary between individuals and communities. Worship can take place anywhere, from large temples to private homes. Meditation, or silent reflection, and yoga help many Hindus focus their thoughts. Rituals and ceremonies have always been important in Hinduism. **Samskaras**, rites of passage to prepare a person for a special event or for his or her next stage in life, are still important today.

Hinduism spread throughout Southeast Asia, mostly due to traders exchanging goods. Later it spread through colonization when Hindus went to work in British and Dutch colonies.

THE RISE OF OTHER RELIGIONS IN INDIA

The religions of **Jainism** and **Sikhism** also developed in India. Jainism is based upon the teachings of **Mahavira,** who taught four basic principles: injure no life, tell the truth, do not steal, and own no property. Jains practice **nonviolence**, meaning they avoid violent actions because they believe that everything is alive and part of the cycle of rebirth. The Sanskrit word for nonviolence is *ahimsa* (uh-HIM-sah).

> **Underline the four main teachings of Jainism.**

Sikhism was founded centuries after Jainism, based on the teachings of **Guru Nanak**. It is monotheistic, which means Sikhs believe in one god. Sikhs believe in the equality of all people, regardless of their social class or wealth.

> **What does *monotheistic* mean?**
> _____
> _____
> _____

CHALLENGE ACTIVITY

Critical Thinking: Make Inferences The idea of *ahimsa* has proved popular with reformers through the centuries. Write a one-page essay explaining why this might be so.

DIRECTIONS On the line provided before each statement, write **T** if a statement is true and **F** if a statement is false. If the statement is false, write the correct term on the line after each sentence that makes the sentence a true statement.

_____ 1. The force created by a person's actions is called <u>karma</u>.

_____

_____ 2. <u>Hinduism</u> is based on four major principles: injure no life, tell the truth, do not steal, and own no property.

_____

_____ 3. <u>Hinduism</u>, the largest religion in India, teaches that each person has a *dharma*, or spiritual duties to fulfill in each life.

_____

_____ 4. <u>Nonviolence,</u> the avoidance of violent actions, was practiced by the Jains.

_____

_____ 5. Hindus believe that souls are born and reborn many times, each time into a new body, in a process called <u>reincarnation</u>.

_____

_____ 6. According to Hindu teachings, everyone has a soul, or *<u>atman</u>*, inside them.

_____

_____ 7. <u>Hinduism</u> is based on the teachings of a man named Guru Nanak.

_____

_____ 8. Many Hindus believe that a person's soul will eventually reunite with <u>karma</u>, the universal spirit.

_____

Ancient India

MAIN IDEA
1. Siddhartha Gautama searched for wisdom in many ways.
2. The teachings of Buddhism deal with finding peace.
3. Buddhism spread far from where it began in India.

Key Terms and People

fasting going without food

meditation focusing the mind on spiritual ideas

the Buddha founder of Buddhism, born an Indian prince named Siddhartha Gautama

Buddhism religion based on the teachings of the Buddha

nirvana a state of perfect peace

missionaries people who spread and teach religious beliefs

Lesson Summary

SIDDARTHA'S SEARCH FOR WISDOM

Not everyone in India accepted Hinduism. In the late 500s BC, a major new religion began to develop from questions posed by a young prince named Siddhartha Gautama (si-DAHR-tuh GAU-tuh-muh). Siddhartha was born to a wealthy family and led a life of comfort, but he wondered at the pain and suffering he saw all around him. By the age of 30, Siddhartha had left his home and family to travel India. He talked to many priests and wise people, but he was not satisfied with their answers.

Siddhartha did not give up. He wandered for years throughout India trying to free himself from daily concerns by **fasting** and **meditating**. After six years, Siddhartha sat down under a tree near the town of Gaya and meditated for seven weeks. He came up with an answer to what causes human suffering. Suffering is caused by wanting what one does not have, wanting to keep what one likes and already has, and not wanting what one dislikes but has. He began to travel and

> Why did Prince Siddhartha leave a comfortable home and loving family?
> _____
> _____
> _____
> _____

> Underline what Siddhartha believed to be the three causes of human suffering.

teach his ideas. He was soon called **the Buddha**, or "Enlightened One." From his teachings sprang the religion **Buddhism**.

TEACHINGS OF BUDDHISM

Buddhism is intent on relieving human suffering. It is based upon the Four Noble Truths. These truths are: suffering and unhappiness are a part of life; suffering stems from our desire for pleasure and material goods; people can overcome their desires and reach **nirvana**, a state of perfect peace, which ends the cycle of reincarnation; and people can overcome desire and ignorance by following an eightfold path to nirvana.

These teachings were similar to some Hindu concepts but went against some traditional Hindu ideas. The Buddha challenged the authority of the Brahmins, the Hindu priests. The Buddha said that each individual could reach salvation on his or her own.

BUDDHISM SPREADS

Buddhism spread quickly throughout India to eventually become a major global religion. With the help of Indian king Asoka, Buddhist **missionaries** were sent to other countries to teach their religious beliefs. Buddhism quickly took hold in neighboring countries like Nepal, Sri Lanka, and China. Buddhism soon became very influential in Japan and Korea. Over time, two branches of Buddhism developed—Theravada and Mahayana.

CHALLENGE ACTIVITY

Critical Thinking: Make Inferences Could you leave your family, home, and everything you know to preach what you believe to be a spiritual truth? What do you think inspired the Buddha to do so? Write a short essay in which you explain his choice.

| Underline the name of the central teachings of Buddhism. |

| What is one difference between Buddhism and Hinduism? _____ _____ _____ _____ |

| Name three countries to which Buddhism spread. _____ _____ _____ |

| Buddha | Buddhism | fasting |
| meditation | missionaries | nirvana |

DIRECTIONS Answer each question by writing a sentence that contains at least one word from the word bank.

1. According to Buddhist teachings, if people can overcome their desires and ignorance, they will reach what?

    _____

2. What did Siddhartha do to free his mind from daily concerns?

    _____

3. Who did Asoka send to spread the religious beliefs of Buddhism?

    _____

4. What is the term that means "Enlightened One"?

    _____

5. What is the religion based on the teachings of Siddhartha Gautama?

    _____

DIRECTIONS On the line provided before each statement, write **T** if a statement is true and **F** if a statement is false. If the statement is false, write the correct term on the line after each sentence that makes the sentence a true statement.

_____ 6. The Buddha taught that anyone could achieve meditation.

    _____

_____ 7. Buddhism split into two major branches called Theravada and Mahayana.

    _____

_____ 8. Nirvana traveled throughout Asia, eventually spreading Buddhism to China, Korea, and Japan.

    _____

Guided Reading Workbook

Ancient India

MAIN IDEA
1. The Mauryan Empire unified most of India.
2. Gupta rulers promoted Hinduism in their empire.

Key Terms and People

Chandragupta Maurya Indian military leader who first unified India and founded the Mauryan Empire

Asoka Chandragupta's grandson and last ruler of the Mauryan Empire

Chandra Gupta II ruler who brought great prosperity and stability to India

Lesson Summary
MAURYAN EMPIRE UNIFIES INDIA

Under Aryan rule, India was divided into several states with no central leader. Then, in the 320s BC, an Indian military leader named **Chandragupta Maurya** seized control of the entire northern part of India. The Mauryan Empire lasted for 150 years.

Chandragupta's complex government included a huge army and a network of spies. He taxed the population heavily for the protection he offered. Eventually, Chandragupta became a Jainist monk and gave up his throne to his son. His family continued to expand the Indian empire.

Chandragupta's grandson, **Asoka**, was the strongest ruler of the Mauryan dynasty. The empire thrived under his rule. But eventually, tired of bloodshed and war, Asoka converted to Buddhism. He devoted the rest of his rule to improving the lives of his people by building roads, hospitals, and even universities. Asoka also sent Buddhist missionaries to other countries. The rest of the family, however, did not follow Asoka's example. When Asoka died, his sons struggled for power and foreign invaders threatened the country. The Mauryan Empire fell

> **Which Indian leader unified northern India in the 320s BC?**
> _____

> **What is the relationship between Chandragupta's government and heavy taxes?**
> _____
> _____
> _____
> _____
> _____

in 184 BC and India divided into smaller states for about 500 years. The spread of Buddhism steadily increased, while Hinduism declined.

GUPTA RULERS PROMOTE HINDUISM

A new dynasty was established in India. During the AD 300s, the Gupta Dynasty once again rose to unite and build the prosperity of India. Not only did the Guptas control India's military, they were devout Hindus and encouraged the revival of Hindu traditions and writings. The Guptas, however, also supported Jainism and Buddhism.

Indian civilization reached a high point under **Chandra Gupta II** (not related to Chandragupta Maurya). He poured money and resources into strengthening the country's borders, as well as promoting the arts, literature, and religion.

The Gupta Dynasty lasted until fierce attacks by the Huns from Central Asia during the late 400s drained the empire of its resources. India broke up once again into a patchwork of small states.

CHALLENGE ACTIVITY

Critical Thinking: Make Inferences Asoka was strongly influenced by Buddhism. Chandra Gupta II followed Hinduism. Choose one of these kings and write an essay explaining how his religion affected his point of view and his decisions during his reign.

> **How did India's government change after the death of Asoka?**
> _____
> _____
> _____
> _____

> **Underline the name of the dynasty that reunited India and revived Hindu traditions.**

Lesson 5, *continued*

| Asoka | Chandra Gupta II | Chandragupta Maurya |
| establish | Gupta Dynasty | Huns |

DIRECTIONS Read each sentence and fill in the blank with the word in the word pair that best completes the sentence.

1. Under Emperor _____, Indian civilization reached a high point. The empire's economy strengthened and people prospered. **(Chandra Gupta II/Chandragupta Maurya)**

2. _____ was the strongest ruler of the Mauryan dynasty. Later, he converted to Buddhism and worked toward improving the lives of his people. **(Asoka/Huns)**

3. The Mauryan Empire was founded by _____, who ruled with a complex government that included a network of spies and a huge army. **(Chandra Gupta II/Chandragupta Maurya)**

4. When the _____ from Central Asia invaded India, it led to the end of the Gupta Dynasty. **(Asoka/Huns)**

5. Under the _____, Hinduism became popular again, but the rulers also supported Buddhism and Jainism. **(Gupta Dynasty/Huns)**

DIRECTIONS Use the vocabulary terms from the word bank to write a summary of the Mauryan Empire and the Gupta Dynasty.

_____

_____

_____

_____

_____

_____

_____

_____

_____

Guided Reading Workbook

Ancient India

Lesson 6

MAIN IDEA
1. Indian artists created great works of religious art.
2. Sanskrit literature flourished during the Gupta period.
3. The Indians made scientific advances in metalworking, medicine, and other sciences.

Key Terms and People

metallurgy the science of working with metals

alloy a mixture of two or more metals

Hindu-Arabic numerals the numbering system invented by Indian mathematicians and brought to Europe by Arabs; the numbers we use today

inoculation a method of injecting a person with a small dose of a virus to help him or her build up defenses to a disease

astronomy the study of stars and planets

Lesson Summary
RELIGIOUS ART

Both the Mauryan and Gupta empires unified India and created a stable environment where artists, writers, scholars, and scientists could thrive. Their works are still admired today. Much of the Indian art from this period was religious, inspired by both Hindu and Buddhist teachings. Many beautiful temples were built during this time and decorated with elaborate wood and stone carvings.

> What was the main inspiration for art and literature during the Mauryan and Gupta empires?
>
> _____
> _____
> _____
> _____

SANSKRIT LITERATURE

Great works of literature were written in Sanskrit, the ancient Aryan language, during the Gupta Dynasty. The best-known works are the *Mahabharata* (muh-HAH-BAH-ruh-tuh) and the *Ramayana* (rah-MAH-yuh-nuh). The *Mahabharata*, a long story about the struggle between two families for control of a kingdom, is considered a classic Hindu text. The most famous passage of the *Mahabharata* is called the

> In what language were literary works from the Gupta period written?
>
> _____
> _____

Bhagavad Gita (BUG-uh-vuhd GEE-tah). The *Ramayana* is the story of the Prince Rama, a human incarnation of one of the three major Hindu gods, Vishnu, who fights demons and marries the beautiful Princess Sita.

SCIENTIFIC ADVANCES

Scientific and scholarly work also blossomed during the early Indian empires. Most prominent was the development of **metallurgy**, the science of working with metals. Indian technicians and engineers made strong tools and weapons. They also invented processes for creating **alloys**. Alloys, such as steel or bronze, may be stronger or more useful than pure metals like iron or copper.

The numbers we use today, called **Hindu-Arabic numerals**, were first developed by Indian mathematicians and brought to Europe by Arabs. They also created the concept of zero, upon which all modern mathematics is based.

Other sciences also benefited from this period of Indian history. In medicine, Indians developed the technique of **inoculation**, which is injecting a person with a small dose of a virus to help him or her build up defenses to a disease. Doctors could even perform certain surgeries. India's fascination with **astronomy**, the study of stars and planets, led to the discovery of seven of the planets in our solar system.

CHALLENGE ACTIVITY

Critical Thinking: Make Inferences Our modern society borrows significantly from the scientific and mathematical achievements of the early Indian empires. Write a short play, story, or essay describing how our modern world might look without these inventions.

> **What is the science of working with metals called?**
> _____

> **What important mathematical concept did Indian's create?**
> _____

> **Indians at this period did not have telescopes. How do you think they discovered planets?**
> _____
> _____
> _____
> _____
> _____
> _____
> _____
> _____
> _____

Lesson 6, *continued*

DIRECTIONS Write a word or phrase that has the same meaning as the term given.

1. alloy _____

_____

2. astronomy _____

_____

3. Hindu-Arabic numerals _____

_____

4. inoculation _____

_____

5. metallurgy _____

_____

DIRECTIONS Read each sentence and fill in the blank with the term in the word pair that best completes the sentence.

6. Identifying seven of the planets in our solar system is one accomplishment early Indians made in the field of _____. **(astronomy/metallurgy)**

7. Indian doctors knew how to protect people against disease through _____. **(alloy/inoculation)**

8. Ancient Indians were masters of _____ and knew processes for mixing metals to create an _____. **(astronomy/metallurgy); (alloy/inoculation)**

9. The _____ is one of Hinduism's most famous texts. (***Bhagavad Gita/*Hindu-Arabic numerals)**

10. The numbers we use today are called _____ because they were created by Indian scholars and brought to Europe by the Arabs. (***Bhagavad Gita/*Hindu-Arabic numerals**)

Ancient China

MAIN IDEAS
1. China's physical geography made farming possible but travel and communication difficult.
2. Civilization began in China along the Huang He and Chang Jiang rivers.
3. China's first dynasties helped Chinese society develop and made many other achievements.

Key Terms and People

jade a hard gemstone

oracle a prediction

Lesson Summary
CHINA'S PHYSICAL GEOGRAPHY

China is a large country—about the same size as the United States. It has many geographical features that affected Chinese civilization. Some features separated China from the rest of the world. An example is the Gobi, a desert that spreads over much of China's north. Some features separated groups of people within China. These include rugged mountains on the western frontier.

> **In which part of China is the Gobi?**
> _____

Low-lying plains in the east form one of the world's largest farming regions. Weather patterns vary widely across China. Two great rivers flow from west to east, the Huang He, or Yellow River, and the Chang Jiang, or Yangzi River. These rivers helped connect people in the east with the west.

> **Underline the names of the features that helped connect people in the eastern part of China with those in western China.**

CIVILIZATION BEGINS

Like other ancient peoples, people in China first settled along rivers. By 7000 BC, farmers grew rice in the Chang Jiang Valley. Along the Huang He, they grew millet and wheat. They also fished and hunted and raised pigs and sheep.

> **Where did the Chinese first grow rice?**
> _____
> _____

Guided Reading Workbook

Separate cultures developed along the rivers. As populations grew, villages spread. A social order developed. Graves of the rich often had objects made from **jade**.

CHINA'S FIRST DYNASTIES

Societies along the Huang He grew larger and more complex. Around 2200 BC, a legendary emperor called Yu the Great is said to have founded the Xia (SHAH) dynasty. It is believed that the first flood control channels were built during the Xia dynasty.

Under which dynasty were the first flood control channels built in China?

_____

The first dynasty for which there is clear evidence is the Shang. It was established by the 1500s BC. The Shang ruler and his family were at the top of the social order. Nobles and warrior leaders also had high rank. Artisans came next. They lived in groups depending on what they did for a living. Farmers were below artisans. They worked hard but had little wealth. Slaves, the lowest rank, provided an important source of labor.

The Shang made many advances, including China's first writing system. The Chinese symbols that are used today are based on the pictographs and symbols of the Shang period. Priests carved questions about the future on bones or shells, which were then heated, causing them to crack. The priests believed they could "read" these cracks to predict the future. So the bones were called **oracle** bones.

Which dynasty created China's writing system?

_____

Artisans made bronze containers for cooking and religious ceremonies. They made ornaments, knives, and axes from jade. The military developed war chariots and bronze body armor. Shang astrologers developed a calendar based on sun and moon cycles.

Underline some achievements of Shang artisans.

CHALLENGE ACTIVITY

Critical Thinking: Interpret Using the library
or online resources, study ancient Chinese
writing. Use some of these symbols to illustrate
something you have learned about China and
its culture.

DIRECTIONS Read each sentence and fill in the blank with the term
in the word pair that best completes the sentence.

1. One of the physical barriers that separates China from the outside world is a
   desert called the _____. **(Gobi/Huang He)**

2. Farmers grew millet and wheat along the _____, or
   Yellow River. **(Gobi/Huang He)**

3. An indication of a social order was that the graves of many rich people had
   objects made of _____. **(oracle/jade)**

4. A legendary emperor, Yu the Great, is believed to have founded the
   _____ dynasty around 2200 BC. **(Xia/Shang)**

5. The _____ dynasty made many advances, including
   China's first writing system. **(Xia/Shang)**

6. _____ bones were pieces of bone or shell that Chinese
   priests believed they could "read" to predict the future. **(Oracle/Jade)**

7. The Shang social order had the ruler and nobles at the top and
   _____ in the middle. **(warrior leaders/artisans)**

8. China's first writing system used _____, symbols that
   express words or ideas. **(pictographs/jade)**

DIRECTIONS Look at each set of three vocabulary terms following
each number. On the line provided, write the letter of the term that
does not relate to the others.

_____ 9. a. Chang Jiang   b. jade   c. Huang He

_____10. a. Gobi   b. Shang   c. Xia

Ancient China

MAIN IDEAS
1. The Zhou dynasty expanded China but then declined.
2. Confucius offered ideas to bring order to Chinese society.
3. Daoism and Legalism also gained followers.

Key Terms and People

lords people of high rank

peasants farmers with small farms

Confucius the most influential teacher in Chinese history

ethics moral values

Confucianism the ideas of Confucius

Daoism an early Chinese belief that stressed living in harmony with the guiding force of all reality

Laozi the most famous Daoist teacher

Legalism an early Chinese belief that people were bad by nature and needed to be controlled

Lesson Summary
THE ZHOU DYNASTY

The Zhou (JOH) came from an area west of the Shang kingdom. The Zhou overthrew the Shang during the 1100s BC. The Zhou expanded its territory east and northwest. Then its army moved south to the Chang Jiang river. The Zhou established a new political order. The king granted land to **lords**, or people of high rank. They paid taxes and provided soldiers to the king. **Peasants**, farmers with small farms, received a small plot of land and had to farm additional land for a noble. The social system brought order for a time. However, the loyalty of the lords gradually lessened. Eventually, they began to fight each other. Family structure, which had been the foundation of Chinese life for centuries, was severely weakened. By the 400s BC, China had entered an era called the Warring States period.

> **How did the Zhou establish their rule throughout China?**
> _____
> _____
> _____

> **What kind of wars existed during the Warring States period? Why?**
> _____
> _____
> _____
> _____

CONFUCIUS AND SOCIETY

Toward the end of the Zhou period, the most influential teacher in Chinese history, **Confucius**, traveled through China. He taught that order in society stems from **ethics**, or moral values. He wanted China to return to the ideas and practices from a time when people knew their proper roles in society. **Confucianism** has been a guiding force in human behavior and religious understanding in China through the centuries.

What was Confucius's goal?
_____ _____ _____ _____

DAOISM AND LEGALISM

Around the same time as Confucianism, other influential beliefs arose in China. **Daoism** (DOW-ih-ZUM) stressed living in harmony with the Dao, the guiding force of all reality. Daoists believed that people should be like water and simply let things flow in a natural way. They regarded humans as just a part of nature, not better than any other thing. **Laozi** was the most famous Daoist teacher.

Underline the sentence that describes the way Daoists regard human life.

Legalism is different from both Daoism and Confucianism. Legalists believed that society needed strict laws to control people. They believed in unity, efficiency, and punishment for bad conduct. They wanted the empire to continue to expand, so they urged the state to always be prepared for war. Legalists were the first to put their ideas into practice throughout China.

Why did Legalists want the state to always be prepared for war?
_____ _____

CHALLENGE ACTIVITY

Critical Thinking: Summarize Write a short play with two characters, a Daoist and a Legalist. Make sure each character clearly expresses his or her views on behavior, society, and government.

Confucianism	Confucius	Daoism	ethics
Laozi	Legalism	lords	peasant

DIRECTIONS Choose five of the vocabulary words from the word bank. On a separate sheet of paper, use these words to write a letter that relates to the lesson.

DIRECTIONS Look at each set of three vocabulary terms following each number. On the line provided, write the letter of the term that does not relate to the others.

_____ 1. a. ethics   b. Confucius   c. lords

_____ 2. a. lords   b. Daoism   c. Laozi

_____ 3. a. peasant   b. lords   c. Confucianism

DIRECTIONS On the line provided before each statement, write **T** if a statement is true and **F** if a statement is false. If the statement is false, write the correct term on the line after each sentence that makes the sentence a true statement.

_____ 4. <u>Peasants</u>, or farmers with small farms, were at the bottom of the social order during the Zhou dynasty.

_____

_____ 5. <u>Daoism</u> was the belief that people were bad by nature and needed to be controlled through strict laws and punishments.

_____

_____ 6. <u>Confucianism</u> stressed living in harmony with the Dao, the guiding force of all reality.

_____

Ancient China

MAIN IDEAS
1. The first Qin emperor created a strong but strict government.
2. A unified China was created through Qin policies and achievements.

Key Terms and People

Shi Huangdi the first emperor of the Qin dynasty

Great Wall a barrier across China's northern frontier

Lesson Summary

THE QIN EMPEROR'S STRONG GOVERNMENT

The Warring States period marked a time in China when several states battled each other for power. One state, the Qin (CHIN), built a strong army that defeated the armies of the other states. In 221 BC, the Qin king Ying Zheng unified China. He gave himself the title **Shi Huangdi** (SHEE hwahng-dee), which means "first emperor."

Shi Huangdi was a follower of Legalist beliefs. He created a strong government with strict laws and severe punishments. He ordered the burning of all writings that did not agree with Legalism.

Shi Huangdi took land and power away from the lords. He made commoners work on government building projects. He divided China into districts, each with its own governor. This helped Shi Huangdi enforce taxes and a strict chain of command.

A UNIFIED CHINA

Qin rule brought other major changes to China. Under Shi Huangdi, new policies and achievements united the Chinese people. The emperor set up a uniform system of law. Rules and punishments were to be the same in all parts

> How did Shi Huangdi's rule demonstrate his Legalist beliefs?
>
> _____
> _____
> _____
> _____

> List three ways Shi Huangdi unified China.
>
> _____
> _____
> _____
> _____
> _____
> _____

Lesson 3, continued

of the empire. He also standardized the written language. People everywhere were required to write using the same set of symbols. People from different regions could now communicate with one another in writing. This gave them a sense of shared culture and a common identity.

Shi Huangdi also set up a new monetary system. Standardized gold and copper coins became the currency for all of China. Weights and measures were also standardized. With all these changes and the unified writing system, trade became much easier. A new network of highways connected the capital to every part of the empire. Workers built canals to connect the country's rivers. Goods could be shipped faster and easier from north to south. Also, an irrigation system was built to make more land good for farming. Parts of the Qin irrigation system are still used today.

Shi Huangdi wanted to keep fierce nomads from the north from invading China. So he completed the **Great Wall**, a barrier across China's northern frontier. This was a major Qin achievement. The Qin connected earlier pieces of the wall to form a long, unbroken structure. Building the wall required years of labor from hundreds of thousands of soldiers and workers. Many of them died building the wall.

Although he unified China, many Chinese people hated Shi Huangdi's harsh ways. When he died in 210 BC, rebel forces formed across the country. One group attacked the Qin capital, and the new emperor surrendered. The Qin palace burned to the ground. Qin authority had disappeared. With no central government, China fell into civil war.

> **Give three reasons why trade became easier under the Qin.**
>
> _____
> _____
> _____
> _____
> _____
> _____
> _____

> **What was the purpose of the Great Wall?**
>
> _____
> _____
> _____

Lesson 3, *continued*

CHALLENGE ACTIVITY

Critical Thinking: Make Judgments If you had lived in China during the Qin dynasty, would you have joined a rebel group to overthrow the government? Be sure to consider the ideas of Confucianism and Daoism in your answer.

DIRECTIONS On the line provided before each statement, write **T** if a statement is true and **F** if a statement is false. If the statement is false, write the correct term on the line after each sentence that makes the sentence a true statement.

_____ 1. The emperor who unified China gave himself the title <u>Qin dynasty</u>, which means "first emperor."

_____

_____ 2. <u>Shi Huangdi</u> was a follower of Legalist political beliefs. He created a strong government with strict laws and severe punishments.

_____

_____ 3. Under the <u>Qin dynasty</u>, China was unified, a network of roads and canals was built, and the written language was standardized.

_____

Great Wall	Qin dynasty	Shi Huangdi

DIRECTIONS Answer each question by writing a sentence that contains at least one word from the word bank.

4. Who ordered the destruction of all the writings that did not agree with Legalism?

_____

_____

5. What was the massive building project undertaken that required the labor of hundreds of thousands of soldiers and workers?

_____

_____

Ancient China

 MAIN IDEAS
1. Han dynasty government was based on the ideas of Confucius.
2. Family life was supported and strengthened in Han China.
3. The Han made many achievements in art, literature, and learning.
4. Buddhism spread to China along the trade routes from other lands.

Key Terms and People

sundial a device that uses the position of shadows cast by the sun to tell time

seismograph a device that measures the strength of an earthquake

acupuncture the practice of inserting needles through the skin at specific points to cure disease or relieve pain

silk a soft, light, highly valued fabric

diffusion the spread of ideas, goods, and technology from one culture to another

Lesson Summary

HAN DYNASTY GOVERNMENT

After the end of the Qin dynasty, Liu Bang (LEE-OO BANG) won control of China. He lowered farmers' taxes and made punishments less severe. His government was based on that of the Qin. His successor, Wudi (WOO-DEE), made Confucianism the official government policy. A person had to pass a test based on Confucianism to get a government job.

> What was one aspect of the Qin government that the Han changed?
> _____
> _____
> _____
> _____
> _____
> _____

FAMILY LIFE

A class structure took hold during Han rule. Peasants were the second class in this Confucian system. Merchants were the lowest class because they only bought and sold what others made. This social division did not indicate wealth though. Peasants were still poor and merchants were still rich.

> Underline the sentence that explains why Confucian thinking devalues merchants.

Lesson 4, *continued*

During Wudi's reign, children were taught to respect their elders and the father had absolute power. Chinese parents valued boys more highly than girls. Some women, however, gained power and could influence their sons' families. An older widow might become the head of the family.

> Underline the sentence that explains which women could become heads of families.

HAN ACHIEVEMENTS

During Han rule, art and literature thrived and inventors developed many useful devices. Artists painted portraits. Poets developed new styles of verse. A historian wrote a history of China up to the Han dynasty. The Han Chinese also invented paper. Other innovations were the **sundial,** the **seismograph**, and the Chinese medical practice of **acupuncture** (AK-yoo-punk-cher). These and other Han inventions and advances are still used today.

> Which Han dynasty invention made books possible?
> _____

Advances in manufacturing, such as the iron plow and wheelbarrow, increased productivity. **Silk** production also increased. Weavers used foot-powered looms to weave fabric. Silk garments were expensive. The Chinese were determined to keep their process for making silk a secret.

> Why do you think it was important to keep the silk production process a secret?
> _____
> _____
> _____
> _____

BUDDHISM COMES TO CHINA

Over time, the Han government became less stable. Buddhism seemed to offer more hope than Confucianism or Daoism. It offered a rebirth and a relief from suffering.

Buddhism caught on in China with both the poor and the upper classes. Buddhism's introduction to China is an example of **diffusion**, the spread of ideas from one culture to another. Chinese culture changed in response to it.

> Why did Buddhism become popular in China?
> _____
> _____
> _____
> _____
> _____

CHALLENGE ACTIVITY

Critical Thinking: Evaluate Do you think the Han dynasty would have flourished as well if the Qin had not set up a strong government? Write a brief essay providing your point of view.

DIRECTIONS Write a word or phrase to describe the term given.

1. acupuncture _____

   _____

2. seismograph _____

3. sundial _____

4. diffusion _____

5. silk _____

DIRECTIONS Read each sentence and fill in the blank with the word in the word pair that best completes the sentence.

6. _____ became the first Han emperor by winning control of China after the fall of the Qin dynasty. **(Wudi/Liu Bang)**

7. Under the _____ dynasty, the Chinese made advances in art, literature, medicine, and science. **(Qin/Han)**

8. The spread of ideas, goods, and technology from one culture to another is _____. **(diffusion/innovation)**

9. A soft, light, highly valued fabric is called _____. **(silk/acupuncture)**

DIRECTIONS Look at each set of three vocabulary terms following each number. On the line provided, write the letter of the term that does not relate to the others.

_____10. a. acupuncture   b. paper   c. Great Wall

_____11. a. Buddhism   b. diffusion   c. Liu Bang

_____12. a. Han   b. Qin   c. iron plow

Ancient China

MAIN IDEAS
1. Trade routes linked China with the Middle East and Rome.
2. The most famous trade route was known as the Silk Road.

Key Terms and People

Silk Road a network of trade routes between China and the Mediterranean Sea

Lesson Summary
EXPANSION OF TRADE

During the Han dynasty, Chinese goods, especially silk fabric and fine pottery, were highly valued by people in other lands. So the value of these goods outside China helped increase trade.

Powerful Han armies expanded into Central Asia, Vietnam, and Korea. Han rulers believed that other ethnic groups outside of China were inferior to the Chinese. So Han armies brought Chinese culture into these societies. They also stabilized the region, which made the transport of goods over trade routes safer. Trade increased as China's leaders realized they could make a profit by bringing silk to Central Asia. Then they traded it for horses. The Central Asian people then took the silk west and traded it for other products.

In 139 BC, Emperor Wudi wanted to establish alliances with an enemy group. He sent one of his generals to these western lands. However, the general was imprisoned and did not return for 13 years. Then he told of great wealth and large horses in Central Asia. Wudi sent an army there to conquer the lands. The empire grew, and trade routes developed to the west. The Chinese extended the Great Wall to protect their land and trade routes. Along the trade routes, trading

> **What led to an increase in trade outside China?**
> _____
> _____
> _____

> **Underline the sentence that explains why Han armies brought Chinese culture into areas outside of China.**

> **What caused cities to grow in western China?**
> _____
> _____
> _____
> _____

posts and farming settlements developed. This
led to the rise of cities in western China.

TRADE ALONG THE SILK ROAD

Traders used a series of overland routes to take
Chinese goods to distant lands. The most famous
trade route was known as the **Silk Road**. Most
merchants traveled only a small part of the Silk
Road, selling their goods along the way to other
traders. Then when they reached Central Asia,
these traders sold their goods to other local
traders who took the goods the rest of the way.

> **What was the most famous overland trade route that the Chinese used to take goods to distant lands?**
>
> _____

Traveling the Silk Road was difficult and risky,
so traders formed groups for protection. Traders
also faced icy blizzards, desert heat, and
sandstorms. However, the Silk Road was worth
the many risks. Silk was so popular in Rome, for
example, that China grew wealthy just from
trading with Romans. Traders also returned from
Rome with gold, silver, precious stones, and
horses.

> **Underline the sentences that explain why traveling the Silk Road was worth the risks traders faced.**

The exchange of goods along the Silk Road led
to a wider world economy. Goods from Europe
and Africa went to China, and Chinese goods
went west. In addition to goods, the Silk Road
also caused people to exchange knowledge and
inventions. People had to learn new languages to
communicate with traders from different cultures.
People from different places talked to one
another and exchanged knowledge of the arts
and science.

Advanced technologies such as paper making
and irrigation systems spread across Asia and
beyond by way of the Silk Road. Religion also
spread because of trade routes. Buddhism came
from India to China by way of the Silk Road.

During the Han period, few foreigners traveled
to China. However, trade brought foreign ideas
and technology.

> **List three examples that demonstrate the spread of knowledge and technology along the Silk Road.**
>
> _____
>
> _____
>
> _____
>
> _____

CHALLENGE ACTIVITY

Critical Thinking: Summarize Imagine that you are an experienced Chinese trader on the Silk Road. Write a short advertisement for an assistant trader. Be sure to include the benefits of the job.

DIRECTIONS Use the vocabulary term *Silk Road* to write a poem about what you learned in the lesson.

_____

_____

_____

_____

_____

_____

DIRECTIONS On the line before each statement, write **T** if the statement is true and **F** if the statement is false. If the statement is false, change the underlined term to make the sentence true. Then write the correct term on the line after the sentence.

_____ 1. The Chinese extended the Silk Road to protect its land and trade routes.

_____

_____ 2. During the Han dynasty, silk and pottery were highly valued by Romans.

_____

_____ 3. The <u>Silk Road</u> was a network of routes westward between China and the Mediterranean Sea.

_____

_____ 4. Traders returned from Vietnam with gold, silver, precious stones, and horses.

_____

The Hebrews and Judaism

MAIN IDEAS
1. Abraham led the Hebrews to Canaan and to a new religion, and Moses led the Israelites out of slavery in Egypt.
2. Strong kings united the Israelites to fight off invaders.
3. Invaders conquered and ruled the Israelites after their kingdom broke apart.
4. Some women in Israelite society made great contributions to their history.

Key Terms and People

Judaism the religion of the Hebrews

Abraham the biblical father of the Hebrew people

Moses Hebrew leader who led the Israelites out of slavery in Egypt

Exodus the journey the Israelites made from Egypt to Canaan, led by Moses

Ten Commandments moral code of laws that God handed down to Moses

David former shepherd who became king after the death of Saul, Israel's first king

Solomon David's son; became king of the Israelites

Diaspora the dispersal of the Jews outside of Israel and Judah

Lesson Summary
ABRAHAM AND MOSES LEAD THEIR PEOPLE

A people called the Hebrews (HEE-brooz) appeared in Southwest Asia sometime between 2000 and 1500 BC. Their writings describe the laws of their religion, **Judaism** (JOO-dee-i-zuhm). The Hebrew Bible, or Torah, traces the Hebrews back to a man named **Abraham**. The Hebrew Bible says that God told Abraham to leave his home. God promised to lead him to a new land and to make his children into a mighty nation. Abraham moved to Canaan (KAY-nuhn) where the Hebrews lived for many years.

Some of Abraham's descendents, the Israelites, later moved to Egypt. In time, Egypt's ruler, the pharaoh, made them slaves. In the 1200s BC, God told a leader named **Moses** to lead the Israelites out of Egypt. Moses went to the pharaoh and demanded that the Israelites be freed.

> Circle the name of the people who appeared in Southwest Asia sometime between 2000 and 1500 BC.

> Underline the promise that God made to Abraham. Where did Abraham move?
>
> _____

Lesson 1, *continued*

The pharaoh agreed only after a series of plagues, or disasters, struck Egypt.

Moses led his people on a journey called the **Exodus**. The Israelites believed that they had been set free because God was watching over them. The Bible says that during this journey, God gave Moses two stone tablets with laws written on them. They were known as the **Ten Commandments**. According to them, the Israelites were to worship only one God and were to value human life, self-control, and justice. After 40 years in exile, the Israelites reached Canaan.

> **Why was Moses an important Israelite leader?**
> _____
> _____

> **What three basic values are emphasized in the Ten Commandments?**
> _____
> _____

KINGS UNITE THE ISRAELITES

Saul, after fighting the Philistines (FI-li-steenz), became the first king of Israel. After he died, a former shepherd named **David** became king. David was well-loved. He defeated the Philistines and other enemies. He captured the city of Jerusalem. It became Israel's new capital. David's son **Solomon** (SAHL-uh-muhn) became the next king around 965 BC. He was a strong king. He built a great temple in Jerusalem. It became the center of the Israelites' religious life.

> **Circle the names of the first three kings of Israel. Which king built a temple?**
> _____
> _____

INVADERS CONQUER AND RULE

Soon after Solomon's death in 930 BC, Israel split into two kingdoms, Israel and Judah (JOO-duh). The people of Judah were known as Jews. Over the centuries, the Jewish people were often conquered and enslaved. Jerusalem was conquered by the Greeks during the 330s BC. Judah regained independence for a time, but was conquered again in 63 BC, this time by the Romans. The dispersal of the Jews outside of Israel and Judah is known as the **Diaspora**.

Guided Reading Workbook

WOMEN IN ISRAELITE SOCIETY

Although men dominated Israelite society, some Israelite and Jewish women made great contributions to the culture.

CHALLENGE ACTIVITY

Critical Thinking: Make Inferences Write a set of ten commandments that reflects the responsibilities and rights of students and faculty for your school.

DIRECTIONS Read each sentence and fill in the blank with the word in the word pair that best completes the sentence.

1. After King Saul died, _____ became the new king of Israel. **(David/Solomon)**

2. _____ led the Israelites out of Egypt, which freed them from slavery under the pharaoh. **(Moses/Abraham)**

3. The _____, a code of moral laws, has helped shape the development of Israelite and Jewish society over time. **(Judaism/ Ten Commandments)**

4. The Hebrews trace their ancestry back to a man named _____. **(Abraham/David)**

DIRECTIONS Write three adjectives or a descriptive phrase to describe the term or person.

5. Diaspora _____

6. Exodus _____

7. Judaism _____

8. Solomon _____

9. Ten Commandments _____

The Hebrews and Judaism

Lesson 2

> **MAIN IDEAS**
> 1. Belief in God, commitment to education and justice, and observance of the law anchor Jewish society.
> 2. Jewish beliefs are listed in the Torah, the Hebrew Bible, and the Commentaries.
> 3. The Dead Sea Scrolls reveal many past Jewish beliefs.
> 4. The ideas of Judaism helped shape later cultures.

Key Terms and People

monotheism belief in only one god

Torah the sacred text of Judaism

synagogue Jewish house of worship

prophets people said to receive messages from God to be taught to others

Talmud commentaries, stories, and folklore recorded to explain Jewish laws

Dead Sea Scrolls writings by Jews who lived about 2,000 years ago

Lesson Summary
JEWISH BELIEFS ANCHOR THEIR SOCIETY

Jewish society is founded upon religion. Judaism's central concepts are belief in God, education, justice and righteousness, and observance of religious and moral law.

> Underline the four core values of Judaism.

Judaism is the oldest known religion to practice **monotheism**, the belief in only one God. The Hebrew name for God is YHWH. The Jews say their history was guided through God's relationship with Abraham, Moses, and other leaders. Moral and religious laws, believed to be handed down from God, have guided Jewish society throughout their history and continue to do so today.

> What is monotheism?
> _____
> _____

Besides the Ten Commandments, Jews believe that Moses recorded a whole set of laws governing Jewish behavior. These are called Mosaic laws. They set down rules for everything, including what to eat, when to work, and how to pray.

Guided Reading Workbook

Today, Orthodox Jews continue to follow all of the Mosaic laws. Reform Jews choose not to follow many of the ancient rules. Conservative Jews fall in between.

TEXTS LIST JEWISH BELIEFS

The laws and principles of Judaism are written down in sacred texts. The most important text is the **Torah**. The five books of the Torah record most of the laws and the history of Judaism until the death of Moses. Every **synagogue**, or place of Jewish worship, has at least one Torah.

Circle the name of the most important sacred Jewish text.

The Torah is one of the three parts of the Hebrew Bible, or Tanakh (tah-NAKH). The second part contains messages from **prophets**, people who are said to have received messages directly from God. The third part is a collection of poems, songs, stories, lessons, and histories.

The **Talmud** is a collection of commentaries, folktales, and stories written by scholars. These are intended to help people understand and analyze the laws described in the Hebrew Bible.

What is in the Talmud?
_____
_____
_____
_____

SCROLLS REVEAL PAST BELIEFS

Another set of ancient texts, the **Dead Sea Scrolls**, was discovered in 1947. These scrolls, written by Jewish scholars about 2,000 years ago, contain commentaries and stories, and they offer more information about ancient Jewish life.

JUDAISM AND LATER CULTURES

Jewish ideas helped shape two other major world religions, Christianity and Islam. In addition, the Ten Commandments are reflected in our laws and in modern society's rules of behavior.

CHALLENGE ACTIVITY

Critical Thinking: Draw Inferences Pretend you
are a writer contributing to a modern-day
Talmud of American life. Write a short story
illustrating how one of the Ten Commandments
is followed today.

DIRECTIONS On the line provided before each statement, write **T** if
a statement is true and **F** if a statement is false. If the statement is
false, change the underlined term to make the statement true. Write
the correct term on the line provided.

_____ 1. The <u>Talmud</u> is a sacred text of Judaism and one of the three parts of
the Hebrew Bible.

_____

_____ 2. Historians have learned much about the ancient laws and history of
Judaism by studying the <u>Torah</u>.

_____

_____ 3. Orthodox Jews strictly follow a set of laws, known as <u>Mosaic</u> law, that
guide many areas of their daily lives.

_____

_____ 4. <u>Prophets</u> are people who are said to have received messages from God
to be taught to others.

_____

_____ 5. Texts related to Judaism include the Torah, the Talmud, and the <u>Dead
Sea</u> Scrolls.

_____

DIRECTIONS Write a word or short phrase that has the same
meaning as the term given.

6. monotheism _____

7. sacred _____

8. synagogue _____

Guided Reading Workbook

The Hebrews and Judaism

MAIN IDEAS
1. Revolt, defeat, and migration led to great changes in Jewish culture.
2. Because Jews settled in different parts of the world, two cultural traditions formed.
3. Jewish traditions and holy days celebrate the history and religion of the Jews.

Key Terms and People

Zealots Jews who rebelled against their Roman rulers

rabbis teachers who guide Jews in their religious lives

Passover a time for Jews to remember the Exodus

High Holy Days the two most sacred Jewish holidays, Rosh Hashanah and Yom Kippur

Lesson Summary
REVOLT, DEFEAT, AND MIGRATION

The teachings of Judaism helped unite the ancient Jews. But many Jews were unhappy with the Roman rule of Jerusalem. Tensions increased. Some Jews refused to obey Roman officials. In AD 66, a group called the **Zealots** (ZE-luhts) led a rebellion against Rome. After four years of fierce fighting, the rebellion failed. The Jews' Second Temple of Jerusalem was destroyed in AD 70. The Romans put down another Jewish rebellion 60 years later. After this uprising, Jews were banned from living in Jerusalem, so they migrated to other parts of the world.

> **Why did the Zealots revolt?**
> _____
> _____
> _____
> _____

TWO CULTURAL TRADITIONS

Because Jews could not worship at a central temple anymore, their traditions changed. Everywhere Jews went, they built local temples. They also appointed **rabbis**, religious leaders responsible for teaching Judaism. Even with a similar culture and background, Jewish traditions grew differently depending on where they moved. Two major Jewish cultures developed that still exist today.

> **Underline the definition of** *rabbis* **in the summary.**

Lesson 3, *continued*

The Ashkenazim (ahsh-kuh-NAH-zuhm) are descended from Jews who moved to France, Germany, and Eastern Europe. These Jews maintained separate customs from the region's other residents. They even developed Yiddish, their own language.

The Sephardim (suh-FAHR-duhm) moved to Spain and Portugal. Unlike the Ashkenazim, these Jews mixed with their non-Jewish neighbors. This melding of language and culture produced a Jewish golden age in Spain and Portugal when many Jews contributed to artistic achievement and scientific discovery.

What was the main difference between the Ashkenazim and the Sephardim?
_____
_____
_____
_____

TRADITIONS AND HOLY DAYS

No matter where Jews live, common traditions and holy days help them maintain and celebrate their long history. Many of these holidays honor the Jews' freedom. **Passover**, for example, celebrates the Jews' flight from slavery in Egypt during the Exodus. Hanukkah commemorates the rededication of the Temple of Jerusalem during the Maccabbees' successful revolt against the Greeks in 160 BC.

The most important holidays are the **High Holy Days**. These days are Rosh Hashanah (rahsh uh-SHAH-nuh), which celebrates the Jewish New Year, and Yom Kippur (yohm ki-POOHR), when Jews ask God to forgive their sins.

What is the proper name for the Jewish New Year?
_____

CHALLENGE ACTIVITY

Critical Thinking: Draw Inferences Imagine that you are living in Jerusalem during Roman rule. Write a letter to your relatives explaining the difficulties the Zealots faced and why they rebelled.

Lesson 3, *continued*

| Hanukkah | High Holy Days | Masada | Passover |
| Rabbis | Rosh Hashanah | Yom Kippur | Zealots |

DIRECTIONS Choose the correct term from the word bank to replace the underlined phrase in each sentence below. Write the term in the space provided and then define the term in your own words.

1. The rebellion led by <u>this group</u> resulted in the destruction of the Second Temple of Jerusalem and in the death or enslavement of many Jews. _____
   Your definition: _____

2. <u>This event</u> commemorates the Jews' flight from slavery. _____.
   Your definition: _____

3. After the Romans banned Jews from Jerusalem, <u>these individuals</u> helped shape how Judaism was practiced for the next several centuries. _____
   Your definition: _____

4. During <u>this sacred period</u>, Jews celebrate the start of a new year in the Jewish calendar and ask God to forgive their sins. _____
   Your definition: _____
   _____

Guided Reading Workbook

Ancient Greece

MAIN IDEAS
1. Geography helped shape early Greek civilization.
2. Trading cultures developed in the Minoan and Mycenaean civilizations.
3. The Greeks created city-states for protection and security.

Key Terms and People

polis Greek word for city-state

acropolis a fortress atop a tall hill in the center of the city-states

Lesson Summary
GEOGRAPHY SHAPES GREEK CIVILIZATION

The Greeks lived on rocky, mountainous lands, located on a peninsula surrounded by the Mediterranean, Ionian, and Aegean seas. The peninsula has an irregular shape. Many islands lie off the mainland. This area was the home of one of the world's greatest civilizations.

The few small valleys and plains of Greece provided farmland, and that is where people settled. These communities were separated by steep mountains, so there was little contact between groups. The villages created separate governments.

Because they were surrounded by water, the Greeks became skilled shipbuilders and sailors. The Greeks were exposed to other cultures when they sailed to other lands.

> Underline the names of the three seas that surrounded the Greek peninsula.

> Why did separate governments develop in ancient Greece?
>
> _____
> _____
> _____
> _____
> _____

TRADING CULTURES DEVELOP

Many cultures settled and grew in early Greece. The earliest, with the greatest influence, were the Minoans and the Mycenaeans. By 2000 BC, these two cultures had built advanced societies on the island of Crete. The Minoans were known as the best shipbuilders of their time. They used ships mainly for trading purposes. A volcano that erupted in the 1600s BC may have led to the end of the Minoan civilization.

The Mycenaeans spoke the language that became Greek. While the Minoans were building ships, the Mycenaeans were building fortresses on the Greek mainland. The Mycenaeans eventually took over the trade routes once sailed by the Minoans. The Mycenaeans set up a powerful trading network on the Mediterranean and Black seas. In the 1200s BC, Mycenaean society also fell prey to earthquakes and invaders. Greece entered a period called the Dark Age.

> While the Minoans built
> _____ ,
> the Mycenaeans built
> _____ .

GREEKS CREATE CITY-STATES

After 300 years of war and disorder, communities began to band together for stability and protection. They created the **polis**, or city-state. This marked the beginning of the Greek classical era, a time when some city-states became more powerful.

The Greeks often built a city-state around a fortress perched atop a high hill called an **acropolis**. Walls surrounded many of these cities. Much of daily life centered on the agora, or marketplace, where politics and shopping shared the stage. As stability returned, some of the Greek city-states formed colonies in foreign lands. Early colonies included the locations of modern-day Istanbul in Turkey, Marseilles in France, and Naples in Italy. This created further independence for these city-states, and some city-states became great trading centers.

> What features of the polis made it a safe, protected place to live and conduct business?
>
> _____
> _____
> _____
> _____
> _____
> _____

CHALLENGE ACTIVITY

Critical Thinking: Make Inferences You are a leader of an ancient Greek polis dealing with all the same problems and circumstances the real city-states of the time faced. Write your own set of laws that would improve both security and quality of life for the citizens who live there.

Lesson 1, *continued*

DIRECTIONS Read each sentence and fill in the blank with the word in the word pair that best completes the sentence.

1. After the Dark Age, Greeks began to set up city-states and entered a period of great achievements known as Greece's _____ era. **(classical/peninsula)**

2. The town around the _____ was surrounded by walls for protection. **(acropolis/colony)**

3. The _____ often served as a central place for Greeks to meet and hold assemblies. **(acropolis/agora)**

4. The mainland of Greece is a _____, land surrounded by water on three sides. **(peninsula/polis)**

5. The Greek _____ provided security, stability, and identity to the people who lived there. **(acropolis/polis)**

DIRECTIONS Write a word that has a similar meaning to the term given.

6. acropolis _____

7. agora _____

8. polis _____

DIRECTIONS Write three adjectives or a descriptive phrase to describe the term given. _____

9. influence _____

10. peninsula _____

Guided Reading Workbook

Ancient Greece

 MAIN IDEAS
1. Aristocrats and tyrants ruled early Athens.
2. Athens created the world's first democracy.
3. Ancient democracy was different from modern democracy.

Key Terms and People

democracy type of government in which people rule themselves

aristocrats rich landowners

oligarchy government in which only a few people have power

aristocracy society ruled by rich landowners

citizens people with the right to participate in government

tyrant leader who rules by the use of force

Pericles Athenian leader who ruled at the height of Athenian democracy

Lesson Summary
ARISTOCRATS AND TYRANTS RULE

The city of Athens in Greece is the birthplace of **democracy**. Democracy is a form of a government in which people rule themselves. Athens was ruled first by kings, and then by an oligarchy of **aristocrats**, or rich landowners. Athenian society was also known as an **aristocracy** because only people in the highest social class had power. In the 600s BC, rebels tried to overthrow the aristocrats and failed. Several rulers followed. First was Draco, who was unpopular due to his overly strict laws. Next was Solon, who ruled that all free men were **citizens** who had a right to participate in government. Then Peisistratus, the first **tyrant,** became a leader of Athens by force. After he died, rebellious aristocrats regained control of the city of Athens.

> Circle two ways that Athens was ruled before democracy.

> Who was the first tyrant of Athens?
> _____

ATHENS CREATES DEMOCRACY

The leader Cleisthenes introduced democracy to Athens in 500 BC when he overthrew the aristocratic leaders by using popular support. Citizens had the right to participate in the assembly that created laws. Assemblies were held outdoors, and anyone could give a speech before voting. Often, either too many or not enough people would come to an assembly, so Athenians selected city officials to vote. Citizens gradually gained more power.

Athenian democracy reached its height with **Pericles**, who led the government from 460 to 429 BC. Democracy all but ended when Athens was conquered by Macedonia in the 330s BC. The Macedonian king wanted to make his own laws.

> **What do you think is the major disadvantage of allowing every citizen to participate in lawmaking?**
>
> _____
>
> _____
>
> _____
>
> _____

ANCIENT DEMOCRACY DIFFERS FROM MODERN DEMOCRACY

Although citizenship was very limited, Athens had a direct democracy, in which every citizen could participate and the majority ruled. The United States operates as a representative government, in which citizens elect people to represent them.

> **What type of democracy is practiced in the United States today?**
>
> _____
>
> _____

CHALLENGE ACTIVITY

Critical Thinking: Compare Create a chart showing the differences between direct and representative democracy.

Lesson 2, *continued*

DIRECTIONS On the line before each statement, write **T** if the statement is true and **F** if the statement is false. If the statement is false, change the underlined term to make the statement true. Then write the correct term on the line after the statement.

_____ 1. An <u>oligarchy</u> is a government in which only a few people have power.

_____

_____ 2. Greece is considered the birthplace of <u>democracy</u>, which is a type of government in which people rule themselves.

_____

_____ 3. Democracy in Athens reached its height under the rule of a brilliant elected leader named <u>Cleisthenes</u>.

_____

_____ 4. In the 590s BC, a leader named Solon ruled that all free men living in Athens were <u>aristocrats</u>.

_____

_____ 5. The oligarchy in Athens lasted until one noble overthrew the government and ruled it alone as a <u>tyrant</u>.

_____

DIRECTIONS Look at each set of vocabulary terms following each number. On the line provided, write the letter of the term that does not relate to the others.

_____ 6. a. democracy   b. oligarchy   c. tyranny   d. Pericles

_____ 7. a. oligarchy   b. aristocrats   c. democracy   d. aristocracy

Guided Reading Workbook

Ancient Greece

Lesson 3

MAIN IDEAS
1. The Spartans built a military society to provide security and protection.
2. The Athenians admired the mind and the arts in addition to physical abilities.
3. Sparta and Athens fought over who should have power and influence in Greece.

Key Terms and People

alliance an agreement to work together

Peloponnesian War a war between the two great Greek city-states of Athens and Sparta in the 400s BC

Lesson Summary
SPARTANS BUILD A MILITARY SOCIETY

Spartan life was dominated by the army. The city-state of Sparta's social system was created by a man named Lycurgus (ly-KUHR-guhs) after a slave revolt. He increased the military's role. Courage and strength were the highest values. Boys who were healthy at birth were trained from an early age to be soldiers. Boys ran, jumped, swam, and threw javelins to increase their strength. Men between the ages of 20 and 30 lived in army barracks and only occasionally visited their families. Spartan men stayed in the army until they turned 60.

Spartan men were often away at war, so Spartan women had more rights than other Greek women. Women owned much of the land in Sparta and ran their households. Women also learned how to run, jump, wrestle, and throw javelins. Spartans believed this would help women bear healthy children.

> **What were the highest values in Spartan society?**
> _____
> _____
> _____

> **Underline why Spartan women had more rights than other Greek women.**

Guided Reading Workbook

Sparta was ruled by two kings who jointly led the army. Elected officials ran Sparta's day-to-day activities and handled dealings between Sparta and other city-states. Slaves grew the city's crops and did many other jobs. Fear of the army kept slaves from rebelling.

ATHENIANS ADMIRE THE MIND

Sparta's main rival in Greece was Athens. Although Athens had a powerful military and valued physical training, the Athenians also prized education, clear thinking, and the arts. They believed that educated men made the best citizens.

> Underline the sentence that explains why the Athenians valued education.

Many Athenian students learned to read, write, and count as well as sing and play musical instruments. Boys from rich families often had private tutors who taught them philosophy, geometry, astronomy, and public speaking. Boys from poor families, however, did not receive much education, and very few girls were educated. Despite Athens's reputation for freedom and democracy, Athenian women had almost no rights at all.

> Who received the most education in the city-state of Athens and why?
>
> _____
> _____
> _____
> _____
> _____
> _____

SPARTA AND ATHENS FIGHT

After the Persian Wars, many Greek city-states joined an **alliance** to help defend one another and protect trade. With its navy protecting the islands, Athens was the most powerful member of the league. Soon Athenians began to treat other city-states as their subjects. In 431 BC, Sparta and other cities formed the Delian League and declared war on Athens. In the long **Peloponnesian War** that followed, the Athenians won at first but were forced to surrender in 404 BC. For about the next 30 years, the Spartans controlled nearly all of Greece, but resentment from other city-states led to a long period of war that weakened all of Greece and left it open to attack from outside.

> Circle the noun that describes the popular feeling that undermined the power of Sparta.

Guided Reading Workbook

CHALLENGE ACTIVITY

Critical Thinking: Make Inferences Imagine you
live in Sparta or Athens after the Persian Wars.
Write a poem or a song expressing how it feels to
live in that city-state.

| alliance | Athens | city-states | Delian League |
| influence | Peloponnesian League | Peloponnesian War | Sparta |

DIRECTIONS Use the vocabulary terms in the word list above to
write a summary of the conflicts that occurred between Athens and
Sparta.

_____

_____

_____

_____

_____

_____

_____

_____

DIRECTIONS Write three descriptive words or phrases that describe
each term.

1. Athens _____

2. Sparta _____

Ancient Greece

Lesson 4

MAIN IDEAS

1. The Greeks created myths to explain the world.
2. Ancient Greek literature provides some of the world's greatest poems and stories.
3. Greek literature lives on and influences our world even today.

Key Terms and People

mythology body of stories about gods or heroes that tries to explain how the world works

Homer author of two great epic poems, the *Iliad* and the *Odyssey*

Sappho most famous lyrical poet of ancient Greece

Aesop author of the world's most famous set of fables

fables short stories that offer lessons on living

Lesson Summary
MYTHS EXPLAIN THE WORLD

Instead of science, the ancient Greeks used **mythology**—stories about gods or heroes—to try to explain how the world works. The Greeks believed that the gods caused natural events, from the rising of the moon to thunderstorms. Everything was attributed to the gods, from disasters to daily events.

The Greeks believed that Demeter, the goddess of agriculture, caused the seasons. Hades, the god of the underworld, kidnapped Demeter's daughter. He eventually agreed to give her daughter back for half of the year. Because of Demeter's grief, when her daughter was not with her the plants did not grow, causing winter.

Some myths told not of gods but of heroes. Each city had its own hero, real or fictional, who would slay terrible monsters. The most famous Greek hero was Hercules. The Greeks loved to tell these stories.

> Underline what the Greeks believed to be caused by the gods.

> According to Greek mythology, which season was caused by Demeter not having her daughter?
>
> _____
>
> _____

Lesson 4, *continued*

ANCIENT GREEK LITERATURE

Greek writers produced great works of literature and the world's most famous stories. Among the earliest and most influential are the epic poems the *Iliad* and the *Odyssey* by the poet **Homer**. Scholars are not sure if Homer actually existed, but the poems are central to Greek lore and education. The *Iliad* tells the story of the last years of the Trojan War. The *Odyssey* describes the Greek hero Odysseus's long journey home after the war.

Other forms of literature were also popular. Lyric poetry, recited by the poet while playing the lyre, was especially prized. The most famous lyric poet was a woman, **Sappho**. Also popular were **fables**, or short stories that offer lessons on life. The most famous fable writer was **Aesop** (EE-sahp), who may have lived around 500 BC. Aesop's fables are still commonly told today.

If Homer did not exist, how do you think the *Iliad* and the *Odyssey* were composed?
_____
_____
_____
_____
_____

What is lyric poetry?
_____
_____

GREEK LITERATURE LIVES

Greek literature, language, and art have had a great influence on modern culture. The English language contains Greek expressions. A long journey, for example, is called an "odyssey" after Odysseus. Many places are named after Greek gods. Greek myths and stories have inspired painters, writers, and filmmakers for centuries.

Greeks created drama, or plays, as part of religious ceremonies to honor their gods and heroes. Greeks also were among the first to write about history, believing people learn from the past. One early historian, Thucydides, tried to be neutral, not taking sides, in his historical account of a war. Later historians often modeled their works on his.

Titans were large and powerful gods in Greek myth. What word in English is derived from this group of Greek gods?
_____

CHALLENGE ACTIVITY

Critical Thinking: Elaborate Greek literature has
influenced our modern culture. Write a
paragraph describing how Greek literature,
language, or art may have influenced you.

Achilles	Aesop	fables	Hercules
Homer	mythology	neutral	Zeus

DIRECTIONS Answer each question by writing a sentence that
contains at least one word from the word bank. Not all words
are used.

1. What is the modern expression that refers to a person's weak spot and is
   based on a figure from Greek mythology?

   _____

   _____

2. What was one way that Greek writers taught people important lessons about
   life?

   _____

   _____

3. How did the ancient Greeks explain weather, seasons, and natural disasters?

   _____

   _____

4. What famous Greek hero fought monsters and killed the nine-headed hydra?

   _____

   _____

5. What was special about the historical work of the Greek historian
   Thucydides?

   _____

   _____

   _____

Ancient Greece

Lesson 5

> **MAIN IDEA**
> 1. The Greeks made great contributions to the arts.
> 2. The teachings of Socrates, Plato, and Aristotle are the basis of modern philosophy.
> 3. In science, the Greeks made key discoveries in math, medicine, and engineering.

Key Terms and People

Socrates the first of the great Greek thinkers and teachers

Plato teacher and thinker, student of Socrates, and founder of the Academy

Aristotle philosopher who taught that people should live lives of moderation based on reason

reason clear and ordered thinking

Euclid great and influential mathematician

Hippocrates great Greek doctor who taught how to treat disease by understanding what caused illness

Lesson Summary

THE ARTS

The ancient Greeks were master artists. Their paintings and statues have been admired for thousands of years. Greek sculptors studied the human body, especially how it looks when it is moving. They used what they learned when they carved stone and marble statues. Greek artists painted detailed scenes on vases, pots, and other vessels. The remains of Greek architecture show how much care the Greeks took in designing their buildings so they would reflect the beauty and greatness of their cities.

> **Which three art forms are mentioned in this paragraph?**
> _____
> _____
> _____

PHILOSOPHY

The ancient Greeks worshipped gods and goddesses whose actions explained many of the mysteries of the world. But around 500 BC a few people began to think about other explanations.

We call these people philosophers. Philosophers believe in the power of the human mind to think, explain, and understand life.

> Underline the sentence that explains what philosophers believe in.

Three Greek philosophers' teachings are at the root of modern philosophy and science. These men thought about the world and searched for knowledge, wisdom, and truth. **Socrates** (SAHK-ruh-teez) believed that people must never stop looking for knowledge. He taught by asking questions. When people answered, he challenged their answers with more questions. This style of teaching is now called the Socratic method. His student **Plato** (PLAYT-oh) created a school called the Academy to which students, philosophers, and scientists could come to discuss ideas. Plato's student **Aristotle** (ar-uh-STAH-tuhl) taught that people should live lives of moderation, or balance. He believed that moderation was based on **reason.** Aristotle also made great advances in the field of logic, the process of making inferences.

> What would Socrates say about learning?
> _____
> _____
> _____
> _____

SCIENCE

Many of the rules we still use today to measure and calculate were first developed by Greek mathematicians like **Euclid** (YOO-kluhd), who is best known for his work in geometry. Greek doctors like **Hippocrates** (hip-AHK-ruh-teez) wanted to cure diseases and keep people healthy. He is known today for his ideas about how doctors should behave. Greek inventors also made many discoveries that are still in use, such as practical devices like water screws, which bring water up from a lower level to a higher one.

> Do you think doctors today have the same basic beliefs about medicine as Hippocrates did? Why or why not?
> _____
> _____
> _____
> _____
> _____
> _____
> _____

CHALLENGE ACTIVITY

Critical Thinking: Summarize Create a list showing contributions ancient Greeks made to modern culture. Include the name or names of people who are credited with each contribution.

DIRECTIONS On the line provided before each statement, write **T** if
a statement is true and **F** if a statement is false. If the statement is
false, write the correct term on the line after each sentence that
makes the sentence a true statement.

_____ 1. The <u>Parthenon</u>, a beautiful temple to the goddess Athena, was one of
the most impressive of all ancient Greek buildings.

_____

_____ 2. The Greek philosopher <u>Archimedes</u> taught by asking questions that
challenged people to think about their beliefs.

_____

_____ 3. The Greek philosopher <u>Plato</u> taught that people should live lives of
moderation, or balance, based on reason.

_____

_____ 4. The Greek scientist <u>Hippocrates</u> devoted his life to studying
mathematics and developed many of the geometry rules used today.

_____

DIRECTIONS Write three words or descriptive phrases that describe
each person.

5. Socrates _____

_____

6. Plato _____

_____

7. Aristotle _____

_____

8. Euclid _____

_____

The Hellenistic World

 MAIN IDEAS
1. Macedonia conquered Greece in the 300s BC.
2. Alexander the Great built an empire that united parts of Europe, Asia, and Egypt.
3. Alexander spread Greek cultural influences throughout his empire.

Key Terms and People

Philip II powerful king of Macedonia

phalanx a group of warriors who stood close together in a square

Alexander the Great king of Macedonia who built the largest empire the world had ever seen

Hellenistic name for the blended culture that developed in Alexander's empire

Lesson Summary
MACEDONIA CONQUERS GREECE

About 360 BC, **Philip II** of Macedonia invaded Athens and won easily. The rest of Greece surrendered. Philip's victory resulted from his military strategy and weaponry. For instance, he extended the Greek idea of the **phalanx** (FAY-langks) by giving each soldier spears longer than their opponents'. Philip planned to conquer Persia, but he was murdered in 336 BC and his throne passed to his 20-year-old son Alexander.

How was Philip II able to conquer Athens so easily?
_____
_____
_____
_____

ALEXANDER BUILDS AN EMPIRE

When Philip died, the people of the Greek city of Thebes rebelled. Alexander attacked Thebes and enslaved the Theban people. He used Thebes as an example of what would happen if any other Greek cities rebelled against him. Alexander went on to defeat the Persians time after time and to conquer Egypt. He became ruler of what had been the Persian empire. Before his death at 33 years of age, **Alexander the Great** (as he came to be called) had built an empire stretching from

How did Alexander respond to the Theban rebellion?
_____
_____
_____
_____

Asia Minor west to India and to Egypt in the south. This was the largest empire the world had ever seen. He ruled as an absolute dictator—whatever he said was law. With no individual rights under a dictatorship, Alexander often punished people with death. Leaders who governed poorly or were dishonest were executed.

SPREADING GREEK CULTURE

Alexander admired Greek culture and worked to spread Greek influence by founding cities in the lands he conquered. He modeled the cities after the cities of Greece, and he encouraged Greek settlers to move to these new cities. As a result, Greek became a common language throughout Alexander's empire. Even as he supported the spread of Greek culture, however, Alexander encouraged common people to keep their own customs and traditions. The new, blended culture that developed is called **Hellenistic.** It was not purely Greek. It combined elements of Persian, Egyptian, Syrian, and other cultures with Greek ideas.

Literature remained a popular art form during the Hellenistic period. Menander was the leading poet and dramatist of the Hellenistic period. He wrote over 100 plays, most of which were comedies. Another important and well-educated poet was Callimachus, who lived in the Egyptian city of Alexandria. Writers of this period wrote histories, biographies, and novels.

> Underline the sentence that explains why Greek became a common language throughout Alexander's empire.

> Why is Hellenistic culture called a "blended" culture?
> _____
> _____
> _____
> _____
> _____
> _____

CHALLENGE ACTIVITY

Critical Thinking: Make Inferences Write a short essay that characterizes the United States as a blended culture.

Guided Reading Workbook

Name _____ Class _____ Date_____

Alexander the Great	elements	Macedonians
Hellenistic	Persia	phalanx
Philip II	strategies	spears

DIRECTIONS Answer each question by writing a sentence that contains at least one word from the word bank.

1. How was Philip II able to defeat the Greeks?

_____

_____

_____

2. What advantage did the soldiers in Philip's army have?

_____

_____

_____

3. What Macedonian leader is considered one of the greatest conquerors in history? Why?

_____

_____

_____

4. What new blended culture developed in Alexander the Great's empire, and what did this culture combine?

_____

_____

_____

The Hellenistic World

MAIN IDEAS
1. Three powerful generals divided Alexander's empire among themselves, establishing Hellenistic Macedonia, Hellenistic Syria, and Hellenistic Egypt.
2. A uniform system of trade developed throughout the Hellenistic kingdoms, with a common language, culture, and coinage.

Key People

Antigonus a powerful general of Alexander's who became the king of Macedonia

Seleucus a powerful general who seized most of Alexander's Asian conquests

Ptolemy a powerful general of Alexander's who ruled Egypt and whose dynasty became the most powerful and wealthiest of Hellenistic kingdoms

Cleopatra VII the last and most famous Ptolemaic ruler of Egypt

Lesson Summary
THREE HELLENISTIC KINGDOMS

After Alexander died, there was no obvious heir to his kingdom. So his generals fought for power. The empire was divided among three generals.

Antigonus became the king of Alexander's homeland, Macedonia, which included Greece. It had the weakest government. Macedonia had trouble defending itself from the many revolts of the Greeks. Rome's armies conquered the Antigonid dynasty in the mid-100s BC.

Seleucus seized control of most of Alexander's Asian conquests, including Persia. This empire was larger than Macedonia and was difficult to control. It was spread out and was home to many different people with different customs. The capital was far from some parts of the kingdom, so people ignored the king. Seleucid rulers were eventually conquered by Rome in the 60s BC.

Ptolemy became ruler of Egypt. His dynasty, the Ptolemaic, was the most powerful and wealthiest of the Hellenistic kingdoms. He was called "pharaoh" to gain him the support of the

> Why were Rome's armies able to conquer the Antigonid dynasty?
> _____
> _____
> _____
> _____

> What problems existed in the Seleucid kingdom?
> _____
> _____
> _____
> _____
> _____
> _____
> _____

Egyptians. He ruled from Alexandria, one of the ancient world's greatest cities. It had the world's largest library and the Museum, a place for scholars and artists. Even this stable and prosperous kingdom, though, came into conflict with other powers, especially Rome. It lasted longer than the other kingdoms. But after the death of the last and most famous Ptolemaic ruler, **Cleopatra VII**, the Romans took control of Egypt.

> Underline the sentence that provides some reasons for Alexandria being considered a great city.

GOVERNMENT AND ECONOMY

Alexander had ruled without limits on his power, as did the Hellenistic rulers. Rule passed down within their families. Only men could be kings in Macedonia and the Seleucid kingdom. A few women became pharaohs in Egypt, such as Cleopatra VII.

> How was rule in Egypt different from rule in Macedonia and the Seleucid kingdom?
>
> _____
>
> _____

Hellenistic rulers relied on Greek advisors. Together, they strengthened their economies, built and repaired roads and irrigation systems, promoted manufacturing and trade, and supported the arts. Large cities grew as kings became wealthy from the taxes.

Throughout the Hellenistic region, the people followed a uniform system of trade. They shared a common culture and used a form of Greek as their common language. They continued to use standard coins from Alexander's time. They built trade networks with other civilizations. For example, China could send silk to the Hellenistic kingdoms, and they could send other goods back to China.

> What made trade so successful throughout the Hellenistic region?
>
> _____
>
> _____
>
> _____
>
> _____
>
> _____

CHALLENGE ACTIVITY

Critical Thinking: Make Judgments Consider the three Hellenistic kingdoms Alexander's successors ruled. Choose the kingdom that you believe was the most successful. Write a short essay that supports your choice.

Antigonus	Cleopatra VII
Ptolemy	Seleucus

DIRECTIONS Answer each question by writing a sentence that contains at least one word from the word bank.

1. Who was a female pharaoh who was the last and the most famous ruler of Egypt?

   _____

   _____

2. Who took control of most of Alexander's Asian conquests?

   _____

   _____

3. Who formed the most powerful and wealthiest of Hellenistic kingdoms?

   _____

   _____

4. Who became king of Macedonia?

   _____

   _____

DIRECTIONS Use the vocabulary terms from the lesson to write a short summary of the Hellenistic World after Alexander.

_____

_____

_____

_____

_____

_____

_____

The Hellenistic World

Lesson 3

> **MAIN IDEAS**
> 1. Greek-influenced culture was most noticeable in the cities, while rural areas tended to be more traditional.
> 2. Hellenistic art and architecture demonstrated Greek influences but had their own unique touches.

Key People

Aristarchus an astronomer who was the first person to propose that the earth moves around the sun

Lesson Summary
SOCIETY AND DAILY LIFE

Alexander introduced Greek customs into his empire, but he did not force people to follow them. So his kingdoms had a blended Hellenistic, or Greek-inspired, culture. Hellenistic Egypt was a blend of Greek and traditional Egyptian cult...

Greek influence was found in cities. The Greek language was used for government. People followed Greek-type laws. Buildings resembled ones found in Greek city-states. The upper class wore Greek-style clothing and followed Greek philosophy.

Alexandria, Egypt, was an example of a Greek-style Hellenistic city. It had buildings that reflected Greek taste and technological skill. The Pharos, a lighthouse more than 350 feet tall, towered over the city. It was one of the wonders of the ancient world. Alexandria also had the greatest collection of Greek and Hellenistic knowledge in its library.

Rural areas showed little Greek influence, though. People spoke their own native languages and followed their own religions. Their dress and buildings remained the same. These areas followed traditional Egyptian laws.

> Why did Alexander's kingdoms have a Greek-inspired, or blended, Hellenistic culture?
> _____
> _____
> _____
> _____

> How were rural areas different from Hellenistic cities?
> _____
> _____
> _____
> _____
> _____
> _____

In Greek city-states, women had few rights. Over time, women in Hellenistic culture could be educated, own property, and run businesses.

CULTURE AND ACHIEVEMENTS

Hellenistic art and architecture were inspired by Greek works. However, artists added their own unique style. For example, Hellenistic buildings were larger than Greek buildings had been. These large buildings were symbols of the rulers' power.

> Underline the sentence that offers a reason why Hellenistic buildings were so large.

Hellenistic artists wanted their works to appear more natural than Greek works. A Greek statue might show a formal pose such as a king seated on a throne. In contrast, a Hellenistic sculpture might show a subject in an active and natural pose.

Religion inspired artistic expression in the Ptolemaic kingdom. The people worshipped both Greek and Egyptian gods, so artists made statues of both sets of gods. Hellenistic philosophers considered ways people could be happy and other worldly issues. Diogenes founded Cynicism, which said people should live according to nature. Pyrrho founded Skepticism, which said people can never know how things really are. Epicurus founded Epicureanism, which said people should avoid pain and pursue pleasure. Zeno founded Stoicism, which said that all people have a role to play in society.

> Hellenistic artists made statues of both Greek and Egyptian gods. What does this fact indicate?
>
> _____
> _____
> _____

Some Hellenistic thinkers were interested in the physical world, so they studied science. They conducted experiments and invented items to make people's lives easier. The greatest Hellenistic inventor, Archimedes, created a device to help farmers bring water uphill to their fields. Some scientists made advances in mathematics and astronomy. Euclid described basic ideas about geometry. Astronomer **Aristarchus** first proposed that the earth moves around the sun.

> What made Aristarchus an important Hellenistic scientist?
>
> _____
> _____
> _____
> _____

CHALLENGE ACTIVITY

Critical Thinking: Contrast Hellenistic art and architecture took its inspiration from the Greeks. However, the Hellenistic style incorporated its own ideas. Write a short essay that describes what made Hellenistic works different from Greek style.

DIRECTIONS Write a word or descriptive phrase to describe each place, term, group, or person.

1. Greek-style Hellenistic city _____

_____

_____

2. Hellenistic rural areas _____

_____

_____

3. Hellenistic women _____

_____

_____

4. Hellenistic art _____

_____

5. The Pharos _____

_____

_____

6. Archimedes_____

_____

_____

7. Aristarchus _____

_____

8. Hellenistic philosophers _____

_____

Ancient Rome

MAIN IDEAS
1. The geography of Italy made land travel difficult but helped the Romans prosper.
2. Ancient historians were very interested in Rome's legendary history.
3. Once a monarchy, Rome created a republic.

Key Terms and People

Aeneas great Trojan hero who fled Troy for Italy in a journey told in Virgil's *Aeneid*

Romulus and Remus legendary twin brothers who are said to have founded Rome

republic government in which people elect leaders to govern them

dictator ruler with almost absolute power, elected during time of war

Cincinnatus famous dictator who defeated a powerful enemy and then resigned his powers

plebeians common people of Rome

patricians powerful nobles of Rome

Lesson Summary

THE GEOGRAPHY OF ITALY

Rome grew from a small town on the Tiber River to become a great power. Rome conquered Greece, Egypt, and Asia Minor. Rome's central location and good climate were factors in its success. Because most of Italy is surrounded by water, Romans could easily travel by sea. The mountains in the north made it difficult to travel over land, so it was hard for others to invade. The warm dry weather resulted in high crop yields, so the Romans had plenty of food.

> How did Italy's geography help the rise of Rome?
> _____
> _____
> _____
> _____

ROME'S LEGENDARY ORIGINS

Rome's beginnings are a mystery. Some ruins suggest that people lived there as early as 800 BC. Romans wanted a glorious past, so they created stories and legends about their history.

> Why did the Romans make up stories and legends about their history?
> _____
> _____

The Romans believed their history began with the great Trojan hero **Aeneas** (i-NEE-uhs). Aeneas fled Troy when the Greeks destroyed the city during the Trojan War. He formed an alliance with a people called the Latins and went to Italy. This story is told in the *Aeneid* (i-NEE-id), an epic poem written by a poet named Virgil (VUHR-juhl) around 20 BC.

According to legend, Rome was founded by twin brothers, **Romulus** (RAHM-yuh-luhs) and **Remus** (REE-muhs). Romulus killed Remus. Then he built Rome and became its first king. Historians believe Rome was founded sometime between 800 and 700 BC. Early Rome was ruled by kings until 509 BC.

> **Which of the two brothers named the city of Rome after himself?**
> _____
> _____

THE EARLY REPUBLIC

The Romans created a **republic** so people could elect leaders to govern them. They voted once a year to prevent any one person from having too much power. However, most officials were wealthy, so other people had little say in the republic.

Rome faced many challenges, such as being at war with nearby countries. To lead the country during war, the Romans chose **dictators**, rulers with almost absolute power. Dictators stayed in power for only six months. The most famous dictator was **Cincinnatus** (sin-suh-NAT-uhs), a farmer elected to defeat a major enemy. He resigned as dictator right after the war and went back to his farm.

Within Rome, the **plebeians**, or common people, worked for change. Only the city's **patricians**, the wealthy citizens, could be elected to rule Rome. When the plebeians elected their own officials, the patricians changed the government to avoid a split.

> **Why do you think Rome's patricians were so concerned when the plebeians elected their own council?**
> _____
> _____
> _____

CHALLENGE ACTIVITY

Critical Thinking: Summarize Imagine you are a Roman plebeian. Write a campaign speech saying why people should elect you to office—even though your position has no official power. Your speech should be historically accurate.

DIRECTIONS On the line provided before each statement, write **T** if a statement is true and **F** if a statement is false. If the statement is false, write the correct term on the line after each sentence that makes the sentence a true statement.

_____ 1. According to legend, <u>Cincinnatus</u> was chosen as dictator to lead the Roman army and quickly defeated his foes.

_____

_____ 2. The Romans chose <u>patricians</u> to lead the city during difficult wars; however, these officials could remain in power for only six months.

_____

_____ 3. <u>Romulus</u> was a legendary hero from Troy who fled to Italy and allied himself with a people called the Latins.

_____

_____ 4. In a <u>republic</u>, people elect leaders to represent them in government.

_____

_____ 5. The richer, more powerful citizens of Rome were called <u>patricians</u> and were originally the only ones who could be elected to office.

_____

_____ 6. <u>Plebeians</u> were the common people of Rome, a group that wanted more of a say in how Rome was run.

_____

_____ 7. A ruler with almost unlimited power is called a <u>dictator</u>.

_____

_____ 8. After <u>Cincinnatus</u> killed his brother, he named the city they built after himself.

_____

Ancient Rome

MAIN IDEAS
1. Roman government was made up of three parts that worked together to run the city.
2. Roman life was shaped by laws, government, and social order.
3. Written laws helped keep order in Rome.
4. The late republic period saw the growth of territory and trade.
5. Rome expanded its territory by conquering other lands.

Key Terms and People

magistrates elected officials

consuls two most powerful elected officials

Roman Senate council of wealthy and powerful Romans that advised officials

majority rule the largest group has the power to decide government actions

veto to prohibit an official action

Latin language spoken by the ancient Romans

checks and balances methods of balancing power

Forum Rome's public meeting place

legions groups of up to 6,000 soldiers

Punic Wars a series of wars between Rome and Carthage

Hannibal brilliant Carthaginian general who attacked the city of Rome

Lesson Summary
ROMAN GOVERNMENT

During the 400s BC, so the plebeians did not overthrow the government, the patricians created positions for them. A three-part, or tripartite, government was formed. First, there were elected officials, or **magistrates**. The two most powerful magistrates were **consuls.** The second part was the **Roman Senate,** a council of wealthy and powerful Romans that advised leaders. The third part was assemblies and tribunes. The assemblies' primary job was to elect magistrates. The tribunes governed by **majority rule**, so the group with the most members made the decisions. They could

> **Why might the Romans have created a tripartite government?**
>
> _____
> _____
> _____

> **Underline the name given to the most powerful magistrates in Rome.**

veto, or prohibit, government actions. *Veto* means
"I forbid" in **Latin**, the Romans' language.
Checks and balances kept any part from being
too powerful.

| Underline what the word *veto* means in Latin. |

WRITTEN LAWS KEEP ORDER

Rome's officials followed the rule of law, the
belief that all people must follow set rules. In
450 BC, Rome's law code was written on twelve
tablets and displayed in the **Forum**, Rome's public
meeting place. The Law of the Twelve Tables
became the basis of Roman law.

| What was the official name of Rome's first set of written laws? _____ _____ |

LIFE IN ANCIENT ROME

Women in ancient Rome ran the household and
took care of children. Children played games and
had pets. Generally, only the children in rich
families went to school.

The Roman Forum was the heart of Rome.
Government buildings and temples were there.

GROWTH OF TERRITORY AND TRADE

Roman territory grew as the Romans fought off
attacks. Rome's soldiers were organized into
legions, or groups of up to 6,000 men. The army
could fight together or break up into smaller
groups. This contributed to Rome's success.

Trade grew around Rome. Rome coined copper
and silver money, which was used in the region.

| What might be the military advantage of an army with both small units and large units? _____ _____ _____ _____ |

ROME GROWS BEYOND ITALY

The Roman army fought the **Punic Wars** with
Carthage, the capital of a Phoenician civilization.
Carthage's brilliant general **Hannibal** led an
attack, but Rome conquered Carthage. It also
took over Gaul, Greece, and parts of Asia. The
Romans adopted much of the Greek culture.

| How did the Romans benefit from conquering Greece? _____ _____ _____ _____ |

Guided Reading Workbook

CHALLENGE ACTIVITY

Critical Thinking: Evaluate Use reference sources
to find some Roman laws. Rewrite any laws you
think are unfair. Then explain why you made the
changes. Discuss whether those laws should apply
today.

checks and balances	consuls	Forum	Hannibal
Latin	legions	magistrates	majority rule
Punic Wars	rule of law	Roman Senate	veto

DIRECTIONS Read each sentence and fill in the blank with a word
from the word bank that best completes the sentence.

1. The first tables of Rome's written law code were displayed in the public
   square called the _____.

2. The tribunes had the ability to _____, or prohibit, actions
   by other government officials.

3. Rome's elected officials were called _____.

4. Through the use of _____, one part of government
   cannot become more powerful than other parts of the government.

5. The most powerful officials in Rome were called _____.

6. The Romans' language was _____.

7. The _____ was a council of wealthy and powerful
   Romans that advised the city's leaders.

8. The brilliant general from Carthage who led an attack against Rome during
   the Punic Wars was _____.

9. Rome's soldiers were organized into _____, which were
   groups of up to 6,000 men.

10. The largest group of tribunes had the power to decide government actions
    because that part of government was governed by _____.

11. Wars fought by the Roman army against Carthage were the
    _____.

12. The belief that all people must follow an established set of rules is known as
    the _____.

MAIN IDEAS
1. Several crises struck the republic in later years.
2. As Rome descended into chaos, many called for change in government.
3. Julius Caesar rose to power and became the sole ruler of Rome.
4. Augustus became Rome's first emperor after defeating Caesar's killers and his own former allies.

Key Terms and People

Gaius Marius consul and general who encouraged poor people to join the army, creating a force more loyal to him than to Rome

Lucius Cornelius Sulla rival of Marius who raised his own army to defeat Marius and take control of Rome

Spartacus slave and former gladiator who led an uprising of slaves

Cicero a gifted philosopher and orator

orator a public speaker

Julius Caesar Roman general who became dictator for life

Pompey a powerful man in Rome who fought against the Roman Senate

Brutus a young Senator who was once a friend and ally of Caesar's

Marc Antony Caesar's former assistant who took control of Roman politics

Augustus the first emperor of Rome

Cleopatra the queen of Egypt

Lesson Summary
CRISES STRIKE THE REPUBLIC

As Rome's territory grew, so did its problems. Some leaders tried to ease tensions between the rich and poor, but wealthy citizens opposed their ideas. **Gaius Marius**, a consul, encouraged poor people to join the army. The purpose of his decision was to keep poor citizens happy. The troops became more loyal to Marius than to Rome. Then **Lucius Cornelius Sulla** also raised an army. He and Marius fought, which led to civil war. Sulla killed Marius and became dictator. A former gladiator, **Spartacus**, led a slave uprising. He was eventually killed.

> **Why do you think the poor and unemployed respected Gaius Marius?**
>
> _____
> _____
> _____
> _____

> **What effect did conflicts and a slave uprising have on Rome?**
>
> _____
> _____

Lesson 3, *continued*

THE CALL FOR CHANGE

Rome in the 70s BC was dangerous. Generals and politicians went to war to gain more power. People who were unemployed rioted for food. Some Romans tried to stop the chaos in the government. For example, **Cicero**, an **orator**, asked Romans to limit the generals' power and return power to the Senate. But Rome's government stayed the same.

> **What actions did Cicero ask Romans to take?**
> _____
> _____
> _____

CAESAR'S RISE TO POWER

Then another powerful general, **Julius Caesar**, made an agreement with **Pompey**, a powerful Roman, to fight the Senate. Eventually, Caesar became dictator for life. People resented his rise to power. On March 15 in 44 BC, a group of senators stabbed him to death. **Brutus**, a young senator and former ally of Caesar's, was one of the attackers.

AUGUSTUS THE EMPEROR

Caesar's former assistant, **Marc Antony,** and Octavian, later renamed Augustus, took charge of Roman politics. They defeated Caesar's killers, who then killed themselves. Octavian returned to Italy while Antony headed east to fight Rome's enemies. Antony met **Cleopatra**, the queen of Egypt, and the two fell in love. Octavian and Antony soon became enemies. In 31 BC, Octavian defeated Antony's fleet. Antony escaped and returned to Cleopatra. They killed themselves to avoid capture. Then Octavian ruled Rome. He claimed that he was giving his power to the Senate. But he took the name **Augustus** and became the Roman emperor.

> **Underline the name of the person with whom Antony fell in love.**

> **Who was Augustus and how did he come to power?**
> _____
> _____
> _____
> _____
> _____
> _____
> _____

Guided Reading Workbook

CHALLENGE ACTIVITY

Critical Thinking: Make Inferences Spartacus's
rebellion had an impact on Roman history. Use
the Internet to learn more about it. Then write an
essay evaluating how one person can affect the
course of history, using Spartacus as an example.

DIRECTIONS Read each sentence and fill in the blank with the
name in the pair that best completes the sentence.

1. Slaves led by _____ fought against the Roman army but
   were eventually defeated. **(Cicero/Spartacus)**

2. To help grow an army, _____ encouraged poor people to
   join the army. **(Lucius Cornelius Sulla/Gaius Marius)**

3. In hopes of returning power to the Senate, _____ asked
   Romans to limit the generals' power. **(Cicero/Pompey)**

4. _____ became dictator for life, but was eventually stabbed
   to death on March 15 in 44 BC. **(Brutus/Julius Caesar)**

5. After civil war, _____ named himself dictator of Rome.
   (Spartacus/Lucius Cornelius Sulla)

6. The former ally of Caesar, _____, betrayed Caesar when
   he joined other senators in attacking the ruler. **(Brutus/Marc Antony)**

7. Caesar's former assistant who took control of Roman politics and then fell in
   love with the queen of Egypt was _____. **(Octavian/Marc
   Antony)**

8. _____ changed his name from Octavian when he became
   the Roman emperor. **(Augustus/Julius Caesar)**

DIRECTIONS Look at each set of three vocabulary terms following
each number. On the line provided, write the letter of the term that
does not relate to the others.

_____ 9. a. Gaius Marius   b. Lucius Cornelius Sulla   c. Spartacus

_____ 10. a. Julius Caesar   b. Cicero   c. Augustus

Ancient Rome

MAIN IDEAS
1. The Roman Empire expanded to control the entire Mediterranean world.
2. Trade increased in Rome, both within the empire and with other people.
3. The Pax Romana was a period of peace and prosperity in the cities and the country.
4. The Romans were very religious and worshipped many gods.

Key Terms and People

Hadrian the emperor under whom the Romans conquered most of the island of Britain

provinces the areas outside of Italy that the Romans controlled

currency money

Pax Romana the Roman Peace, a peaceful period in Rome's history

villas country homes belonging to rich Romans

Lesson Summary
THE EMPIRE EXPANDS

Rome ruled most of the Mediterranean world when it became an empire. Within 150 years it controlled large areas of Europe, Africa, and Asia. The empire expanded through military might. It expanded to control hostile neighbors and prevent attacks. It also conquered for economic reasons, because conquered people had to pay taxes. In addition, many territories had gold, good farmland, and other resources.

The empire grew after Augustus died. By the early 100s, the Romans had taken over Gaul and much of central Europe. By the time of the emperor **Hadrian**, the Romans had conquered most of Britain. Its people, the Celts, had fought fiercely but lost. The Romans had also taken over Asia Minor, the eastern coast of the Mediterranean, and all of the northern African coast. Romans called the Mediterranean *Mare Nostrum*, meaning "Our Sea."

> Underline the sentence that tells the areas that Rome controlled.

> What are three reasons why the empire expanded?
>
> _____
> _____
> _____
> _____
> _____
> _____

Guided Reading Workbook

TRADE INCREASES

As the empire expanded, Romans wanted foreign goods. Traders went to the **provinces** to bring back metals, cloth, and food. In return, the Romans traded jewelry, glass, and clothing. Traders went to eastern Africa, India, and what is now Vietnam for other goods. Some went to China for silk. Romans used money, or **currency.** The empire had a uniform currency so trade could grow.

> **What did traders find in the provinces?**
> _____

THE PAX ROMANA

The **Pax Romana**, or Roman Peace, lasted about 200 years. It was a time of peace and prosperity, and the population grew. An effect of the time was an improvement in the people's quality of life.

Many people in cities were wealthy, but others lived in crowded apartment buildings. Many people lived in rural areas and were farmers. Some spoke languages other than Latin and did not follow Roman customs. **Villas**, or country homes, were scattered among the farms. Wealthy Romans used villas when they wanted a break from the city.

> **Why do you think a uniform currency helped trade grow?**
> _____
> _____
> _____

ROMANS ALLOW MANY RELIGIONS

The Romans were religious. Myths about Rome's founding and rulers often connected past rulers to a god or goddess. Many of Rome's most popular gods came from people they had conquered. For example, many Romans worshipped Greece's Olympian gods because they had learned about Greek mythology. These gods became Rome's main gods, but with different names. Roman mythology influences culture today, as evidenced by our planets being named after Roman gods.

> **Where did many of Rome's most popular gods originate?**
> _____

> **Underline a way in which Roman mythology influences culture today.**

CHALLENGE ACTIVITY

Critical Thinking: Elaborate Use reference sources
to find out more about Hadrian. Write an essay
describing his achievements and their effect on
the Roman Empire.

DIRECTIONS Write a descriptive phrase to describe each term.

1. Hadrian _____

    _____

2. provinces _____

    _____

3. currency _____

    _____

4. Pax Romana _____

    _____

5. villas _____

    _____

DIRECTIONS Use at least three of the vocabulary words **provinces,**
Hadrian, villas, currency, and **Pax Romana** to write a letter that
relates to the lesson.

_____

_____

_____

_____

_____

_____

_____

_____

Ancient Rome

MAIN IDEAS
1. Many problems threatened the Roman Empire, leading one emperor to divide it in half.
2. Barbarians invaded Rome in the 300s and 400s.
3. Many factors contributed to Rome's fall.

Key Terms and People

Diocletian emperor who divided the Roman Empire into two parts

Clovis Frankish king who built a huge kingdom in Gaul

Attila fearsome Hun leader who attacked Rome's eastern empire

corruption decay in people's values

Lesson Summary

PROBLEMS THREATEN THE EMPIRE

At its height, the Roman Empire included all the land around the Mediterranean Sea. But by the end of the 100s, emperors had to give up some land.

Rome had to defend itself from attacks from the north and the east. Problems came from within the empire, too. Disease killed many people. Taxes were high. Food was scarce because many farmers went to war. To increase food production, Germanic farmers were invited to work on Roman lands, but they were not loyal to Rome.

The emperor **Diocletian** took power in the late 200s. He divided the empire and ruled the east while a co-emperor ruled the west. The emperor Constantine reunited the empire. He moved the capital from Rome to Constantinople in the east. Constantinople had strategic importance because trade routes passed through it. Also, the city was hard to attack because it could be reached by land from only one direction.

> Name three problems facing the Roman Empire in the late 100s.
>
> _____
> _____
> _____
> _____

> Which emperor divided the Roman Empire? Which emperor reunited it?
>
> _____
> _____

BARBARIANS INVADE ROME

Once the capital moved to the east, barbarians attacked Roman territory in the north. During the late 300s, a fierce group from Central Asia called the Huns began attacking a group called the Goths. The Goths were forced into Roman territory. The Roman rulers kept the Goths in control and even paid them not to attack. However in the end, the Goths destroyed Rome.

After the destruction of Rome, the Vandals invaded Spain. The Angles, Saxons, and Jutes invaded Britain. The Franks invaded Gaul. The Frankish king **Clovis**, who was a Christian, was one of the most powerful German kings. He built a large kingdom in Gaul. Meanwhile, the Huns were under a new leader named **Attila**. He was a brilliant leader and raided Roman territory in the east. Rome's leaders were too weak to survive the attacks. In 476, a barbarian leader overthrew the Roman emperor and declared himself king. This ended the western empire.

> What role might the Huns have played in the Goths' destruction of Rome?
> _____
> _____
> _____
> _____

> Underline the name of the leader of the Huns.

FACTORS IN ROME'S FALL

Barbarian invasions are often considered the cause of Rome's decline. However, the vast size of the empire contributed to its fall as well. Its government suffered from **corruption**, or the decay of people's values. As problems continued, wealthy landowners left Rome. Life became more difficult for those who remained. The population decreased, and schools closed. However, taxes and prices soared, so more people became poor. By the end of the 400s, Rome was not the city it had once been. The empire collapsed around it.

> What are two factors that led to the weakening of the Roman Empire?
> _____
> _____
> _____

CHALLENGE ACTIVITY

Critical Thinking: Evaluate Do you think the rulers of the Roman Empire could have done anything to stop the empire's collapse? Write a one-page essay explaining your answer.

Attila	Clovis
corruption	Diocletian

DIRECTIONS Answer each question by writing a sentence that contains at least one word from the word bank.

1. Who divided the Roman Empire in the late 200s?

   _____

   _____

2. Who was the fearsome leader of the Huns?

   _____

   _____

3. What do we call the decay of people's values?

   _____

   _____

4. Who was the Frankish king who built a huge kingdom in Gaul?

   _____

   _____

DIRECTIONS Look at each set of vocabulary terms following each number. On the line provided, write the letter of the term that does not relate to the others.

_____ 5. a. Constantine   b. Diocletian   c. Clovis

_____ 6. a. Franks   b. Attila   c. Huns

Ancient Rome

MAIN IDEAS
1. The Romans looked for ways to use science and engineering to improve their lives.
2. Roman architecture and art were largely based on Greek ideas.
3. Roman literature and language have influenced how people write and speak.
4. Roman law serves as a model for modern law codes around the world.
5. Romans made important contributions to philosophy and history.

Key Terms and People

Galen Greek doctor who lived in the Roman Empire in the AD 100s

aqueduct a raised channel used to carry water from mountains into cities

Virgil an author who wrote a great epic about the founding of Rome, the *Aeneid*

Ovid a poet who wrote about Roman mythology

satire style of writing that pokes fun at people or society

Romance languages the languages that developed from Latin, including Italian, French, Spanish, Portuguese, and Romanian

civil law a legal system based on a written code of laws

Lesson Summary
ROMAN SCIENCE AND ENGINEERING

Romans used engineering and science for practical purposes so they could improve their lives. They studied stars to produce a calendar. They studied plants to grow better crops. A Greek surgeon living in the empire, **Galen**, made discoveries about the body. Doctors based their ideas on his work for centuries. The Romans developed materials such as cement to make their structures last. They used arches in **aqueducts,** or channels that carry water from mountains to cities. Builders combined the arch to create a vault, a set of arches that supports a building's roof. They created large, open spaces within buildings. Roman buildings were larger than any created before.

> For what reason did the Romans use engineering and science?
>
> _____
>
> _____
>
> _____

> Underline the sentence that explains what helped Roman buildings last a long time.

Name _____ Class _____ Date _____

ARCHITECTURE AND ART

Roman architecture was influenced by earlier Greek designs. Similar to the Greeks, Romans used columns to make public buildings look stately and impressive. However, Roman engineering allowed them to create much larger buildings.

Roman artists used mosaics for decoration on walls or floors. Frescoes also decorated walls. Roman sculptures were either original or copies of older Greek works. Since many original Greek works were destroyed, Roman copies provided the world with knowledge of the Greek masterpieces.

How did Roman engineering improve on Greek architecture?
_____
_____
_____
_____
_____

LITERATURE AND LANGUAGE

Virgil wrote a great epic, the *Aeneid*, about the founding of Rome. **Ovid** wrote poems about Roman mythology. Romans excelled in **satire**, writing that pokes fun at people or society. Many works served as models for modern works. Roman poets wrote in Latin. Today, languages that developed from Latin are called **Romance languages** because they share many elements with each other and with Latin.

What might have happened if the Romans had not been influenced by Greek sculptures?
_____
_____
_____
_____

THE BEGINNINGS OF CIVIL LAW

Civil law, a legal system based on a written code of laws, was inspired by Roman law, which was enforced throughout the empire. Most European nations today are ruled by civil law.

Why do you think civil law continues today in most of Europe?
_____
_____
_____

PHILOSOPHY AND HISTORY

Greek philosophy and the way Greeks wrote about history influenced the Romans. They also studied about their own history. They documented the way the republic and the empire changed over time.

CHALLENGE ACTIVITY

Critical Thinking: Make Judgments Which of the following was the greatest Roman contribution to today's world: engineering, science, architecture, poetry, language, or law? Write a speech defending your view.

DIRECTIONS Match the terms in the first column with the correct definition from the second column by placing the letter of the correct definition in the space provided before each term.

_____ 1. civil law

_____ 2. Galen

_____ 3. satire

_____ 4. Romance languages

_____ 5. Virgil

_____ 6. aqueduct

_____ 7. vault

_____ 8. Ovid

a. style of writing that pokes fun at people or society

b. author who wrote a great epic about the founding of Rome

c. Greek doctor who lived in the Roman Empire and made discoveries about the body

d. a set of arches that supports the roof of a building

e. a legal system based on a written code of laws

f. poet who wrote about Roman mythology

g. a raised channel used to carry water from mountains into cities

h. the languages that developed from Latin

DIRECTIONS Look at each set of vocabulary terms following each number. On the line provided, write the letter of the term that does not relate to the others.

_____ 9. a. Galen   b. Virgil   c. Ovid

_____ 10. a. vault   b. aqueduct   c. satire

The Growth of Christianity

Lesson 1

MAIN IDEAS
1. The Romans allowed many religions to be practiced in their empire.
2. Jews and Romans clashed over religious and political ideas.
3. The roots of Christianity had appeared in Judea by the end of the first century BC.

Key Terms and People

Christianity religion based on the life and teachings of Jesus of Nazareth

Jesus of Nazareth founder of Christianity

Messiah leader Jews believed would return and restore the greatness of Israel

John the Baptist famous Jewish prophet who traveled throughout Judea to announce the Messiah was coming

Lesson Summary
ROMAN IDEAS ABOUT RELIGION

Roman religion had many gods, but the Roman Empire did allow most conquered people to keep their own religions. The empire often built temples to honor Roman gods. These structures were called pantheons. Romans also built temples to the gods of new religions, so religious knowledge spread through the empire.

> **Which two groups of gods had temples built for them?**
> _____
> _____
> _____

JEWS AND ROMANS CLASH

Roman leaders thought Judaism was a problem for both religious and political reasons. The Jews only worshiped one god and thought their God was the only god. Some Romans thought these ideas insulted their own religious beliefs.

Many Jews were unhappy about the way Rome ruled Judea, a Jewish territory. The Jews wanted their rulers to be Jewish and follow their beliefs. Some Jews rebelled several times. In the 100s, the Roman emperor Hadrian banned Jews from practicing some Jewish rituals.

> **Why did some Romans think Judaism insulted their own religious beliefs?**
> _____
> _____
> _____
> _____

Lesson 1, *continued*

This meant that Jews could not do certain things that were part of their religion. Hadrian thought this would make the Jews give up and follow Roman religion, rules, and laws.

He was wrong. Hadrian's actions upset the Jews even more, and they rebelled again. After the last revolt, the Romans destroyed Jerusalem and forced all Jews out of the city. Jews moved throughout the Roman world.

What did the Romans do after the last Jewish revolt?
_____
_____
_____

THE ROOTS OF CHRISTIANITY

At the start of the first century AD, a new religion appeared. **Christianity** had roots in Judaism, but it was based on the life and teachings of **Jesus of Nazareth**. During this time, many Jews were waiting for the **Messiah** (muh-SY-uh).

Underline two ideas that Jews believed about the Messiah.

The Messiah was a savior chosen by God that had been foretold by Jewish prophets. One of the most famous prophets was **John the Baptist**. He traveled throughout Judea to announce the Messiah was coming. Jews believed the Messiah would lead their people. He would be a descendent of King David and would restore the greatness of the ancient kingdom of Israel.

No one knew when the Messiah would come. To encourage him to appear, some Jews followed strict religious rules that Moses had given them. When the Romans took over Judea in 63 BC, many Jews hoped the Messiah would arrive soon.

Why did some Jews follow strict religious rules that Moses had given them?
_____
_____
_____

CHALLENGE ACTIVITY

Critical Thinking: Summarize Jews who follow the strict religious rules of Moses are called Orthodox Jews. Use print or digital resources to research two rules of this type of Judaism. Write a short summary that explains each rule and tells what makes it strict.

DIRECTIONS Read each sentence and fill in the blank with the word in the word pair that best completes the sentence.

1. A savior chosen by God that had been foretold by Jewish prophets was _____. **(John the Baptist/Messiah)**

2. _____ founded a religion based on his life and teachings. **(John the Baptist/Jesus of Nazareth)**

3. The religion of _____ had roots in Judaism. **(Messiah/Christianity)**

4. _____ was a famous prophet who traveled throughout Judea to announce the Jewish leader was coming. **(John the Baptist/Jesus of Nazareth)**

The Growth of Christianity

Lesson 2

MAIN IDEAS
1. In Christian belief, Jesus was the Messiah and the son of God.
2. Jesus taught about salvation, love for God, and kindness.
3. Jesus' followers spread his teachings after his death.

Key Terms and People

Bible the holy book of Christianity

crucifixion a type of execution that involved being nailed to a cross

Resurrection Christian belief that Jesus rose from the dead after his death

disciples followers

Apostles the 12 disciples whom Jesus chose to receive special teaching

Lesson Summary

THE LIFE AND DEATH OF JESUS OF NAZARETH

Jesus of Nazareth was born at the end of the first century BC. Much of what we know about Jesus is from the **Bible**, the holy book of Christianity. This book has two parts. The Old Testament tells the history and ideas of the Hebrew people. The New Testament is the second part of the Bible. It is about the life and teachings of Jesus and the early history of Christianity.

The Bible states that Jesus was born in a small town called Bethlehem (BETH-li-hem). His birth marked the shift from BC to AD in our dating system. Jesus' mother, Mary, was married to a carpenter named Joseph. But Christians believe God, not Joseph, was the father of Jesus.

Roman leaders thought Jesus' teachings challenged their authority. He was arrested and executed by **crucifixion**. Christians believe Jesus rose from the dead in an event called the **Resurrection**. Many of Jesus' **disciples** claimed to see him again.

> How did Jesus' birth affect our dating system?
> _____
> _____

> What did many disciples claim after the Resurrection?
> _____
> _____

ACTS AND TEACHINGS

Jesus spread his message among the Jewish people. People who liked what he did and said became the first Christians.

Many acts that Jesus performed were miracles. These events cannot normally be performed by a human. The New Testament describes a miracle where Jesus fed an entire crowd with just a small amount of bread and fish.

Jesus told stories known as parables to give lessons about his teachings. There are many parables in the New Testament. Parables helped Jesus explain complicated ideas by connecting them to people's daily lives. Then people could understand the lessons.

The main message Jesus talked about was that people should love God and each other. He also taught about salvation.

JESUS'S FOLLOWERS

Jesus chose 12 of his disciples, the **Apostles**, to spread his teachings. Peter brought Christianity to the people of Rome after Jesus died. Matthew, Mark, Luke, and John wrote the four Gospels of the New Testament. The tradition of baptism came from the Gospel account of John the Baptist immersing Jesus in water to clean him of sin.

The Apostles also shared a special prayer with others. It was one that Jesus had taught them. The Lord's Prayer is now a common prayer for many Christians, and the act of saying prayers is an important tradition in the Christian faith.

CHALLENGE ACTIVITY

Critical Thinking: Analyze Find and read an example of a parable in the New Testament. Then write a short essay that explains the lesson the parable teaches.

> How did Jesus perform a miracle with bread and fish?
>
> _____
> _____
> _____
> _____

> What did parables allow Jesus to do?
>
> _____
> _____
> _____
> _____
> _____
> _____
> _____
> _____

> Circle the names of the people who wrote the four Gospels.

Bible	crucifixion	Resurrection
disciples	Apostles	

DIRECTIONS Answer each question by writing a sentence that contains at least one word from the word bank.

1. Who were the 12 people whom Jesus chose to receive special teaching?

   _____

   _____

2. Which Christian belief states that Jesus rose from the dead after his death?

   _____

   _____

3. What is the name of the holy book of Christianity?

   _____

   _____

4. Who were followers of Jesus?

   _____

   _____

5. What type of execution involves being nailed to a cross?

   _____

   _____

The Growth of Christianity

MAIN IDEAS
1. Paul, one of Jesus' followers, spread his teachings after his death.
2. Christianity spread quickly in Rome, but its growing strength worried some emperors.

Key Terms and People

Paul follower whose letters defined Christianity as separate from Judaism

saint a person known and admired for his or her holiness

monotheism belief in the existence of only one god; central feature of Christianity

martyrs people who die for their religious beliefs

persecution punishing people for their beliefs

Lesson Summary

PAUL OF TARSUS

Paul of Tarsus was most important in spreading Christianity. Even though he had never met Jesus, Paul traveled and wrote letters explaining Christian ideals. Many Christians think of Paul as another Apostle, and he was named a **saint** after he died. Paul helped Christianity break away from Judaism.

> Underline two details that show that Paul was an important person in the Christian Church.

At first, Paul did not like Christianity. He was born Jewish and thought Jesus' ideas would threaten Judaism. Paul tried to stop the Christian message from spreading. The Bible states that Paul then saw a blinding light while he was traveling one day. Jesus' voice called out to him. After that, Paul became a Christian.

> While he was traveling, what happened to Paul that caused him to become a Christian?
> _____
> _____
> _____
> _____

He traveled to many major Mediterranean cities so that he could share Christian teachings with others. Paul also wrote long letters and sent them to communities throughout the Roman world. These letters helped to explain Jesus' teachings and give more details about them.

Lesson 3, *continued*

Paul mentioned the Trinity in his letters. Christians believe that three persons—God the Father, Jesus the Son, and the Holy Spirit—all make up one God. **Monotheism** is the belief that only one god exists.

CHRISTIANITY SPREADS QUICKLY IN ROME

People like Paul wanted to share Christian teachings with as many people as possible, not just with people who were Jewish. Christians began to write down the Gospels and other writings about their religion. This information helped Christians strengthen their faith, and Christianity spread throughout the Roman Empire.

As this religion became more popular, Roman leaders began to worry. Some local leaders arrested and killed Christians. These **martyrs** died for their religious beliefs. Some Roman emperors outlawed Christianity and **persecuted** Christians. This did not stop followers from practicing their faith. Christians began to hold secret meetings. They used secret symbols so they could identify other Christians and gather together safely. One of the most common symbols was a fish, and this image is still used as a Christian symbol today.

CHALLENGE ACTIVITY

Critical Thinking: Make Judgments Paul of Tarsus has been called the most influential person in the history of Christianity besides Jesus. Do you agree with this statement? Why or why not?

In Christianity, who are the three persons who make up the Trinity?

_____

_____

_____

What risks did early Christians face in spreading their religion?

_____

_____

Guided Reading Workbook

DIRECTIONS Use at least three of the vocabulary words **Paul, saint, monotheism, martyrs,** and **persecution** to write a letter that relates to the lesson.

_____

_____

_____

_____

_____

_____

_____

_____

_____

_____

_____

_____

_____

_____

_____

_____

_____

_____

_____

_____

_____

_____

_____

_____

The Growth of Christianity

MAIN IDEAS
1. The Pope influenced the growth of the early Christian Church.
2. As the church grew, new leaders and ideas appeared and Christianity's status in the empire changed.

Key Terms and People

bishops local leaders in Christian communities

Eucharist central Christian ceremony that honors the last supper Jesus shared with his Apostles

pope the head of the whole Christian Church; comes from the Greek word for "father"

Augustine of Hippo writer who linked the ideas of classical philosophers with Christian beliefs

Constantine Roman emperor who became a Christian

Lesson Summary
THE CHURCH GROWS

Early Christians had to meet in secret, so the church did not have a single leader. Each Christian community had a **bishop**, or local leader. Most bishops lived in cities. Bishops helped people understand Christian teachings and live by them. One of their most important duties was to lead Christians during the celebration of the **Eucharist** (YOO-kuh-ruhst).

> **Where did most bishops live?**
> _____
> _____

The Eucharist was the central ceremony of the Christian Church. It honored the last supper Jesus shared with his Apostles. Christians ate bread and drank wine in memory of Jesus' death. This is still how the Eucharist is celebrated in Christian churches today.

By the late 100s, the bishops in large cities had become very powerful. They had great influence over Christians and other bishops. The Apostle Peter had been the first bishop of Rome. He was an important leader in the early church.

> **What did Christians do during the Eucharist?**
> _____
> _____
> _____
> _____

Christians considered anyone who was the bishop of Rome to be the most honored bishop of all. This church leader became known as the **pope**, a word that means "father" in Greek.

NEW TEACHINGS AND EMPERORS

As Christianity spread through the Roman world, Christian teachings began to mix with the works of classical philosophers like Plato. In the late 300s and early 400s, Christian writers like **Augustine** (AW-guhs-teen) **of Hippo** had begun to read classical works. After studying Plato's writings, Augustine felt that Christians should focus on God's plan for the world instead of on material goods. Augustine's ideas helped shape Christian beliefs for hundreds of years.

In the early 300s, emperor **Constantine** (KAHN-stuhn-teen) became a Christian and removed the bans on Christians. He created a council of Christian leaders, and his government had a close relationship with the church. Constantine had several great Christian churches built in the empire. He believed that God had helped him have a successful life. Later, Emperor Theodosius I (theeuh-DOH-shuhs) made Christianity the official religion of Rome.

CHALLENGE ACTIVITY

Critical Thinking: Elaborate Sometimes popes choose names that are different from the ones their parents gave them. Use an encyclopedia or other reference source to do research on some of the popes of the early church. Write three facts that you think are interesting or unusual about their names.

> **Why did Christians consider the bishop of Rome the most honored bishop of all?**
>
> _____
> _____
> _____
> _____

> **What did Augustine of Hippo think Christians should focus on?**
>
> _____
> _____

> **Circle the name of the emperor who made Christianity the official religion of Rome.**

DIRECTIONS Match the terms in the first column with their correct definition from the second column by placing the letter of the correct definition in the space provided before each term.

_____ 1. pope

_____ 2. Augustine of Hippo

_____ 3. bishops

_____ 4. Constantine

_____ 5. Eucharist

a. local leaders in Christian communities

b. Roman emperor who became a Christian

c. Christian ceremony that honors the last supper Jesus had with the Apostles

d. writer who linked classical philosophy with Christian beliefs

e. Greek word for "father"

Civilizations of Eastern Europe

> **MAIN IDEAS**
> 1. The physical geography of eastern Europe varies widely from place to place.
> 2. The climate and vegetation of eastern Europe also vary greatly from place to place.
> 3. The early history of eastern Europe was shaped by the movement of different groups of people into the region from other areas.

Key Terms and People

Ural Mountains used by most modern geographers as the solid eastern boundary between Asia and Europe

Carpathians low, rugged mountains that are an extension of the Alps

Balkan Peninsula one of the largest peninsulas in Europe; extends south into the Mediterranean Sea

Danube river that begins in Germany and flows east

Volga river that flows south through western Russia to the Caspian Sea

taiga huge forest of evergreen trees that covers about half of Russia

Rus Vikings from Scandinavia

Lesson Summary
PHYSICAL FEATURES

Eastern Europe is a region with a variety of landforms, water features, and climates. Geographically, eastern Europe's boundary with Asia are the **Ural Mountains,** in western Russia.

Several other mountain ranges are also in the eastern Europe. The **Carpathians** are a low mountain range that stretch in a long arc from the Alps of west-central Europe to the Black Sea. East of the Black Sea are the Caucasus Mountains. Two more mountain ranges, the Dinaric Alps and Balkan Mountains, cover most of the **Balkan Peninsula**. This landform is one of Europe's largest peninsulas. It extends south into the Mediterranean Sea.

Eastern Europe has many seas and rivers. Many rivers are vital to trade and transportation. The

> Underline the name of the landform that is eastern Europe's boundary with Asia.

> The Carpathians stretch to what body of water?
>
> _____
>
> _____

Danube begins in Germany and flows east through nine countries before flowing into the Black Sea. The **Volga** is Europe's longest river and flows south through western Russia. It forms the center of Russia's river network. Canals connect the Volga to the Don River and the Baltic Sea.

CLIMATE AND VEGETATION

The climate is cold and harsh in the far north of eastern Europe. Winters are long. There is less rain than in other parts of the region and not that much sun. Huge forests of evergreen trees are able to grow, including **taiga** in Russia. Frozen soil, or tundra, is also found here.

Winter is still cold in the interior plains, but the summers are pleasant. The grassland of the steppe is Russia's most important farming area.

Temperatures are warm in the Mediterranean climate along the Balkan coast. Hardy trees and shrubs grow in this area that gets little rain.

EASTERN EUROPEAN PEOPLES

Throughout history, many different peoples have moved into eastern Europe. They all brought their customs and cultures. For example, the word *Russia* probably comes from the name of the **Rus**. These Vikings were from Scandinavia.

The Slavs created kingdoms and traded. The Balts farmed land and raised cattle. One people, the Magyars, even helped establish the Hungarian language. By the 600s BC, areas of eastern Europe would become colonies of ancient Greece and later be part of the Roman Empire.

> **Why is the Volga an important river in Europe?**
> _____
> _____
> _____
> _____
> _____

> **What are the climate and vegetation like along the Balkan coast?**
> _____
> _____
> _____
> _____

> **Circle the name of the language that the Magyars helped establish in eastern Europe.**

Lesson 1, *continued*

CHALLENGE ACTIVITY

Critical Thinking: Rank Use an almanac, atlas, or
other source to research the mountains, rivers, or
seas of eastern Europe. Choose a category (like
length, depth, or height), and rank five examples.
List them by least to most or most to least. Use
at least one example not found in the text.

DIRECTIONS Read each sentence and fill in the blank with the
word in the word pair that best completes the sentence.

1. The _____ forms the center of Russia's river network.
   (Danube/Volga)

2. The _____ is one of the largest of these landforms in
   Europe. **(Ural Mountains/Balkan Peninsula)**

3. Vikings named the _____ came to eastern Europe from
   Scandinavia. **(Carpathians/Rus)**

4. Evergreen trees of the _____ cover about half of Russia.
   (taiga/Volga)

5. Flowing east, the _____ goes through nine countries
   before flowing into the Black Sea. **(Rus/Danube)**

6. Most modern geographers use the _____ as the solid
   eastern boundary between Asia and Europe. **(Ural Mountains/Balkan
   Peninsula)**

7. The _____ are low, rugged mountains that are an
   extension of the Alps. **(Danube/Carpathians)**

Civilizations of Eastern Europe

MAIN IDEAS
1. Eastern emperors ruled from Constantinople and tried but failed to reunite the whole Roman Empire.
2. The people of the eastern empire created a new society that was different from society in the west.
3. Byzantine Christianity was different from religion in the west.

Key Terms and People

Justinian last ruler of the Roman Empire

Theodora Justinian's wife, a wise woman who advised her husband during his reign

Byzantine Empire civilization that developed in the eastern Roman Empire

mosaics pictures made with pieces of colored glass and stone

Lesson Summary

EMPERORS RULE FROM CONSTANTINOPLE

After Diocletian divided the Roman Empire into east and west, Constantinople became its center. Located on a peninsula between the Black and Mediterranean Seas, it was protected from attack. The city had a natural harbor, and it was located along major trade routes, such as the Silk Road. So Constantinople controlled trade between Europe and Asia.

After Rome fell in AD 476, the emperor **Justinian,** who ruled in the 500s, wanted to reunite the Roman Empire. His armies recaptured Italy. He was respected for making laws fairer. But he made enemies who tried to overthrow him. Groups led riots and set fire to buildings. Justinian feared for his life and planned to leave Constantinople. He was stopped by his wife, **Theodora.** She persuaded him to stay and helped him rule successfully. Together, they ended the riots. Justinian was able to keep his throne. Despite Justinian's success, later emperors could not fight off attacks or hold onto the land.

> Why was Constantinople an important center?
> _____
> _____
> _____
> _____
> _____

> Who was Justinian's most trusted advisor?
> _____

Lesson 2, *continued*

The eastern empire lasted for several hundred years, but it never regained its former strength. After Justinian's death, Constantinople was defeated by the Ottoman Turks in 1453.

A NEW SOCIETY

People began to follow Greek culture instead of Roman culture. The cultural ties to Rome were slowly lost.

Constantinople was a major trade route among Europeans, Africans, and Asians. Because of this, the people were exposed to new ideas from other cultures. They blended those ideas with their own Roman and Greek roots. Historians call the new society that developed in the east the **Byzantine Empire**. Byzantine culture developed its own distinct features. An eastern emperor, for example, was head of both the church and the government. In the west, popes and bishops ruled the church, but the emperor held political power.

> What name was given to the society that developed out of the eastern Roman Empire?
>
> _____

BYZANTINE CHRISTIANITY

Christianity was central to the Byzantine Empire. Byzantine artists showed their devotion to God and the Christian church by creating religious art. **Mosaics**, pictures made with pieces of colored stone or glass, were grand. The Byzantine churches were magnificent.

For hundreds of years, church leaders of the east and west worked together. In the 1000s, the church split in two. Christians in the east formed the Eastern Orthodox Church. As a result, eastern and western Europe were divided by religion.

> Underline the way in which Byzantine artists showed their devotion to Christianity.

Guided Reading Workbook

CHALLENGE ACTIVITY

Critical Thinking: Explain Imagine that you are
Theodora, the wife of Roman Emperor Justinian.
Your husband wants to leave his kingdom
because his enemies have started a riot and
threaten to kill him. You think he is wrong. Write
a short speech that you would make to Justinian
to persuade him to stay and solve his problems.

Byzantine Empire	Justinian
mosaics	Theodora

DIRECTIONS Answer each question by writing a sentence that
contains at least one word from the word bank.

1. Who was the emperor who wanted to reunite the Roman Empire?

   _____

   _____

2. What are pictures made with pieces of colored stone or glass known as?

   _____

   _____

3. Who advised Justinian to solve his problems rather than give up the throne?

   _____

   _____

4. What do historians call the society that developed in the eastern Roman Empire?

   _____

   _____

Civilizations of Eastern Europe

MAIN IDEAS
1. Russia was invaded by Mongol armies and later freed by Prince Ivan III.
2. Trade played an important part in Russian daily life.
3. Orthodox Christianity greatly influenced Russian culture.

Key Terms and People

Ivan III prince of Muscovy who broke away from the Mongol Empire

czar title of Russian emperors

principalities small states ruled by princes

icons religious images painted on wood

Lesson Summary
EARLY RUSSIAN HISTORY

As Christianity spread throughout eastern Europe, a people called the Rus formed the kingdom that would become Russia. The Rus were Vikings. They set up a capital near Kiev, which formed part of a trade route that stretched from Scandinavia to the Byzantine Empire. Kiev became powerful, and the rulers formed alliances with other kingdoms. However, after the death of powerful ruler Yaroslav, Kiev was invaded by the Mongols. For 200 years, Russia was under Mongol rule. Then in Muscovy, which is now Moscow, **Ivan III** began to strengthen his rule. He worked with the Mongols and gained additional power. In 1480, Prince Ivan broke away from the Mongol Empire and made himself **czar**, or emperor of Russia. He successfully fought the Mongols for Russia's independence.

> Which group ruled Russia for 200 years?
> _____
> _____

> Underline the title Prince Ivan gave himself after freeing Russia.

RUSSIAN SOCIETY AND DAILY LIFE

During its early history, Russia was a cluster of **principalities**, small states ruled by princes. These princes had great power. Even when the Mongols invaded, the princes remained in power if they

Guided Reading Workbook

Lesson 3, *continued*

swore allegiance to the Mongols. After Ivan III won Russia's independence, he was the most powerful Russian prince. He launched a series of wars to conquer other Russian states. He was able to unify much of Russia into a single state.

Russian culture remained the same even with government changes. For example, Christianity stayed Russia's official religion. Russia had close ties to the Byzantine Empire. As a result, when the Roman Catholic and Eastern Orthodox churches split, Russia became part of the Eastern Orthodox Church.

Russia's economy was based on trade, and its most important trading partner was the Byzantine Empire. Trade goods from Russia were fur, wax, and honey. In return, Russians received wine, silk, art objects, and spices. Trade brought wealth to Russia. In fact, traders were ranked just below princes and nobles. Clergy were also respected.

Why was Russia part of the Eastern Orthodox Church?
_____
_____
_____
_____
_____
_____

RUSSIAN CULTURE AND ACHIEVEMENTS

Most of Russia's culture reflects a religious influence. Early Russians designed churches with multiple domes. Inside Russian churches were mosaics and paintings. **Icons**, religious images on wood, showed figures from the Bible so that people could focus on their prayers.

What is an icon?
_____
_____

Music was important in Russian church celebrations. Choirs from later periods sang in complex harmonies. Russian music and religious texts were created in Slavonic. At first, it could not be written down. Then missionaries developed a Slavonic alphabet called Cyrillic. It is still used to write Russian and other related languages, but its characters are not familiar to English speakers.

Underline the sentence that explains the reason for the Slavonic language in Russia.

Lesson 3, *continued*

CHALLENGE ACTIVITY

Critical Thinking: Summarize Use the Internet or
other resources to gather information about
Prince Ivan III. Write a biography about how he
became prince, his role in Russia's independence,
and his importance to the country's growth.

DIRECTIONS Write a word or descriptive phrase to describe
each term.

1. Ivan III _____

   _____

2. czar _____

   _____

3. principalities _____

   _____

4. icon _____

   _____

DIRECTIONS Write a vocabulary term that has a *similar* meaning to
the word or words given.

5. strong ruler _____

6. religious symbol _____

7. small, independent area _____

The Rise of Islam

MAIN IDEAS
1. Arabia is a mostly a desert land.
2. Two ways of life—nomadic and sedentary—developed in the desert.

Key Terms

sand dunes hills of sand shaped by the wind

oasis a wet, fertile area in the desert

sedentary settled

caravan a group of traders that travels together

souk a market or bazaar

Lesson Summary
A DESERT LAND

The Arabian Peninsula is a mostly hot and dry desert of scorching temperatures and little water. Yet people have lived there for thousands of years.

Arabia, located in the southwest corner of Asia, is the crossroads for three continents— Africa, Europe, and Asia. Trade routes cross the region by both land and sea. These routes have brought many different people and customs through Arabia, influencing the people who live there.

The world's largest sand desert, the Rub'al-Khali, which means "Empty Quarter," lies in Arabia. There is little life there. **Sand dunes**, or hills of sand shaped by the wind, can rise to 800 feet and stretch for hundreds of miles. Water is scarce and exists mainly in oases throughout the desert. An **oasis** is a wet, fertile area in the desert. Oases have always been key stops along Arabia's trade routes.

Deserts cover much of Arabia's interior, but other landforms are along its edges. Mountains border the southern and western coasts, and

Arabia was the trading crossroads for what three continents?

_____

_____

Why would oases be important to people traveling along trade routes?

_____

_____

Lesson 1, *continued*

marshy land is near the Persian Gulf. Most people have settled in the milder coastal regions.

TWO WAYS OF LIFE

People developed two main ways to live in the desert: nomadic and **sedentary**, or settled. Nomads moved from place to place. They lived in tents and raised goats, sheep, and camels. They traveled with their herds across the desert, moving along regular routes as seasons changed. They depended on camels for transportation and milk. Nomads traveled in tribes, or groups of people. Tribe membership was important to nomads. It offered protection from desert dangers and reduced competition for grazing lands.

Other people settled in oases and farmed. Settlements in oases along the trade routes became towns, where most people in Arabia lived. Merchants and craftspeople lived there too and worked with people in caravans. A **caravan** is a group of traders that travel together. Most town centers featured a **souk**, which is a market or bazaar. Both nomads and caravans used these centers of trade. Nomads traded animal products and desert herbs for cooking supplies and clothing. Merchants sold spices, gold, leather, and other goods brought by the caravans.

Arabian towns were important places along the trade routes. They linked India with Northeast Africa and the Mediterranean. Trade made it possible for Arabs to come in contact with people and ideas from different cultures around the world.

CHALLENGE ACTIVITY

Critical Thinking: Elaborate If you lived in Arabia, would you choose a nomadic or sedentary life? Write a one-page description of what your life would be like based on the lifestyle you would prefer to live.

> **Why did nomads want to travel in a tribe?**
> _____
> _____
> _____

> **Underline the sentence that tells where most people in Arabia lived.**

> **What are some things that could be found at a souk?**
> _____
> _____
> _____

Guided Reading Workbook

Lesson 1, *continued*

DIRECTIONS Write a descriptive phrase to describe each term.

1. sand dunes _____

_____

2. souk _____

_____

3. caravan _____

_____

4. oasis _____

_____

5. sedentary _____

_____

DIRECTIONS Look at each set of vocabulary terms. On the line provided, write the letter of the term that does not relate to the others.

_____ 6. a. sand dunes
          b. souk
          c. oasis

_____ 7. a. souk
          b. sedentary
          c. sand dunes

Guided Reading Workbook

The Rise of Islam

MAIN IDEAS
1. Muhammad became a prophet and introduced a religion called Islam in Arabia.
2. Muhammad's teachings had similarities to Judaism and Christianity, but they also presented new ideas.
3. Islam spread in Arabia after being rejected at first.
4. The Qur'an is the holy book of Islam.
5. Along with the Qur'an, the Sunnah guide Muslims' lives.
6. Islamic law is based on the Qur'an and the Sunnah.

Key Terms and People

Muhammad an Arabian man whose teachings became the basis for a new religion

Islam religion based on messages Muhammad received from God

Muslim a person who follows Islam

Qur'an the holy book of Islam

shrine a place where people worship a saint or god

pilgrimage journey to a sacred place

mosque a building for Muslim prayer

jihad literally means "to make an effort" or "to struggle"

Sunnah a collection of actions or sayings by Muhammad

Five Pillars of Islam the five acts of worship required of all Muslims

Lesson Summary

MUHAMMAD BECOMES A PROPHET

Muhammad brought a new religion to Arabia. What is known about him is from religious writings. He was born in the city of Mecca around 570.

Muhammad became upset that Mecca's rich people did not help the poor. According to Islamic teachings, when he was 40, an angel revealed God's messages to him. These form the basis of **Islam**. A follower of Islam is a **Muslim**. Islam's messages were written in the **Qur'an**, the holy book of Islam.

> Underline the name of Islam's founder.

> What did the messages Muhammad received from God form?
> _____

Lesson 2, *continued*

MUHAMMAD'S TEACHINGS

Some of Muhammad's ideas came from
Judaism and Christianity, including monotheism,
or belief in one god. This was a new idea for
many Arabs who prayed to gods at a **shrine**. The
most important shrine was in Mecca. People
traveled there on a **pilgrimage**.

> **Why did people travel to Mecca on a pilgrimage?**
> _____
> _____
> _____
> _____

ISLAM SPREADS IN ARABIA

Mecca's rulers felt threatened by Muhammad. So
he left and went to Medina. His house became
the first **mosque**, or Muslim prayer building.
Many Arab tribes accepted Islam. After years of
fighting, Meccans welcomed back Muhammad
and accepted Islam.

> **Underline the name for a Muslim prayer building.**

THE QUR'AN

Muslims believe that the Qur'an is the word of
God as told to Muhammad. Muslims believe that
God wishes them to follow rules. These rules
affect Muslims' everyday life.

   Jihad is an important Islamic concept, which
means "to make an effort" or "to struggle." It
refers to the internal struggle of a Muslim trying
to follow Islamic beliefs. It can also mean the
struggle to defend the Muslim community or
convert people. The word has also been
translated as "holy war."

> **Why is the Qur'an so important?**
> _____
> _____
> _____
> _____

> **What two struggles does jihad refer to?**
> _____
> _____
> _____
> _____
> _____

THE SUNNAH

Another important Islamic holy book is the
Sunnah, a written record of Muhammad's words
and actions. It spells out the five acts of worship
required of Muslims—the **Five Pillars of Islam**.

ISLAMIC LAW

The Qur'an and the Sunnah form the basis of
Islamic law, or Shariah. This sets punishments
or rewards. It makes no distinction between
religious and secular life. Most Islamic countries

> **How is Shariah law used in Islamic countries today?**
> _____
> _____
> _____

Guided Reading Workbook

Lesson 2, *continued*

today blend Islamic law with a legal system like
that in the United States.

CHALLENGE ACTIVITY

Critical Thinking: Summarize Suppose you
had to explain Islam to someone who knew
nothing about it. Write a one-page paper that
includes important information about the religion.

Five Pillars of Islam	Islam	jihad
Mosque	Muhammad	Muslim
pilgrimage	Qur'an	shrine
Sunnah		

DIRECTIONS Read each sentence and fill in the blank with a word
from the word bank that best completes the sentence.

1. The first acts of worship required of all Muslims are known as
   the _____.

2. The inner struggle people go through in their effort to obey God or to
   convert others to Islam is known as _____.

3. The religion based on messages sent by God through an angel to an Arabian
   man is _____.

4. A collection of actions or sayings by an Arabian man who founded a religion
   is the _____.

5. A person who follows Islam is a(n) _____.

6. A building for Muslim prayer is known as a(n) _____.

7. The holy book of Islam is the _____.

8. A place where people worship a saint or god is a(n) _____.

9. A journey to a sacred place is a(n) _____.

10. The Arabian man whose teachings became the basis for a new religion
    was _____.

The Rise of Islam

MAIN IDEAS
1. Muslim armies conquered many lands into which Islam slowly spread.
2. Trade helped Islam spread into new areas.
3. A mix of cultures was one result of Islam's spread.
4. Islamic influence encouraged the growth of cities.

Key Terms and People

Abu Bakr one of Islam's first converts, appointed caliph after Muhammad's death

caliph title of the highest Islamic leader

tolerance acceptance

Lesson Summary
MUSLIMS ARMIES CONQUER MANY LANDS

After Muhammad's death, his followers chose **Abu Bakr** to be the next leader of Islam. He was one of Muhammad's first converts. Abu Bakr became the first **caliph**, a title that Muslims use for the highest Islamic leader.

Abu Bakr directed battles against Arab tribes who did not follow Muhammad's teachings. He unified Arabia as a Muslim state. Muslim leaders who followed Abu Bakr conquered the Persian and Byzantine empires. Muslim leaders made treaties with non-Muslims that listed rules conquered people had to follow. For example, non-Muslims could not build places of worship in Muslim cities. In return, Muslims would not attack them.

During this time, the conflict between different groups of Muslims led to the Shia-Sunni split. The conflict stemmed from a disagreement about who should be caliph. Shias said caliphs should be descended from Muhammad's family. Sunnis believed that religious leaders should elect caliphs. Today, most Muslims are Sunni. Shia Muslims live in Iran, Iraq, Pakistan, and India.

> **Who was the first caliph?**
> _____

> **Underline the sentence that describes Abu Bakr's major contribution as a caliph.**

> **What was the source of the conflict between different groups of Muslims?**
> _____
> _____

Many caliphs came from the Umayyad family. They conquered lands in Central Asia, northern India, and North Africa. They controlled eastern Mediterranean trade routes. After many years of fighting, the Berbers of North Africa converted to Islam. A combined Arab and Berber army conquered Spain and ruled for 700 years.

> **How were the Arabs able to conquer Spain?**
> _____
> _____
> _____
> _____

TRADE HELPS ISLAM SPREAD

Arab merchants took Islamic beliefs and practices with them to new lands. They brought back products such as cotton and rice. They learned of inventions such as paper and gunpowder. Coastal trading cities grew into large Muslim communities.

> **Why do you think trade flourishes in coastal cities?**
> _____
> _____
> _____

A MIX OF CULTURES

Muslims generally practiced religious **tolerance**, or acceptance. More people began speaking Arabic and practicing Islam. The Arabs also took on non-Muslim customs. Cultural blending changed Islam from a mostly Arab religion into a religion of many different cultures.

> **Underline the sentence that explains how cultural blending affected Islam.**

THE GROWTH OF CITIES

The growing Muslim cities reflected this blending of cultures. For example, the wealthy city of Baghdad was a major trading center. It attracted artists and writers. Córdoba, in Spain, was the largest, most advanced European city during the early 900s. It was a center of learning. People from across the Muslim world came there to study. It was also a center of Jewish culture. Jewish poets, philosophers, and scientists made contributions to Córdoba's growth.

> **In addition to Muslims, what other religious group had a thriving culture in Islamic Spain?**
> _____
> _____

CHALLENGE ACTIVITY

Critical Thinking: Draw Conclusions Consider the benefits to Islam from cultural blending. Write a one-page paper that demonstrates how this practice helped Islam become a more universal faith.

Lesson 3, *continued*

DIRECTIONS Write a word or phrase that defines or describes the name or term given.

1. Abu Bakr _____

2. caliph _____

3. tolerance _____

DIRECTIONS Use the two vocabulary words **caliph** and **tolerance** and the name **Abu Bakr** to write a short summary that relates to the lesson.

_____

_____

_____

_____

_____

_____

_____

_____

_____

_____

_____

_____

_____

_____

_____

_____

_____

_____

The Rise of Islam

MAIN IDEAS
1. Muslim scholars made advances in various fields of science and philosophy.
2. Islam influenced styles of literature and the arts.

Key Terms and People

Ibn Battutah Muslim explorer and geographer

Sufism a movement of Islam, based on the belief that one must have a personal relationship with God

Omar Khayyám famous Sufi poet who wrote *The Rubáiyát*

patrons sponsors

minaret a narrow tower on a mosque from which Muslims are called to pray

calligraphy decorative writing

Lesson Summary
SCIENCE AND PHILOSOPHY

Islamic scholars made great advances in many fields. These included astronomy, geography, math, and science. At Baghdad and Córdoba, Greek and other writings were translated into Arabic. A common language helped scholars share research.

> **In which two cities were scholarly writings translated into Arabic?**
> _____
> _____

Muslim scientists built observatories to study the sun, the moon, and stars. They also improved the astrolabe. The Greeks had invented this tool to chart the position of the stars. The astrolabe would later be used in sea exploration. Also, it helped Muslim explorers spread Islam to different parts of the globe, which expanded the Islamic world.

It was a Muslim mathematician who invented algebra. Muslims found better ways to calculate distance and make precise maps. They also used the stars to navigate. Muslim merchants and explorers traveled wide and far. One great explorer was **Ibn Battutah**. He traveled to Africa, India, China, and Spain in the 1320s.

> **Why do you think the astrolabe would be useful in sea exploration?**
> _____
> _____
> _____
> _____

Lesson 4, *continued*

Muslims were also known in medicine. They added to Greek and Indian medicine. Muslim doctors created tests for doctors to pass before they could treat people. They wrote descriptions of diseases, started the first school of pharmacy, and built public hospitals. A Baghdad doctor found out how to detect and treat smallpox. Another doctor, known in the West as Avicenna, wrote a medical encyclopedia widely used in Europe for centuries.

> Underline advances in medicine made by Muslims.

Some Muslims developed a new philosophy called **Sufism**. People who practice Sufism are Sufis. Sufis seek a personal relationship with God. Sufism has brought many followers to Islam.

LITERATURE AND THE ARTS

Poetry and short stories were popular among Muslims. The collection of stories called *The Thousand and One Nights* includes tales about legendary heroes and characters. The most famous Sufi poet was **Omar Khayyám**. He wrote about faith, hope, and other emotions in *The Rubáiyát*.

> What is the name of Islam's great collection of stories?
> _____
> _____

There were many achievements in architecture. Rulers liked to be **patrons**. Patrons helped fund the design and construction of mosques. The main part of a mosque is a huge hall where thousands of people gather to pray. Often mosques have a large dome and a **minaret**, or narrow tower from which Muslims are called to prayer.

Muslims believe only Allah (God) can create humans and animals or their images, so artists did not show them in religious art. In part for this reason, Muslim artists turned to **calligraphy**. This decorative writing became an art form.

> Underline the sentence that helps to explain why Muslim artists developed calligraphy as an art form.

Guided Reading Workbook

CHALLENGE ACTIVITY

Critical Thinking: Explain Islamic culture made many advances in science, medicine, and art that people still use today. Choose the advancement that you think is the most important to our modern society. Then write a one-page paper explaining your position.

DIRECTIONS Read each sentence and fill in the blank with the word in the word pair that best completes the sentence.

1. Decorative writing that became a Muslim art form is known as _____. **(minaret/calligraphy)**

2. The famous Sufi poet who wrote *The Rubáiyát* was _____. **(Ibn Battutah/Omar Khayyám)**

3. People who helped sponsor the design and construction of mosques in the Muslim Empire were known as _____. **(patrons/Sufis)**

4. A narrow tower on a mosque from which Muslims are called to pray is called a(n) _____. **(patron/minaret)**

5. The great explorer who traveled to Africa, India, China, and Spain in the 1320s was _____. **(Omar Khayyám/Ibn Battutah)**

6. A movement of Islam that is based on the belief that one must have a personal relationship with God is known as _____. **(Sufism/Calligraphy)**

Early African Civilizations

MAIN IDEAS
1. The landforms, water, climate, and plant life affected history in West Africa.
2. West Africa's resources included farmland, gold, and salt.
3. Family and religion influenced daily life in early West African society.
4. Iron technology changed life in West Africa.

Key Terms and People

rifts long, deep valleys formed by the movement of the earth's crust

sub-Saharan Africa Africa south of the Sahara

Sahel a strip of land in West Africa that divides the desert from wetter areas

savannah open grassland with scattered trees

rain forests moist, densely wooded areas near the equator

kinship system a system of social organization based on family ties

extended family a father, mother, children, and close relatives

patrilineal leadership passed down from the father's family

matrilineal leadership passed down from the mother's family

animism the belief that bodies of water, animals, trees, and other natural objects have spirits

Lesson Summary
LANDFORMS, WATER, CLIMATE, AND PLANT LIFE

Africa is the world's second-largest continent. The Sahara, a desert, stretches across North Africa. In eastern Africa, mountains extend along **rifts**. These are long, deep valleys formed by movements of the earth's crust. Large rivers cross the plains of **sub-Saharan Africa**, or Africa south of the Sahara.

Great civilizations grew up near the Niger River. Its regions are warm and rainfall varies, which has an impact on plant life. The southern Sahara is hot and dry. The **Sahel** divides the desert from wetter areas and has grazing animals. So does the **savannah**, or open grasslands. Near the equator

> **What caused the great rift valleys of eastern Africa?**
> _____
> _____

Name _____ Class _____ Date _____

are **rain forests**. These are moist, densely wooded
areas with many plants and animals.

WEST AFRICA'S RESOURCES

West Africa's farmland is a major resource. Its
different climates help grow many traditional
crops such as dates and medicinal kola nuts.
Minerals such as gold and salt are also important
resources.

How has rainfall impacted plant life in the Sahel, savannah, and rain forests?
_____

FAMILIES, RELIGION, AND DAILY LIFE

People once were organized according to a
kinship system, which is based on family ties. An
extended family—a father, mother, children, and
close relatives—lived in villages. Usually,
leadership was hereditary. It could be **patrilineal**,
or passed through the father's family. It could be
matrilineal, or passed through the mother's
family. Within the community, men hunted and
farmed. Women took care of the children,
farmed, and did other chores.

Religion was central to West African life.
People believed their ancestors' spirits stayed
nearby. They believed in **animism**, or that
animals, trees, bodies of water, and other natural
objects have spirits.

Underline the sentences that tell the differences between patrilineal and matrilineal.

Explain how religion was central to West African life.
_____

TECHNOLOGY AND CHANGE

Around 500 BC, West Africans learned how to
make iron tools. These tools meant they could
clear land more quickly and grow more food.
They had better weapons for hunting and
defense. They could live in more places so the
population grew.

Underline three effects of iron tools.

CHALLENGE ACTIVITY

Critical Thinking: Compare and Contrast Write a
one-page essay explaining any similarities and
differences between the ways the early West
Africans lived and the way you live.

DIRECTIONS Write a word that has the same meaning as the term given or a definition of the term.

1. animism _____

_____

2. extended family _____

_____

3. rain forests _____

_____

4. rifts _____

_____

5. Sahel _____

_____

6. savannah _____

_____

7. sub-Saharan Africa _____

_____

8. kinship system _____

_____

9. matrilineal _____

_____

10. patrilineal _____

_____

Early African Civilizations

> **MAIN IDEAS**
> 1. Ghana grew as larger populations settled on desert trade routes.
> 2. Ghana controlled trade and became wealthy.
> 3. Through its control of trade, Ghana built an empire.
> 4. Ghana's decline was caused by attacking invaders, overgrazing, and the loss of trade.

Key Terms and People

silent barter a process in which people exchange goods without ever contacting each other directly

income taxes, tributes, and gold

Tunka Manin Ghana's king who ruled the empire at the height of its power

Lesson Summary
AN EMPIRE AT THE DESERT'S EDGE

Ghana (GAH-nuh), a West African empire, profited from Saharan trade because it gained control of the trade routes. This made it a powerful state.

Ghana lay between the Niger and Senegal rivers in sub-Saharan Africa, northwest of the nation now called Ghana. Historians think the first people were farmers. Starting around 300, these farmers were threatened by nomadic herders. The herders wanted the water and pastures. For protection, small groups banded together. These groups grew stronger with the introduction of farming tools and weapons made of iron.

How did Ghana become powerful?
_____
_____
_____

TRADE IN GHANA AND WEST AFRICA

Ghana lay between the desert and the forests. These were areas rich with gold and salt. The gold and salt trade sometimes followed a **silent barter** process. In this process, people exchange goods without contacting each other directly. This kept business peaceful and the location of

Underline the sentence that describes what was found in the desert and forest areas.

gold mines secret. As gold and salt trade increased, Ghana's rulers gained power. Their armies took control of the trade routes.

Ghana was influenced by Islam in its written language, currency, architecture, and business practices. Muslims were government officials too.

GHANA BUILDS AN EMPIRE

By 800, Ghana was firmly in control of West Africa's trade routes. As a result, trade became safer and Ghana's influence increased. Traders and Ghana's people were charged a tax. Conquered tribes paid tribute. The kings made gold their property. Taxes, tributes, and gold were **income**.

The kings built a powerful army and conquered other tribes. However, Ghana's kings allowed former rulers to keep their own power. They acted as governors of their territories. Ghana reached its peak under **Tunka Manin** (TOOHN-kah MAH-nin). He had a splendid court with many luxuries.

GHANA'S DECLINE

By the end of the 1200s, Ghana had collapsed. Three major factors contributed to its decline. A Muslim group called the Almoravids attacked and tried to force Ghana's leaders to convert to Islam. The attacks weakened the empire. Also, the Almoravids brought herds of animals with them. Their animals overgrazed and ruined the farmland. Many farmers left. At around the same time, internal rebellion occurred. People took over trade routes. However, they could not keep order. Ghana was attacked and defeated by a neighbor. The empire fell apart.

How was Ghana influenced by Islam?
_____
_____
_____

Who owned gold in Ghana?
_____

List two reasons for the decline of Ghana's empire.
_____
_____
_____
_____
_____
_____
_____
_____
_____

Lesson 2, *continued*

CHALLENGE ACTIVITY

Critical Thinking: Analyze Imagine that you are a
gold or salt trader. Work with your classmates to
recreate the silent barter system. Then write a
one-page paper detailing the advantages and
disadvantages of silent barter.

DIRECTIONS Use the vocabulary words **silent barter, income,** and
Tunka Manin to write a letter that relates to the lesson.

_____

_____

_____

_____

_____

_____

_____

_____

_____

_____

_____

_____

_____

_____

_____

_____

Early African Civilizations

MAIN IDEAS
1. A ruler named Sundiata made Mali into an empire.
2. Mali reached its height under the ruler Mansa Musa.
3. Mali fell to invaders in the late 1400s.
4. Songhai regained power from Mali.
5. Askia the Great ruled Songhai as an Islamic empire.
6. Songhai fell to Moroccan invaders, ending the great era of West African empires.

Key Terms and People

Sundiata ruler that led the Mali Empire's rise to power

Mansa Musa Muslim king who ruled the Mali Empire at the height of its power and spread Islam through a large part of Africa

Sunni Ali first leader of Songhai, the last of the great West African empires

Askia the Great Muslim ruler who led Songhai to the height of its power

Lesson Summary

SUNDIATA MAKES MALI AN EMPIRE

Like Ghana, Mali lay along the upper Niger River. Mali's location on the Niger allowed its people to control trade on the river. Mali's rise to power began under its first strong leader, **Sundiata**.

A cruel ruler conquered Mali when Sundiata was a boy. When Sundiata grew older, he built an army and won Mali's independence. He conquered nearby kingdoms, including Ghana. He took over the salt and gold trades and religious and political authority held by local leaders.

> **What river flowed through both Ghana and Mali?**
>
> _____
>
> _____

MANSA MUSA

Mali's most famous ruler was a Muslim named **Mansa Musa**. He made Mali wealthy and powerful and ruled for about 25 years. He captured trading cities, including Timbuktu, and made the Islamic world aware of Mali on his pilgrimage to Mecca.

Mansa Musa stressed the importance of learning Arabic in order to read the Qur'an. He spread Islam through West Africa by building mosques in cities.

THE FALL OF MALI

Mali's success depended on strong leaders, but after he died, poor leadership weakened the empire. Invaders destroyed Timbuktu's schools and mosques. Rebel groups seized the city. By 1500, nearly all of the empire's lands were lost.

THE SONGHAI BUILD AN EMPIRE

During the 1300s, Songhai lands were part of the Mali Empire. As Mali weakened, the Songhai leader, **Sunni Ali,** worked to unify, strengthen, and enlarge the empire. He took part in both Muslim and local religions to build peace between religions.

ASKIA THE GREAT

After Sunni Ali's death, Sunni Baru became ruler. Unlike his father and most of the people, he was not Muslim. Fearing that if Sunni Baru did not support Islam they would lose trade and power, the people rebelled. The leader of the rebellion became known as **Askia the Great**. During his reign, Muslim culture and education thrived.

SONGHAI FALLS TO MOROCCO

Morocco invaded Songhai so it could control the salt mines and gold trade. It used a weapon that was an early form of a gun and destroyed Timbuktu and other cities. Other fighters carried various other weapons, too. Songhai never recovered from losing its cities and its overland trade declined. The period of great West African empires ended.

Why did Mansa Musa stress the importance of learning Arabic?

_____

_____

_____

Why was Sunni Baru overthrown?

_____

_____

_____

_____

_____

_____

Underline the sentence that explains why Morocco was successful in it invasion of Songhai.

CHALLENGE ACTIVITY

Critical Thinking: Summarize You are a reporter
who is unfamiliar with Africa. You meet a Mali
or Songhai ruler. Write an article about this
person.

Askia the Great	Mansa Musa	Sundiata
Sunni Ali		

DIRECTIONS Answer each question by writing a sentence that
contains at least one name from the word bank.

1. Who was the leader of the Songhai people that rebelled against the king
   because the people feared that if the king did not support Islam they would
   lose their trade with Muslim lands?

   _____

   _____

   _____

2. Mali's rise to power began under what ruler?

   _____

   _____

   _____

3. As the Songhai gained in wealth, the Songhai people expanded their territory
   and built an empire under which ruler?

   _____

   _____

   _____

4. Who was Mali's most famous ruler?

   _____

   _____

   _____

Lesson 4

MAIN IDEAS

1. Storytellers helped maintain the oral history of the cultures of West Africa.
2. Visitors to West Africa from other lands wrote histories and descriptions of what they saw there.
3. Traditionally, West Africans have valued the arts.

Key Terms and People

oral history a spoken record of past events

griots West African storytellers

proverbs short sayings of wisdom or truth

kente a hand-woven, brightly colored fabric

Lesson Summary
STORYTELLERS MAINTAIN ORAL HISTORY

Although cities like Timbuktu and Djenné were known for their universities and libraries, writing was not common in West Africa. None of the major early West African civilizations developed a written language. Arabic was the only written language used. However, West Africans passed along information about their civilization through **oral history**, a spoken record of past events.

West Africa's history was entrusted to storytellers called **griots**. Griots' stories were entertaining and informative. Some acted out past events like scenes in a play. Griots also told **proverbs**, or short sayings of wisdom or truth. Griots had to memorize hundreds of names and events. However, some griots confused names and events in their heads, so some stories became distorted. Still, the griots' stories tell a lot about life in West African empires.

Some griot poems are epics, long poems about kingdoms and heroes. Many of these poems were collected in the *Dausi* and the *Sundiata*. The *Dausi* tells the history of Ghana, but it also

> Underline the sentence that tells about a similarity among major early West African civilizations.

> Why might the history of the griots not be perfectly accurate?
>
> _____
> _____
> _____

includes myths and legends. The *Sundiata* tells the story of Mali's first ruler. A conqueror killed his family, but the boy was spared because he was sick. He grew up to be a great warrior who overthrew the conqueror.

VISITORS WRITE HISTORIES

Although the West Africans left no written histories, visitors from other parts of the world wrote about the region. Much of what we know about early West Africa comes from the writings of travelers and scholars from Muslim lands such as Spain and Arabia. Arab scholar al-Masudi described West Africa's geography, customs, history, and scientific achievements. Ibn Battutah was the most famous visitor to write about West Africa. He described the political and cultural lives of West Africans.

> What role did some visitors play in educating the world about early West Africa?
>
> _____
> _____
> _____
> _____
> _____
> _____

WEST AFRICANS VALUE ARTS

West Africans valued the arts, including sculpture, mask making, cloth making, music, and dance. West African artists made statues and carvings from wood, brass, clay, ivory, stone, and other materials. Some West African sculpture inspired European artists such as Henri Matisse and Pablo Picasso.

> Underline the names of European artists inspired by West African sculptors.

West Africans carved elaborate masks of wood. They show the faces of animals and were worn during rituals. Also, African societies were famous for the cloth they wore. The most famous is **kente**, a hand-woven, brightly colored fabric. Kings and queens wore kente garments for special occasions.

> List three ways in which music and dance had a place in West African culture.
>
> _____
> _____
> _____

In many West African societies, music and dance were important too. Singing and dancing entertained, but they also helped people honor their history and were central to many celebrations.

Guided Reading Workbook

CHALLENGE ACTIVITY

Critical Thinking: Compare and Contrast People know about West Africa from oral histories or visitors' written accounts. Write a one-page paper that compares and contrasts the accuracy of these resources.

DIRECTIONS Read each sentence and fill in the blank with the word in the word pair that best completes the sentence.

1. West African storytellers are known as _____.
   (griots/proverbs)

2. A hand-woven, brightly colored fabric is _____.
   (griot/kente)

3. A spoken record of past events is a(n) _____.
   (kente/oral history)

4. A short saying of wisdom or truth is a(n) _____.
   (proverb/oral history)

DIRECTIONS Look at each set of four vocabulary terms. On the line provided, write the letter of the term that does not relate to the others.

_____ 5. a. spoken record
         b. oral history
         c. griots
         d. kente

_____ 6. a. kente
         b. proverbs
         c. hand-woven
         d. bright colors

Early African Civilizations

MAIN IDEAS

1. African customs blended with Christian religious beliefs to create a new form of Christianity in Ethiopia.
2. Some historians think the migration of the Bantu caused one of the most significant cultural transformations in African history.
3. Sub-Saharan Africans and Muslim merchants, among others, traded precious metals and cattle.

Key Terms and People

Ethiopia powerful East African kingdom formed by the descendants of Aksum

Coptic Christianity form of Christianity that blends Christian teaching with African customs; name comes from Arabic word for "Egyptian"

Bantu name for 400 ethnic groups that come from the eastern, central, and southern regions of Africa; means "people" in many native languages

Great Zimbabwe a Bantu kingdom founded by the Shona in about AD 1000; name means "stone houses"

Swahili blended African-Arab culture common in East Africa

Lesson Summary

THE ETHIOPIAN KINGDOM

Ethiopia was an East African kingdom that formed at the same time that Ghana declined and Mali began growing in importance. The descendants of Aksum created Ethiopia. By 1150, it had become one of Africa's most powerful kingdoms.

King Lalibela was Ethiopia's most famous ruler. He ruled in the 1200s and had 11 Christian churches built during that time. They were carved into solid rock, and many still stand today.

Most Ethiopians believed in Christian teachings and African customs. These two things blended together to form **Coptic Christianity.** Christianity made Ethiopia different from its neighbors because most of them were Muslim.

> By 1150, what had happened to Ethiopia?
>
> _____
> _____
> _____

> What made Ethiopia different from its neighbors?
>
> _____

THE BANTU MIGRATION AND GREAT ZIMBABWE

No one is certain why the **Bantu** migrated. It might have been because the Sahara was becoming a desert. Maybe the Bantu needed new crops for food. Historians think the way these ethnic groups moved caused a great cultural change in Africa.

Most Bantu were farmers or herders who raised cattle. They needed pasture where they could raise animals and fields for their crops. By about AD 300, the Bantu had settled much of Africa that was south of the Sahara.

One Bantu ethnic group called the Shona founded the kingdom of **Great Zimbabwe**. No written records exist about it, but archeologists have found three sets of ruins that are the remains of granite structures. There are many theories about how the structures were used and why they might have been built. However, scholars and experts disagree on these ideas.

> Underline two reasons that might explain why the Bantu migrated.

> Why do scholars and experts only have ideas and theories about Great Zimbabwe?
>
> _____
> _____
> _____

SUB-SAHARAN TRADE

Trade was important to the Bantu. They traded iron tips for weapons to get plants or wild game from hunter-gatherers. Based on artifacts they have found, archaeologists know that Great Zimbabwe was also a trading city.

Cities in East Africa became trading centers for resources like copper and goods like coffee. Muslim traders lived in this area because it was an easy place to do their work, and they made lots of money. Muslim communities grew. **Swahili**, a culture that blended elements of African and Arab life, also developed in East Africa.

> Who lived in East Africa because it was an easy place to do work and make money?
>
> _____
> _____

CHALLENGE ACTIVITY

Critical Thinking: Analyze Use the library or Internet to research a tradition in Swahili life or Coptic Christianity. Then write a short essay that explains how the tradition shows that different cultures or ideas have blended.

DIRECTIONS On the line before each statement, write **T** if the statement is true and **F** if the statement is false. If the statement is false, change the underlined term to make the sentence true. Then write the correct term on the line after the sentence.

_____ 1. Bantu was an East African kingdom created by the descendants of Aksum.

_____

_____ 2. The name of Coptic Christianity comes from the Arabic word for "Egyptian."

_____

_____ 3. The Shona founded a kingdom called Ethiopia in about AD 1000.

_____

_____ 4. Great Zimbabwe is the name for 400 ethnic groups that come from the eastern, central, and southern regions of Africa.

_____

_____ 5. Elements of African and Arab culture are blended together in Swahili.

_____

DIRECTIONS Look at each set of vocabulary terms. On the line provided, write the letter of the term that does not relate to the others.

_____ 6. a. Ethiopia
       b. Swahili
       c. Coptic Christianity

_____ 7. a. Aksum
       b. Bantu
       c. Great Zimbabwe

Guided Reading Workbook

Later Chinese Dynasties

Lesson 1

MAIN IDEAS
1. The Period of Disunion was a time of war and disorder that followed the end of the Han dynasty.
2. China was reunified under the Sui, Tang, and Song dynasties.
3. The Age of Buddhism saw major religious changes in China.

Key Terms and People

Period of Disunion era following the fall of the Han dynasty during which China was split into several competing kingdoms

Grand Canal waterway begun by the Sui dynasty that linked northern and southern China

Empress Wu Tang ruler whose methods were sometimes vicious, but whose reign was stable and prosperous

Lesson Summary
THE PERIOD OF DISUNION
After the Han dynasty collapsed in 220, China was split into several competing kingdoms, each ruled by military leaders. This time is called the **Period of Disunion**. The era lasted for more than 350 years, from 220 to 589. During this period, nomadic tribes settled in northern China, and many northern Chinese moved south. These movements resulted in blended cultures in both north and south China.

> **What was the Period of Disunion?**
> _____
> _____
> _____
> _____

THE SUI, TANG, AND SONG
China then reunified. Under the Sui, Tang, and Song dynasties, China remained a unified nation for almost 700 years.

The Sui (SWAY) dynasty was established by a northern leader called Yang Jian (YANG jee-en). In 589, he led his army to conquer the south and reunified China. The Sui began the **Grand Canal** to link northern and southern China. In 618, the Tang dynasty replaced the Sui. The Tang ruled China for nearly 300 years. During this period,

> **Who was the first Sui ruler?**
> _____

> **How many years did the Sui dynasty last?**
> _____

Lesson 1, *continued*

Chinese power and influence reached most of eastern Asia, as well as much of Central Asia.

Historians view the Tang dynasty as a golden age of Chinese civilization. One Tang leader named Taizong (TY-tzoong) conquered most of Central Asia, reformed the military, and created law codes. In the reign of Xuanzong (SHOO-an-tzoong), culture flourished and many of China's finest poets wrote. **Empress Wu**, the only woman to rule China, ruled with an iron first, but she kept China stable and prosperous.

After the Tang dynasty fell, China became divided again and entered a period known as Five Dynasties and Ten Kingdoms. This lasted 53 years. Then, in 960, China was again unified under the Song dynasty, and another great period of accomplishment began that lasted for about 300 years, until 1279.

> Circle the names of three important Tang rulers.

THE AGE OF BUDDHISM

During the troubled Period of Disunion, many Chinese people turned to Buddhism. They took comfort in the Buddhist teaching that people can escape suffering and achieve a state of peace. During the Sui and Tang dynasties, Buddhism became well established throughout China and Buddhist temples arose across the land.

Buddhism influenced many aspects of Chinese culture, including art, literature, and architecture. Chinese Buddhist missionaries brought the religion to Japan, Korea, and other Asian lands. Despite a Tang emperor's campaign against the religion, Buddhism remained a vital part of Chinese culture.

> Why did many people convert to Buddhism during the Period of Disunion?
> _____
> _____
> _____

CHALLENGE ACTIVITY

Critical Thinking: Sequence Research the development of Buddhism in China during the Period of Disunion. Create an illustrated and annotated timeline showing key events and people in the religion's history.

DIRECTIONS Read each sentence and fill in the blank with the word in the word pair that best completes the sentence.

1. The _____ was a time when China was split into several competing kingdoms that were ruled by military leaders. **(Age of Buddhism/Period of Disunion)**

2. The only woman to rule China, _____ was a ruthless ruler, but under her reign China was stable and prosperous. **(Empress Wu/Yang Jian)**

3. Yang Jian established the _____, during which the _____ began to link China and the Period of Disunion ended. **(Sui dynasty/missionaries) (Grand Canal/Age of Buddhism)**

4. After the Tang dynasty fell, China was divided into separate kingdoms competing for power in a period known as the _____. **(Age of Buddhism/Five Dynasties and Ten Kingdoms)**

5. The period from 400 to 845 can be called the _____ because of the influence Buddhism had on Chinese culture. **(Age of Buddhism/Period of Disunion)**

6. In 960 China was reunified under the _____, which, like the Tang dynasty, was a period of great accomplishments. **(Song dynasty/Period of Disunion)**

7. During the _____, Chinese power and influence reached much of eastern Asia, as well as large parts of Central Asia. **(Tang dynasty/Period of Disunion)**

Later Chinese Dynasties

MAIN IDEAS
1. Advances in agriculture led to increased trade and population growth.
2. Cities and trade grew during the Tang and Song dynasties.
3. The Tang and Song dynasties produced fine arts and inventions.

Key Terms and People

porcelain a thin, beautiful pottery invented by the Chinese

celadon a pale green glaze that covers porcelain items

gunpowder a mixture of powders used in guns and explosives

compass an instrument that uses the earth's magnetic field to indicate direction

woodblock printing a form of printing in which an entire page is carved into a block of wood, which is covered with ink and then pressed against paper to make a copy of the page

Lesson Summary
ADVANCES IN AGRICULTURE

Under the Song dynasty, Chinese agriculture reached new heights. Farmers created elaborate irrigation systems based on new techniques and devices. The amount of land under cultivation increased. Farmers developed a new type of fast-ripening rice that enabled them to grow two or even three crops in the time it used to take to grow just one. They also learned to grow cotton efficiently and processed the fiber to make clothes and other goods.

Merchants traded food crops, so food was abundant not just in the countryside but in the cities, too. The population grew to more than 100 million people, making China the most populous country in the world.

CITIES AND TRADE

Chinese cities grew and flourished as the trade centers of the Tang and Song dynasties. Chang'an (chahng-AHN), with a population of

> What was the advantage of fast-ripening rice?
>
> _____
> _____
> _____

> How were the abundance of food and the growth of cities connected?
>
> _____
> _____
> _____

more than a million people, was by far the largest city in the world at the time. Traders used the Grand Canal to ship goods and agricultural products throughout China.

Foreign trade used both land routes and sea routes. China's Pacific ports were open to foreign traders. A bustling trade was carried on with India, Africa, and Southwest Asia. Chinese exports included tea, rice, spices, and jade. Especially prized by foreigners, however, were silk and **porcelain**. The methods of making these Chinese inventions were kept secret for centuries.

> **Why might foreigners prize Chinese silk and porcelain?**
>
> _____
>
> _____
>
> _____

ARTS AND INVENTIONS

The Tang dynasty produced some of China's greatest artists and writers, including Li Bo and Du Fu—the most famous of all Chinese poets— and the Buddhist painter Wu Daozi (DOW-tzee). The Song dynasty produced Li Qingzhao (ching-ZHOW), perhaps China's greatest female poet. Artists of both dynasties created exquisite objects in clay, particularly porcelain items with a pale green glaze called **celadon** (SEL-uh-duhn).

> **Underline three famous Chinese poets. Circle a famous Chinese artist.**

The Tang and Song dynasties produced some of the most remarkable—and important— inventions in human history, including **gunpowder** and the **compass**.

The world's oldest known printed book, using **woodblock printing**, was printed in China in 868. Later, during the Song dynasty, the Chinese invented movable type for printing. The Song dynasty also introduced the concept of paper money.

> **What printing technology was developed after woodblock printing?**
>
> _____
>
> _____

CHALLENGE ACTIVITY

Critical Thinking: Describe Write a paragraph describing an exchange of goods that could have taken place between a Song dynasty Chinese trader and a foreign merchant.

DIRECTIONS Write a word or phrase that has the same meaning as the term given.

1. compass _____

_____

2. gunpowder _____

_____

3. porcelain _____

_____

4. woodblock printing _____

_____

5. movable type _____

_____

6. celadon _____

_____

7. merchants _____

_____

8. Li Qingzhao _____

_____

DIRECTIONS Look at each set of four vocabulary terms. On the line provided, write the letter of the term that does not relate to the others.

_____ 9. a. compass   b. Li Bo   c. gunpowder   d. movable type

_____ 10. a. tea   b. porcelain   c. silk   d. Li Qingzhao

_____ 11. a. porcelain b. paper money c. movable type   d. block printing

Later Chinese Dynasties

Lesson 3

MAIN IDEAS
1. Confucianism underwent changes and influenced Chinese government.
2. Scholar-officials ran China's government during the Song dynasty.

Key Terms and People

bureaucracy body of unelected government officials

civil service service as a government official

scholar-official an educated member of the government

Lesson Summary

DEVELOPMENT OF CONFUCIANISM

Confucianism is the name given to the ideas of the Chinese philosopher Confucius. Confucius's teachings focused on ethics, or proper behavior, of individuals and governments. He argued that society would function best if everyone followed two principles, *ren* and *li*. *Ren* means concern for others, and *li* means practicing appropriate behavior. Order in society is maintained when people know their place and behave appropriately. Confucius said that order happened when young people obeyed their elders and subjects obeyed their rulers.

During the thousand years after his death, Confucius's ideas went in and out of favor several times. The Period of Disunion was a time when Buddhism became more popular than Confucianism. Buddhism also greatly influenced Chinese society during the Sui and early Tang dynasties.

Early in the Song dynasty, however, a new version of Confucianism, known as neo-Confucianism, was adopted as official government policy. In addition to teaching proper behavior, neo-Confucian scholars and

What is the meaning of *ren* and *li*?

_____

_____

_____

_____

According to Confucius, when is order in society maintained?

_____

_____

_____

_____

Under which dynasty did neo-Confucianism take hold in China?

_____

_____

Lesson 3, *continued*

officials discussed such spiritual questions as what made human beings do bad things even if their basic nature was good.

SCHOLAR-OFFICIALS

The Song dynasty took another major step that would affect China for centuries to come. The Song established a system by which people went to work for the government. These workers formed a large **bureaucracy** by passing a series of written **civil service** examinations.

How did people get government jobs under the Song dynasty?
_____
_____

The tests covered both the traditional teachings of Confucius and spiritual questions. Because the tests were extremely difficult, students spent years preparing for them. Often only very few students passed the exam.

Candidates had a good reason to study hard. Passing the tests meant life as a **scholar-official**, whose benefits included considerable respect and reduced penalties for breaking the law. Scholar-officials were admired for their knowledge and ethics. Many became wealthy because they received gifts from people who wanted their help.

Underline three benefits enjoyed by scholar-officials.

The civil service examination system helped ensure that talented, intelligent people became scholar-officials. This system was a major factor in the stability of the Song government.

CHALLENGE ACTIVITY

Critical Thinking: Elaborate Write a short essay on the relationship between the Confucian ideals of *ren* and *li* and the Chinese development of civil service examinations. Explain why you think that Confucian ethics were valued in government employees.

Lesson 3, *continued*

DIRECTIONS Read each sentence and fill in the blank with the word in the word pair that best completes the sentence.

1. _____ means service as a government official. **(Bureaucracy/Civil service)**

2. A _____ was an elite member of society who was admired for his knowledge and ethics. **(scholar-official/bureaucracy)**

3. People who went to work for the government formed a large _____, a body of unelected government officials. **(bureaucracy/scholar-official)**

4. _____ followed the teachings of Confucius but also emphasized spiritual matters. **(Civil service/Neo-Confucianism)**

5. Confucius's teachings focused on _____, or proper behavior, instead of religious beliefs. **(civil service/ethics)**

6. In order to become a government official, a person had to pass a series of exams based on the teachings of _____ and spiritual questions. **(bureaucracy/Confucius)**

DIRECTIONS On the line provided before each statement, write **T** if a statement is true and **F** if a statement is false. If the statement is false, write the correct term on the line after each sentence that makes the sentence a true statement.

_____ 7. Bureaucracy taught that people should conduct their lives according to two basic principles, *ren* and *li*.

_____

_____ 8. Often, only a small fraction of students passed the civil service examinations.

Guided Reading Workbook

Later Chinese Dynasties

Lesson 4

MAIN IDEAS
1. The Mongol Empire included China, and the Mongols ruled China as the Yuan dynasty.
2. The Ming dynasty was a time of stability and prosperity.
3. China under the Ming saw great changes in its government and relations with other countries.

Key Terms and People

Genghis Khan powerful leader who united the Mongols

Kublai Khan Genghis Khan's grandson, who completed the conquest of China

Zheng He famous seafaring voyager of the Ming dynasty

isolationism a policy of avoiding contact with other countries

Lesson Summary
THE MONGOL EMPIRE

In 1206, a powerful leader known as **Genghis Khan** (JENG-giz KAHN) united the nomadic Mongol tribes. He led huge armies on bloody expeditions of conquest throughout much of Asia and Eastern Europe. Many men, women, and children were killed, and the Mongols caused terrible destruction. By the time of Genghis Khan's death in 1227, all of northern China was under Mongol control.

Kublai Khan (KOO-bluh KAHN), Genghis Khan's grandson, declared himself emperor of China in 1279. He named his new dynasty the Yuan dynasty. This empire, which stretched all the way to Eastern Europe, covered more land than any other empire in world history. Kublai Khan's regime preserved much of the structure of the Song dynasty, including the civil service and trade routes.

The Italian merchant Marco Polo, who traveled in China, wrote about generous leaders and beautiful buildings. This sparked

What were two effects of the Mongol conquest of Asia and Eastern Europe?

_____
_____
_____
_____

Name two Mongol leaders involved in the conquest of China.

_____
_____

Guided Reading Workbook

Europeans' interest in China. However, the Chinese actually thought the Mongols were rude and uncivilized.

Two failed campaigns against Japan and expensive public works projects gradually weakened the Yuan dynasty. Many Chinese groups rebelled. Finally, in 1368, Chu Yuan-Chang (JOO yoo-ahn-JAHNG) took control and founded the Ming dynasty.

How was Marco Polo's view of the Mongols different from the way the Chinese viewed them?
_____
_____
_____
_____
_____

THE MING DYNASTY

The Ming dynasty lasted nearly 300 years, from 1368 to 1644. Ming China proved to be one of the most stable and prosperous times in Chinese history. Great Ming achievements include the fabulous ships and goodwill voyages of **Zheng He** (juhng HUH), the famous Forbidden City at the center of Beijing, and the Great Wall of China.

The Forbidden City is a huge complex of palaces, temples, and government buildings in the middle of Beijing. Ming emperors built it as a symbol of China's glory, but the Forbidden City was only for the emperor, his family and servants, and the emperor's court. Ordinary people were forbidden, or not allowed to enter, the area.

Underline three achievements that happened during the Ming dynasty.

CHINA UNDER THE MING

Around 1400 China's emperor and scholar-officials began to react against the influence of foreign goods, beliefs, and customs, and the increasing wealth and power of merchants. China entered a period of **isolationism**. However, this led to weakness that allowed Westerners to seize considerable power in some parts of China. China's imperial glory faded.

What did China's isolationism allow Westerners to do?
_____
_____
_____

CHALLENGE ACTIVITY

Critical Thinking: Make Judgments Why did Ming rulers prohibit common people from entering the Forbidden City? Imagine that you had lived during the period and write a response to this exclusionary policy.

Genghis Khan	Kublai Khan	isolationism
Ming dynasty	Zheng He	

DIRECTIONS Answer each question by writing a sentence that contains at least one word from the word bank.

1. Who was considered one of the greatest sailors during the history of early China?

_____

_____

2. Who was the powerful leader that first united the Mongols?

_____

_____

3. In the 1430s, what policy did China follow in terms of contact with other countries?

_____

_____

4. Which ruler of the Mongol Empire completed his grandfather's conquest of China?

_____

_____

5. What was the name of the prosperous and stable dynasty that rose after the defeat of the Mongols?

_____

_____

Later Chinese Dynasties

MAIN IDEAS
1. Ideas and philosophies central to life in China spread to other nearby states and took root.
2. The Koryo dynasty of Korea adopted several elements of Chinese culture, including the civil service system.
3. Under Chinese rule, the Vietnamese absorbed many features of Chinese civilization.

Key Terms and People

cultural diffusion the spread of cultural traits from one region to another

Trung sisters Vietnamese sisters who raised an army and briefly drove the Chinese out of Vietnam in AD 39; regarded as heroes in Vietnam today

Lesson Summary
NEIGHBORS TO THE NORTH, EAST, AND SOUTH

Beginning with the Sui dynasty, the Chinese forced civilizations in East Asia to live the way people did in China. Chinese traders brought their cultural ideas and philosophies with them as they traveled widely throughout Asia. This **cultural diffusion** allowed China to become a major influence in the region.

During this period, the Chinese tried to invade and conquer Korea more than once. Most times they were unsuccessful. Traders and missionaries brought elements of Chinese culture such as Buddhism into Korea.

Chinese missionaries brought Buddhism to Japan, too. Several Japanese rulers invited officials and scholars from China to visit them. The rulers wanted the Chinese to share their ideas. Vietnam was one place in Southeast Asia where Chinese culture influenced life for centuries.

Which two groups of people helped spread Chinese influence in East Asia?

_____

_____

Why did Japanese rulers invite officials and scholars from China to visit them?

_____

_____

_____

Guided Reading Workbook

CHINESE INFLUENCE IN KOREA

China's Han dynasty colonized part of Korea in 108 BC. In addition to practicing Buddhism, Koreans began to use Chinese writing, political systems, and farming methods.

By 668, the Silla had become a powerful Korean kingdom. First, it was China's ally, but then the Silla drove the Chinese out of Korea. Eventually, rebels overthrew the Silla and formed the Koryo dynasty. During the time of the Koryo, Korean artisans created beautiful pottery. Printers created metal moveable type. The Koryo did not want Korea to be exactly the same as China. It encouraged people to practice a religion that blended Buddhism with traditional Korean beliefs in nature spirits.

> **Describe the religion that the Koryo encouraged people to practice.**
>
> _____
> _____
> _____
> _____

VIETNAM SEEKS INDEPENDENCE

For about 800 years, northern Vietnam was also ruled by China. The Vietnamese were forced to use the Chinese system of government and wear Chinese clothing styles. Buddhist art and architecture became common in Vietnam.

In AD 39, the **Trung sisters** raised an army. They briefly drove the Chinese out of Vietnam, but China regained its control. In 939, the independent Vietnamese kingdom of Dai Viet was finally established. There was chaos for about 60 years.

The Ly dynasty created the first university in Vietnam. Many great works of Vietnamese literature were written during the reign of the Tran dynasty. In 1400, the Tran dynasty fell, and China took control of Vietnam again.

> **What were the Trung sisters able to do in AD 39?**
>
> _____
> _____
> _____

> **What two things happened when the Ly and Tran dynasties ruled Dai Viet?**
>
> _____
> _____
> _____
> _____
> _____

Lesson 5, *continued*

CHALLENGE ACTIVITY

Critical Thinking: Categorize Create a chart with the categories Japan, Korea, and Vietnam. Find images of ancient or present-day examples of Buddhist influence in these three nations, such as art, temples, or people worshipping. Write a caption for each image that tells what it is and how it is an example of Buddhist influence.

DIRECTIONS Write a word or descriptive phrase to describe each term.

1. cultural diffusion _____

_____

_____

2. Trung sisters _____

_____

_____

Guided Reading Workbook

Japan

MAIN IDEAS
1. Geography shaped life in Japan.
2. Early Japanese society was organized in clans, which came to be ruled by an emperor.
3. Japan learned about language, society, and government from China and Korea.
4. During the Nara period, Buddhism became the official religion of Japan.

Key Terms and People

clans extended families

Shinto the traditional religion of Japan, based on the belief that everything in nature has a spirit

Prince Shotoku popular Japanese ruler who brought many Chinese ideas to Japan

regent someone who rules a country for someone who is unable to rule alone

Lesson Summary
GEOGRAPHY SHAPES LIFE IN JAPAN

The islands of Japan are the tops of undersea mountains and volcanoes. Since it is difficult to live and farm on mountain slopes, most Japanese people lived in the coastal plains because they are flat.

Living on islands near the sea affected Japanese life and culture. Seafood has been a key part of the Japanese diet for thousands of years. They created their own religion and social structure. With Korea and China nearby, Japan isn't totally isolated and those cultures influenced the new culture of Japan.

> **What landforms make up most of Japan's islands?**
> _____
> _____

EARLY JAPANESE SOCIETY

Early Japan was home to two different cultures, neither of which had any contact with the rest of Asia. The Ainu (EYE-noo) had a different look and language from the rest of Asia. They were eventually driven back onto the northern island of Hokkaido. Over time, the Ainu culture almost disappeared.

The people living to the south of the Ainu eventually became the Japanese. Most lived in small farming villages. **Clans**, or extended families, ruled these villages. They practiced rituals that became **Shinto**, the traditional religion of Japan, which teaches that everything in nature has a spirit—*kami*.

Some clans became so powerful that they took over much of Japan. The Yamato rulers were the first clan to call themselves emperors of Japan.

What family groups controlled life in early Japanese villages?
_____

JAPAN LEARNS FROM CHINA AND KOREA

By the mid-500s, Japanese rulers sent emissaries to Korea and China to learn about their cultures. The Japanese had no written language, so they used Chinese characters to spell out Japanese sounds and words. Chinese was actually Japan's official language from about 500 to about 1100.

For about how many years was Chinese the official language of Japan?
_____

Prince Shotoku (shoh-TOH-koo) served as **regent** for his aunt, the empress. Shotoku had advisors introduce the Chinese philosophy of Confucianism to Japan. He also encouraged the spread of Buddhism. Shotoku's attempt to bring a more absolute, Chinese-style of rule to Japan was not as successful. Clan leaders, fearful of giving up power, fought against Shotoku's ideas. So the emperors gained little real power.

Underline the sentence that explains why the clan leaders did not want a Chinese-style rule.

THE NARA PERIOD

Yamato rulers had capitals on their own estates. The capital moved with each new ruler. Eventually, the Japanese followed the Chinese practice of setting up a permanent capital. Nara, in 710, became the permanent governing city. This began the 84 years known as the Nara Period in which Nara grew, built roads, and the emperor collected taxes.

Underline what Chinese practice the Japanese adopted in 710.

Guided Reading Workbook

CHALLENGE ACTIVITY

Critical Thinking: Make Inferences Japanese
rulers wanted to learn from the Chinese and
Koreans. Write a paragraph to explain why.

Buddhism	China	clans	Confucianism
Korea	Prince Shotoku	regent	Shinto
	structure		

DIRECTIONS Read each sentence and fill in the blank with the word
from the word bank that best completes the sentence.

1. The Japanese adopted many ideas about language, society,
   religion, philosophy, and government from China and
   _____.

2. The first Japanese lived mostly in small farming villages that were ruled by
   _____, or extended families.

3. A _____ is a person who rules a country for
   someone who is unable to rule alone.

4. _____ is the traditional religion of Japan.

5. One of the people most influential in bringing Chinese ideas to Japan was
   _____.

6. Among the ideas that the scholars brought back from China was
   _____, which helped shape family life in
   Japan for centuries.

7. Prince Shotoku worked to spread the religion of
   _____ across Japan.

8. The early Japanese created a religion and social
   _____ very different from those in other
   parts of Asia.

9. One of the first things the Japanese learned from
   _____ was their written language.

Japan

Lesson 2

MAIN IDEAS
1. Japanese nobles created great art in their court at Heian.
2. Buddhism changed in Japan during the Heian period.

Key Terms and People

court group of nobles who live near and serve or advise a ruler

Lady Murasaki Shikibu Japanese writer credited with writing the world's first novel

Zen form of Buddhism involving quiet, thoughtful meditation

Lesson Summary

JAPANESE NOBLES CREATE GREAT ART

In 794, the emperor and empress of Japan moved to Heian (HAY-ahn), a city now called Kyoto. The nobles who followed created an imperial **court**. These nobles had little to do with the common people of Heian. They lived apart from poorer citizens and seldom left the city. The nobles had easy lives and more free time than poorer citizens. They loved beauty and made the court at Heian the center of a golden age of art and learning between 794 and 1185.

These nobles dressed in beautiful silk robes and carried decorative fans. They were also lovers of the written and spoken word, and spent many hours writing in journals. Men usually wrote in Chinese, but many women wrote in Japanese. Thus women wrote most of the major works of early Japanese literature. Both men and women did write poetry.

Probably the greatest of these early writers was **Lady Murasaki Shikibu** (moohr-ah-SAHK-ee shee-KEE-boo). Around 1000, she wrote *The Tale of Genji*, often considered the world's first full-length novel. It is the story of a prince named Genji and his long quest for love. During his

> Why do you think the nobles of Heian devoted so much time to the promotion of the arts?
>
> _____
> _____
> _____

> Underline the title of what is considered to be the world's first novel.

search he meets women from many different social classes.

Visual arts were also popular, particularly painting, calligraphy, and architecture. The paintings were made in bright, bold colors. Most Heian architecture was based on that of the Chinese capital, Chang'an. Other architectural styles were simple and airy. Wood houses with tiled roofs featured large open spaces surrounded by elegant gardens. Performing arts also flourished at the Heian court. Eventually a form of drama called Noh developed, which combined music, dance and speaking parts. Noh plays often presented the feats of great Japanese heroes.

> **What were some of the art forms popular among the nobles of Heian?**
>
> _____
> _____
> _____
> _____

BUDDHISM CHANGES

Common Japanese people had no time for the long, elaborate rituals practiced by the court. Both groups were deeply religious, however. The Japanese introduced important changes to the Buddhism that had arrived from China. One very popular Japanese form, called Pure Land Buddhism, did not require any special rituals. Instead, Pure Land Buddhists chanted the Buddha's name over and over again to find enlightenment.

> **What did Pure Land Buddhism require of its followers?**
>
> _____
> _____
> _____
> _____

In the 1100s, a new form of Buddhism called **Zen** developed. Zen Buddhists believed that neither faith nor good behavior led to wisdom. Instead, people should practice self-discipline and meditation, or quiet thinking. These ideas appealed to many Japanese, especially warriors. As these warriors gained more influence in Japan, so did Zen Buddhism.

> **Underline the phrase that defines the central practices of Zen Buddhism.**

CHALLENGE ACTIVITY

Critical Thinking: Make Inferences If you were a noble in the Heian court who did not have to work, what would you do all day? Pretend you're a Japanese noble and write a journal entry describing a typical day.

DIRECTIONS On the line provided before each statement, write **T** if a statement is true and **F** if a statement is false. If the statement is false, write the correct term on the line after each sentence that makes the sentence a true statement.

_____ 1. Noh is a form of drama that combines music, speaking, and dance. Its plays tell about great heroes or figures from Japan's past.

_____

_____ 2. Lady Murasaki Shikibu wrote *The Tale of Genji* and is probably the greatest writer in early Japanese history.

_____

_____ 3. Calligraphy is a form of Buddhism that teaches self-discipline and meditation as the keys to wisdom.

_____

_____ 4. A group of nobles that served and advised a ruler was called a court.

_____

_____ 5. Chang'an is most famous for writing *The Tale of Genji*.

_____

_____ 6. Heian, the city now called Kyoto, was the site of the imperial court and was a great center of the arts.

_____

_____ 7. A popular form of art in Heian was Zen, which is a style of decorative writing.

_____

Japan

MAIN IDEAS
1. Samurai and shoguns took over Japan as emperors lost influence.
2. Samurai warriors lived honorably.
3. Order broke down when the power of the shoguns was challenged by invaders and rebellions.
4. Strong leaders took over and reunified Japan.

Key Terms and People

daimyo large landowners in early Japan

samurai trained professional warriors in early Japan

figurehead a person who appears to rule though real power rests with someone else

shogun a general who ruled Japan in the emperor's name

Bushido the strict samurai code of rules

Lesson Summary
SAMURAI AND SHOGUNS TAKE OVER JAPAN

While the Heian court flourished, order was breaking down in Japanese society. By the late 1100s, powerful nobles were openly at war. Rebels fought against imperial officials. Japan's rulers did not notice the problems growing in their country.

Japan's large landowners, or **daimyo** (DY-mee-oh), decided they could not rely on the emperor to protect them. They hired **samurai** (SA-muh-ry), trained professional warriors, to defend their property. Several noble clans decided to seize power themselves.

> Underline the phrase that explains why the daimyo hired their own protection in the late 1100s.

Two of these clans fought each other fiercely for 30 years. Finally, the head of the Minamoto clan declared himself Japan's new ruler. The Minamoto leader kept the emperor on as a **figurehead**. The Minamoto leader took the title **shogun**. He ruled in the emperor's name. When he died, he passed his title and power on to one of his children. For about the next 700 years, Japan was ruled by shoguns.

> To what clan did Japan's first shogun belong?
>
> _____

> Underline how many years the shoguns ruled Japan.

SAMURAI LIVE HONORABLY

The samurai enjoyed many privileges, but they also had to follow a strict code of rules called **Bushido** (BOOH-shi-doh). Loyalty and honor were central to this code. Both men and women of samurai families learned to fight. Most importantly, Bushido required a samurai be loyal to his lord. The values of loyalty and honor remain very important in modern Japan.

> **To whom were samurai loyal?**
> _____
> _____
> _____

ORDER BREAKS DOWN

The shoguns, with the help of the samurai, kept order in Japan for about a century, but that order broke down. Two foreign invasions by the Mongols were stopped. A storm helped stop the second invasion. The Japanese called it kamikaze (kah-mi-KAH-zee), or "divine wind." After the invasions, the authority of the shoguns weakened. Nobles began to resent the shoguns' power over them. The daimyo fought to limit the power of the shogun.

> **What challenges did the shoguns face to their authority?**
> _____
> _____
> _____
> _____
> _____

STRONG LEADERS TAKE OVER

Eventually, new leaders rose to power. Each fought to unify all of Japan under his control. The first to restore the power of the shogun was Oda Nobunaga (OHD-ah noh-booh-NAH-gah). Later shoguns unified Japanese rule. In 1603, the emperor made Tokugawa Ieyasu (toh-koohg-AH-wuhee e-YAHS-ooh) the shogun. He opened trade with other countries. Others, however, feared the intrusion of foreigners. In 1630, the ruling shogun closed off Japan and the samurai period lasted until the 1800s.

> **Which shogun opened Japan up the world?**
> _____
> _____

CHALLENGE ACTIVITY

Critical Thinking: Make Inferences You are an ordinary Japanese citizen living in the early 1200s. To whom do you pledge the highest allegiance—the emperor, the shogun, or the samurai who work for them? Explain your reasoning in a one-page essay.

DIRECTIONS Match the terms in the first column with their correct definition from the second column by placing the letter of the correct definition in the space provided before each term.

_____ 1. samurai

_____ 2. daimyo

_____ 3. shogun

_____ 4. figurehead

_____ 5. kamikaze

_____ 6. emperor

_____ 7. Bushido

a. person who appears to rule even though the real power rests with someone else

b. samurai code that means "the way of the warrior"

c. powerful landowners who held great power in Japan

d. the title of a general who ruled Japan in the emperor's name

e. trained professional warriors that defended the large landowners and protected their property

f. the head of Japan's government, often with little real power

g. name given to the storm that helped the Japanese soldiers defeat the second Mongol invasion

Guided Reading Workbook

Cultures of South and Southwest Asia

MAIN IDEAS
1. The Ottoman Empire covered a large area in eastern Europe and was a large commercial center.
2. Ottoman society produced lasting scientific and cultural contributions.

Key Terms and People

Janissaries enslaved youths converted to Islam and trained as soldiers

Mehmed II Ottoman ruler who defeated the Byzantine Empire

sultan Ottoman ruler

Suleyman I Ottoman ruler who led the empire to its heights

harem separate area of a household where women lived away from men

Lesson Summary
THE RISE OF THE OTTOMAN EMPIRE

Centuries after the early Arab Muslim conquests, Muslims ruled several powerful empires. One of these empires was the Ottoman Empire. This empire controlled much of Europe, Asia, and Africa. Built on conquest, the Ottoman Empire was a political and cultural force for centuries.

In the mid-1200s, Muslim Turkish warriors took land from the Christian Byzantine Empire. The Ottomans eventually ruled lands from eastern Europe to North Africa and Arabia. **Janissaries**, enslaved youths taken from conquered towns and converted to Islam, were fierce fighters for the Ottomans. The Byzantine Empire came to an end in 1453 when Ottomans led by **Mehmed II** captured Constantinople. The Ottomans named it Istanbul.

Istanbul became the capital and a commercial and cultural center. A later **sultan**, or Ottoman ruler, continued Mehmed's conquests. The Ottoman Empire reached its height under **Suleyman I**. By 1566, the Ottomans took control of the eastern Mediterranean and pushed farther into Europe.

> Underline the phrase that tells where the Ottomans found fierce soldiers.

> What year signifies the final end of the Byzantine Empire?
> _____

Ottoman society was divided into two classes. Judges and others who advised the sultan were part of the ruling class. They had to be loyal to the sultan, practice Islam, and understand Ottoman customs. The other class included Christians and Jews from lands the Ottomans had conquered. Ottoman society limited the freedom of women, especially those in the ruling class. Women had to live apart from men in an area called a **harem**.

> **Which groups were part of the ruling class in Ottoman society?**
>
> _____
>
> _____
>
> _____

SCIENTIFIC AND CULTURAL ADVANCES

The Ottoman Empire is well known for its many scientific advancements. Taqi al-Din was an Ottoman astronomer and mathematician who founded the Istanbul Observatory. He wrote books on astronomy, medicine, and physics. He used mechanical-automatic clocks to make his astronomical observations.

Since the Ottoman Empire controlled parts of different continents, people from many cultures lived under its rule. Parts of these cultures are seen in its art and architecture. Previous buildings in the region influenced Ottoman architecture. For example, the Hagia Sophia was once a Byzantine church from the fourth and fifth centuries. The Ottomans converted it to a mosque. Other mosques share its features, such as large domes. Also, the designs of exteriors, windows, and gates of mosques have features found in Italian buildings.

> **Underline the sentence that explains why elements of many cultures are found in Ottoman art and architecture.**

Literature and poetry were popular too. Yunus Emre introduced a form of mythical poetry. Some later poets imitated his style. Different forms of theater were popular, including mime shows and comedies.

> **What forms of poetry and theater were found throughout the Ottoman Empire?**
>
> _____
>
> _____

CHALLENGE ACTIVITY

Critical Thinking: Make Inferences Suppose you are a visitor to the Ottoman Empire. Write two or three journal entries about what you might see there and your impressions of Ottoman society.

DIRECTIONS Read each sentence and fill in the blank with the word in the word pair that best completes the sentence.

1. The Ottoman used fierce fighters called _____, enslaved youths that converted to Islam. **(harem /Janissaries)**

2. The Ottoman ruler who was responsible for leading the empire to its greatest heights was _____. **(Suleyman I/Mehmed II)**

3. The title given to an Ottoman ruler was _____. **(harem/sultan)**

4. The separate area of a household where women lived away from men was known as a _____. **(sultan/harem)**

5. The Ottoman ruler who was responsible for defeating the Byzantine Empire was _____. **(Suleyman I/Mehmed II)**

Cultures of South and Southwest Asia

MAIN IDEAS
1. The Safavid Empire blended Persian cultural traditions with Shia Islam.
2. The Safavids supported trade networks throughout the region.

Key Terms and People

Shia Muslims who thought that only members of Muhammad's family could become caliphs

Sunni Muslims who believed caliphs did not have to be related to Muhammad as long as they were good Muslims and strong leaders

Lesson Summary
THE SAFAVID EMPIRE

To the east of the Ottoman Empire, the Safavids, a group of Persian Muslims, started gaining power. They came into conflict with the Ottomans and other Muslims. The conflict was about the old disagreement among Muslims over who should be caliph. Since a caliph is someone who leads all Muslims, he is viewed as Muhammad's successor. During the mid-600s, Islam had split into two groups over this issue. The **Shia** were Muslims who thought that only members of Muhammad's family could become caliph. In contrast, the **Sunni** did not think caliphs had to be related to Muhammad as long as they were good Muslims and strong leaders. While the two groups both believed in daily prayer and fasting during Ramadan, some religious differences developed between them.

The Safavid leader Esma'il conquered Persia in 1501 and became shah, or king. He made Shiism, the beliefs of the Shia, the official religion of the empire. However, most people in the empire were Sunnis. Esma'il was committed to conquering other Muslim territories and converting all Muslims to Shiism. After his death, his

> What was the basis for the split between the Sunnis and the Shias?
>
> _____
> _____

> Underline the sentence that tells what Esma'il did after he became shah.

Lesson 2, *continued*

successors struggled to keep the empire together. In 1588, 'Abbas, the greatest Safavid leader, became shah. He strengthened the military and had his soldiers use gunpowder weapons. Similar to the Ottomans, 'Abbas trained foreign enslaved boys to be soldiers. Under his rule, the Safavids defeated the Uzbeks and took back land that had been lost to the Ottomans. 'Abbas also made many contributions to Safavid culture and economy.

> **What made 'Abbas the greatest Safavid leader?**
> _____
> _____
> _____
> _____
> _____

SAFAVID CULTURE AND ECONOMY

The Safavids blended Persian and Muslim traditions. They built beautiful mosques in their capital city of Esfahan. The Shah's mosque, built for 'Abbas, was admired for its colorful tiles and large dome. In the 1600s, Esfahan was considered one of the world's most magnificent cities. It was said to have 162 mosques and more than 1,800 commercial buildings. It had rugs and objects made in silver, gold, and enamel. Poetry, painting, and drawing were popular.

> **Why was Esfahan thought of as a magnificent city?**
> _____
> _____
> _____
> _____
> _____
> _____

Safavid culture was important to the empire's economy because 'Abbas encouraged the manufacturing of traditional products. Major exports included handwoven carpets, silk, and velvet. Also, the Safavids were admired for their skills in making ceramic and metal goods, especially goods made from steel.

The Safavids also built roads and bridges, which made it possible for merchants to come from as far away as Europe to trade. This led to wealth for the Safavid Empire and helped establish it as a major Islamic civilization. It lasted until the mid-1700s.

> **Underline the sentence that explains why the Safavid Empire became wealthy and a major Islamic civilization.**

CHALLENGE ACTIVITY

Critical Thinking: Make Judgments The Safavid
shah made Shiism the official religion of the
empire. Do you think he should have done this?
Write a one-page paper about his action, how it
most likely affected people of other religions, and
your opinion of this kind of rule.

DIRECTIONS Use the vocabulary words **Shia** and **Sunni** to write a
letter that relates to the lesson.

_____

_____

_____

_____

_____

_____

_____

_____

_____

_____

_____

_____

_____

_____

_____

_____

Cultures of South and Southwest Asia

Lesson 3

MAIN IDEAS
1. Sikhs believe in equality and generally reject the caste system.
2. Sikhs have responded to historical and modern-day challenges.

Key Terms and People

langar kitchen

gurdwara places of worship

Lesson Summary

SIKH RELIGIOUS PHILOSOPHIES

Sikhism began in the Punjab in the late 15th century and was started by Guru Nanak. People who follow the religion are Sikhs. Guru Nanak opposed some elements of Indian culture during his time, including the caste system. He thought people from different social classes should be treated fairly. People liked his ideas about equality. After his death, there were nine other gurus. The teachings of the ten gurus form the essential beliefs of Sikhism.

Sikhs believe that the gurus were inhabited by a single spirit. When one guru died, the spirit, or eternal Guru, transferred to the next human guru. After the tenth guru died in 1708, Sikhs believe the spirit transferred itself to the sacred scripture called Guru Granth Sahib. It has the actual words spoken by the gurus. Sikhs believe these words are the word of God, or Waheguru.

Sikhs believe that there is only one God. They believe that everyone has equal access to God and is equal before God. Like Hindus, they believe that humans cycle through life, death, and reincarnation, and they believe in karma.

> **What did Guru Nanak believe about the Hindu social classes?**
> _____
> _____
> _____
> _____

> **Underline the phrase that tells what the Sikhs believe about the ten gurus.**

> **What beliefs do Sikhs and Hindus have in common?**
> _____
> _____
> _____

Sikhs believe in equality between social classes. In Sikh places of worship, or **gurdwaras**, people sit on the floor together as a sign of equality. In addition, all people are welcome to eat together without charge in the kitchen, or **langar**.

SIKH HISTORY

During the 1600s, many Sikhs lived in India's Punjab region, which was controlled by the Mughal Empire. The Sikhs protested unfair taxes and other mistreatment. To stop the protests, the Mughals used war elephants. Violent revolts occurred throughout the region during the 1600s and 1700s.

> **How did the Mughal stop Sikh protests?**
> _____
> _____

As the Mughal Empire began to weaken, Sikh resistance got stronger. By the late 1700s, Sikhs controlled much of the Punjab. In 1799, Ranjit Singh declared himself maharaja, or ruler of the Punjab. The Sikh Empire had begun.

During this time, a gurdwara was rebuilt using marble and gold. It became a symbol of Sikh power. It was called the Golden Temple. Ranjit Singh was a strong ruler and the empire thrived. However, Ranjit Singh died in 1839, and the empire began to weaken. Then after conflict with the British, the Punjab became part of British India in 1849.

> **Who was Ranjit Singh?**
> _____
> _____
> _____
> _____
> _____

Today, there are about 25 million Sikhs worldwide. At first, most migrant Sikhs settled in India close to the Punjab. When the British took control of India in 1858, Sikhs became soldiers and were sent to the British colonies of Malaya and Hong Kong. Over time Sikh migration expanded to Asia, Australia, and North America. Also, many live in the United Kingdom.

CHALLENGE ACTIVITY

Critical Thinking: Draw Conclusions Review what
you know about Sikhism. Write a one-page paper
telling why you think Sikhism developed and
spread.

DIRECTIONS Look up the vocabulary terms **langar** and **gurdwara**
on the Internet or another resource. Write a description of each
word that is closest to the definition used in your textbook.

1. langar _____

   _____

2. gurdwara _____

   _____

Cultures of South and Southwest Asia

MAIN IDEAS
1. Akbar was able to unify the Mughal Empire through his tolerant religious and political policies.
2. Many cultures blended together to create a society unique to the Mughal Empire.

Key Terms and People

Babur founder of the Mughal Empire; the name means "tiger"

Akbar emperor who helped the Mughal Empire to grow

Lesson Summary
THE HISTORY OF THE MUGHAL EMPIRE

The Mughal Empire was to the east of the Safavid Empire in India. The Mughals were Turkish Muslims from Central Asia. **Babur**, or "tiger," was the founder of the Mughal Empire. He established it in 1526. During the mid-1500s, the empire grew under **Akbar**. He conquered new lands. He created a government with four departments and provincial governments. Akbar also had a tolerant religious policy. He stopped the tax on non-Muslims, and he included Hindus in the Mughal governments. These policies helped unite the empire.

The Mughal Empire was located along the center of trade routes that stretched across Asia. This contributed to its growth. It produced quality textiles and became a commercial center.

During the 1600s, Mughal emperors took control of almost all of India. Then a new emperor, Aurangzeb, came to power. He ordered people to obey strict religious laws and destroyed Hindu temples. He ended Akbar's tolerant policies by persecuting non-Muslims and reinstituting the tax.

> **Who was the founder of the Mughal Empire?**
> _____

> **How did Akbar's tolerant religious policies help the Mughal Empire?**
> _____
> _____

> **How was Aurangzeb different from Akbar?**
> _____
> _____
> _____
> _____

Aurangzeb's political and religious intolerance caused problems for the empire. Hindus could not have their own customs, and the entire empire was under Islamic law. Hindus and others revolted, and over time the government declined. The economy weakened and soon the empire fell apart.

The British began to take greater control over political and economic life in India. Great Britain replaced Indian leaders with British officials. Indians were unhappy and in 1857, people in different cities throughout India began a mutiny. However, the British military was strong. It had rifles and cannons, which gave the British an advantage over Indian troops. The mutiny was ended in 1858, and the last Mughal shah had to leave the region. The British had control of India.

> Underline the sentence that tells why the British were able to end the mutiny in India.

CULTURAL ACHIEVEMENTS

When Akbar had been ruler, he welcomed different forms of Hindu culture. Persians and Indians lived and worked in the same areas. So elements of their cultures blended together and formed a culture unique to the Mughal Empire.

Also during Akbar's rule, the Persian language and Persian clothing styles were popular. He also encouraged people to write in Hindi and Urdu. Education was reformed and many buildings blended Persian, Islamic, and Hindu styles.

> What languages were part of the Mughal Empire?
>
> _____

The Mughal Empire is famous for its architecture, especially the Taj Mahal. Built by Akbar's grandson as a tomb for his wife, it brought workers and materials from all over India and Central Asia. The palace buildings include a main gateway and a mosque. Its many gardens with pathways and fountains make the palace beautiful.

> What is the most famous architectural achievement of the Mughal Empire?
>
> _____

CHALLENGE ACTIVITY

Critical Thinking: Make Inferences Akbar
encouraged diversity. The United States is a
diverse society, too. Should a nation encourage
diversity? What can a lack of diversity cause?
Write a one-page paper explaining how diversity
affects you.

DIRECTIONS Write a word or descriptive phrase to describe each
person.

1. Babur _____

_____

2. Akbar _____

_____

3. Aurangzeb _____

_____

The Early Americas

MAIN IDEAS
1. The geography of the Americas is varied, with a wide range of landforms.
2. The first people to arrive in the Americas were hunter-gatherers.
3. The development of farming led to early settlements in the Americas.

Key Terms and People

Mesoamerica region that includes the southern part of what is now Mexico and parts of the northern countries of Central America

maize corn

Lesson Summary
GEOGRAPHY OF THE AMERICAS

The Americas are made up of two continents, North America and South America. These continents have a wide range of landforms. North America has high mountains, desert plateaus, grassy plains, and forests.

Historians call the cultural region in the southern part of North America **Mesoamerica**. Mesoamerica reached from the middle of modern-day Mexico south into Central America. The region's many rain forests and rivers created fertile farmland. The first farmers in the Americas domesticated plants there.

The Andes Mountains run along the western side of South America. Narrow desert runs along the edge of fishing waters in the Pacific Ocean. East of the Andes lies a region with a hot rain forest and a mighty river. The region, the river, and the rain forest all share the same name—Amazon.

> **Where was the region of Mesoamerica located?**
> _____
> _____
> _____
> _____

> **What three geographic elements share the name Amazon?**
> _____
> _____
> _____

THE FIRST PEOPLE ARRIVE

No one is sure how people first arrived in the Americas. Some scientists believe they came from Asia up to 15,000 years ago by walking over a land bridge that crossed the Bering Strait. Other historians think the first Americans arrived by sea.

> **Underline two ways that scientists think people might have come to the Americas.**

Guided Reading Workbook

The earliest people were hunter-gatherers. These people survived on wild buffalo and other animals, as well as fruits, nuts, and wild grains. They moved often, going where food was most plentiful. Some people eventually settled along the coastal areas. They fished and planted different types of seeds.

FARMING AND SETTLEMENT

The experiments with seeds led to farming. This allowed people to live in one place permanently. The first farming settlements were in Mesoamerica. By 3500 BC, Mesoamericans were growing **maize**, or corn. Later they learned to grow squash and beans. South Americans in the Andes started growing potatoes. By about 2000 BC, they were also growing maize and beans. Once people settled, the population grew. Societies began to develop religion, art, and trade opportunities.

> **When did the South Americans start growing maize and beans?**
> _____

Historians believe that the Olmecs (OHL-meks) were the first Mesoamericans to live in villages. Some Olmecs lived in bigger towns, which were centers of government and religion. They developed a large trading network. Archaeological evidence suggests the Olmecs may have created the first written language in the Americas and designed a calendar. The Chavín was the first major civilization in South America. Its city was also a center for religion and trade. The Chavín wove textiles, carved monuments, and created pottery shaped like animals.

> **What were some accomplishments of the Olmecs and the Chavín?**
> _____
> _____
> _____
> _____
> _____
> _____
> _____
> _____

Lesson 1, *continued*

CHALLENGE ACTIVITY

Critical Thinking: Sequence Draw a series of
sketches showing how the first human civilization
developed in the Americas. Start with the two
theories of how humans first arrived to the
Americas, and end with the establishment of the
Olmec and Chavín civilizations.

DIRECTIONS Write a word or descriptive phrase to describe each
term.

1. Mesoamerica _____

   _____

   _____

2. maize _____

   _____

   _____

Amazon	Chavín	Mesoamerica	North America
Olmecs	pottery	South America	textiles

DIRECTIONS Answer each question by writing a sentence that
contains at least one word from the word bank. Not all words are
used.

1. Where are the Amazon region, river, and rain forest all located?

   _____

   _____

2. Which civilization lived in villages or bigger towns that were centers of
   government and religion?

   _____

   _____

3. What did the Chavín create that was shaped like animals?

   _____

   _____

Guided Reading Workbook

The Early Americas

MAIN IDEAS
1. Geography affected early Maya civilization.
2. The Maya Classic Age was characterized by great cities, trade, and warfare.
3. A complex class structure shaped roles in Maya society.
4. The Mayas worshipped many gods and believed their kings communicated with them.
5. The Maya culture made great achievements in art, science, math, and writing.
6. Maya civilization declined, and historians have several theories about why.

Key Terms and People

obsidian a sharp, glasslike volcanic rock found in Mesoamerica

Pacal Maya king who dedicated a temple to record his achievements as ruler

observatories buildings designed to study astronomy and view the stars

Popol Vuh a book containing legends and some history of the Maya civilization

Lesson Summary
GEOGRAPHY AFFECTS EARLY MAYAS

The Maya (MY-uh) civilization developed in the lowlands of Mesoamerica around 1000 BC. Forests were a source of many resources for the Mayas. They lived in villages and traded such items as woven cloth and **obsidian**. By AD 200, the Mayas were building the first large cities in the Americas.

> What were the Mayas doing by AD 200?
>
> _____
> _____
> _____

MAYA CLASSIC AGE

Maya civilization reached its height between AD 250 and 900, a period called the Classic Age. Large stone pyramids, temples, and palaces were built to honor local kings like **Pacal** (puh-KAHL). The Mayas also built canals to bring water to the cities. Hillsides were shaped into flat terraces so crops could be grown on them. The Mayas did not have a central government. Cities often fought each other over territory and resources. This warfare was violent and destructive.

> Underline two sentences that tell how the Mayas were affected by having no central government.

ROLES IN MAYA SOCIETY

Kings held the highest position in Maya social structure. Priests, warriors, and merchants made up the upper class. The Mayas believed that their rulers were related to the gods. Most Mayas belonged to lower-class farming families. Slaves held the lowest position in Maya society.

> **Who made up the upper class in Maya society?**
> _____
> _____

RELIGIOUS TRADITIONS

The Mayas believed that their kings spoke with the gods. Each god represented a different area of life. The Mayas believed the gods could either help them or hurt them, and the gods needed blood. Special rituals of blood giving were held at births, weddings, and funerals. The Mayas made human sacrifices to the gods as well.

> **What did the Mayas believe their gods needed?**
> _____

CULTURAL ACHIEVEMENTS

The Mayas built **observatories** for their priests to study the stars. They learned that the year had about 365 days. They developed a number system and a calendar to record important events. Maya legends and history were written in a book called the *Popol Vuh* (poh-pohl VOO).

MAYA CIVILIZATION DECLINES

Maya civilization began to collapse in the 900s. Historians are not sure why. Some believe that fewer crops grew because of weakened soil and drought. Others think that the Maya people got tired of working for the kings and rebelled.

> **What are two reasons why historians think Maya civilization might have collapsed?**
> _____
> _____
> _____
> _____

CHALLENGE ACTIVITY

Critical Thinking: Evaluate Which of the Mayas' achievements do you think has had the greatest influence on history? Write a paragraph to explain your answer.

DIRECTIONS Read each sentence and circle the term in the word pair that best completes each sentence.

1. _____ is a book containing legends and some history of the Maya civilization. (**Pacal**/*Popol Vuh*)

2. Priests studied the stars in buildings called _____. (**obsidian/observatories**)

3. A Maya king named _____ dedicated a temple to record his achievements as ruler. (**Pacal**/*Popol Vuh*)

4. The Mayas traded _____, which are sharp, glasslike volcanic rocks. (**obsidian/observatories**)

The Early Americas

MAIN IDEAS
1. The Aztecs built an empire through warfare and trade, and created an impressive capital city in Mesoamerica.
2. Aztec society was divided by social roles and by class.
3. Aztec religion required human sacrifice for keeping the gods happy.
4. The Aztecs had many achievements in science, art, and language.
5. Hernán Cortés conquered the Aztec Empire.

Key Terms and People

causeways raised roads across water or wet ground

conquistadors Spanish soldiers and explorers

Hernán Cortés Spanish conquistador leader who conquered the Aztec Empire

Moctezuma II Aztec ruler who mistook Cortés for a god, leading to the Aztec's downfall

codex a written historical record

Lesson Summary

THE AZTECS BUILD AN EMPIRE

By the early 1500s, the Aztecs ruled the most powerful empire in Mesoamerica. War was key to the Aztecs. They also controlled a huge trade network. The capital city Tenochtitlán (tay-NAWCH-teet-LAHN) featured a stunning array of Aztec power and wealth. It had temples, palaces, and a busy market. Three wide **causeways** connected Tenochtitlán's island location to the shore.

> Where was Tenochtitlán located?
> _____

AZTEC SOCIETY

The king was the most important person in Aztec society. He was in charge of law, trade and tribute, and warfare. Young nobles learned to be government officials, military leaders, or priests. Just below the king and his nobles were priests and warriors. Merchants and artisans were just below them. Farmers, pawns, slaves, and captives were in the lower class. Most slaves were sold as laborers. Captives were often sacrificed to the Aztec gods.

> In Aztec society, what did young nobles learn to be?
> _____
> _____
> _____

> What often happened to captives?
> _____
> _____
> _____

AZTEC RELIGION

Like other Mesoamericans, the Aztecs always tried to please their gods. They believed sacrifice was necessary to keep the gods happy, and that the gods literally fed on human blood. Aztec priests led bloody ceremonies and sacrificed nearly 10,000 human victims a year.

SCIENCE, ART, AND LANGUAGE

The Aztecs sometimes borrowed scientific advances from the tribes they conquered. They also studied astronomy and created a calendar much like the Maya calendar. The Aztecs kept written history records in a kind of book called a **codex**. They also had strong oral and artistic traditions.

> **From whom did the Aztecs sometimes borrow scientific advances?**
> _____
> _____

CORTÉS CONQUERS THE AZTECS

Hernán Cortés (er-NAHN kawr-TAYS) led **conquistadors** into Mexico in 1519. The ruler of the Aztecs, **Moctezuma II** (MAWK-tay-SOO-mah), thought Cortés was a god. Moctezuma's motive was to welcome him, but Cortés took the emperor prisoner. Enraged, the Aztecs attacked the Spanish, and Moctezuma was killed. The conquistadors used guns and rode horses. Their attack terrified the Aztecs. The Spanish also carried diseases like smallpox that weakened and killed many Aztecs.

> **How did Cortés respond to Moctezuma's welcome?**
> _____
> _____
> _____

> **Circle the name of a disease that weakened and killed many Aztecs.**

CHALLENGE ACTIVITY

Critical Thinking: Form Opinions What do you think about Hernán Cortés and his actions? Write a one-page opinion paper defending your point of view. Give at least three examples to support your opinion.

Lesson 3, *continued*

DIRECTIONS On the line before each statement, write **T** if the statement is true and **F** if the statement is false. If the statement is false, change the underlined term to make the sentence true. Then write the correct term on the line after the sentence.

_____ 1. <u>Conquistadors</u> are raised roads across water or wet ground.

_____

_____ 2. The Spanish leader who conquered the Aztec Empire was <u>Hernán Cortés</u>.

_____

_____ 3. The Aztecs kept their written history in a book called a <u>codex</u>.

_____

_____ 4. Spanish <u>causeways</u> used guns and rode horses when they attacked the Aztecs.

_____

_____ 5. <u>Moctezuma II</u> was the Aztec ruler who thought a Spanish explorer was a god.

_____

Guided Reading Workbook

The Early Americas

MAIN IDEAS
1. The rise of the Inca Empire was due to conquest and the achievements of the Inca people.
2. For the Incas, position in society affected daily life.
3. The Incas made great achievements in building, art, and in oral literature.
4. Pizarro conquered the Incas and took control of the region.

Key Terms and People

Pachacuti ruler who expanded the Inca Empire in the mid-1400s

Quechua the official language of the Incas

llamas animals related to camels but native to South America

Atahualpa the last Inca ruler

Francisco Pizarro Spanish conquistador leader who conquered the Incas

Lesson Summary
THE RISE OF THE INCA EMPIRE

The Chavín, Nazca, Moche, and Chimú cultures influenced the development of the Inca civilization. In the mid-1400s, the ruler **Pachacuti** (pah-chah-KOO-tee) led the Incas to expand their territory. The Incas formed a strong central government and established an official language, **Quechua** (KE-chuh-wuh).

Instead of taxes, Incas had to "pay" their government in a labor tax system called the *mita* (MEE-tah). Most Incas raised **llamas**, provided grain for the army, or worked on government-owned farms and mines. There were no merchants or markets. Government officials distributed goods collected through the *mita*.

> **What four cultures influenced the development of the Inca?**
> _____
> _____
> _____

> **What was the name of the Inca labor tax system?**
> _____

SOCIETY AND DAILY LIFE

The king, priests, and government officials were the upper class in Inca society. Most Incas belonged to the lower class. This included farmers, artisans, and servants. There were no slaves in Inca society. Most children worked and did not go to school. People from conquered lands were part of the lower class.

Incas believed that Inca rulers were related to the sun god and never really died. Inca religious ceremonies often included sacrifice, but humans were rarely harmed.

> **Circle the group that was not part of Inca society.**

BUILDING, ART, AND ORAL LITERATURE

Inca workers built massive buildings and forts of huge stone blocks. The blocks were cut so precisely that no cement was needed to hold them together. The Incas also built a good system of roads. Artisans did beautiful metalwork and produced brightly colored textiles.

The Incas had no written language. Instead, they passed down stories and songs orally. After the conquistadors came, some Incas learned Spanish and wrote about Inca legends.

> **Why did the Inca not use cement to build buildings and forts?**
>
> _____
>
> _____
>
> _____

PIZARRO CONQUERS THE INCAS

On his way to be crowned king after a civil war, **Atahualpa** (ah-tah-WAHL-pah) heard that conquistadors led by **Francisco Pizarro** were in Peru. He agreed to meet with them. The Spanish tried to convert Atahualpa to Christianity, but he refused. He was captured, and the Spanish killed thousands of Inca soldiers. The Incas brought gold and silver for Atahualpa's return, but the Spanish killed him, too. They ruled the Inca lands for the next 300 years.

> **What caused the Spanish to capture Atahualpa and kill Inca soldiers?**
>
> _____
>
> _____
>
> _____

CHALLENGE ACTIVITY

Critical Thinking: Evaluate The Inca used labor as a form of currency instead of money or trading markets. What are the advantages and disadvantages of this type of economic system? Write a brief essay explaining your answer.

DIRECTIONS Write two descriptive phrases that describe the term given.

1. Quechua _____

_____

2. llamas _____

_____

3. Francisco Pizarro _____

_____

DIRECTIONS Read each sentence and fill in the blank with the word in the word pair that best completes the sentence.

4. The Incas brought gold and silver because _____ had been captured, but the Spanish killed him. **(Pachacuti/Atahualpa)**

5. _____ was the leader who expanded Inca territory. **(Francisco Pizarro /Pachacuti)**

The Early Americas

MAIN IDEAS

1. The earliest North American cultures developed in the Southwest and eastern woodlands.
2. North America's different geographical features led to the development of varied cultures.

Key Terms and People

adobe clay that the Anasazi used to make roofs for houses

potlatch social event and feast of the Northwestern Native American peoples; used to increase trade or improve relationships with others

wampum strings of beads that many Native American groups used as currency

Iroquois Confederacy powerful alliance of the Cayuga, Mohawk, Oneida, Onondaga, and Seneca Native American peoples

Lesson Summary
THE EARLIEST NORTH AMERICAN CULTURES

The Anasazi were a society that thrived in what is now the southwestern United States. They survived because they adapted to the dry environment and harsh desert conditions. For example, they built irrigation canals to bring water to their fields and villages. The Anasazi also dug pit houses into the ground. These houses had **adobe** roofs that were made of clay. A new form of architecture developed called pueblo. Pueblo structures were like modern apartment buildings. They were several stories tall and had many rooms.

> **Why were the Anasazi able to survive and thrive in the Southwest?**
> _____
> _____
> _____

Historians are not sure why, but the Anasazi began to abandon their villages after AD 1300. Drought, disease, or attacks might have caused them to leave the area. Descendants of the Anasazi still live in the Southwest.

> **What three reasons might have caused the Anasazi to abandon their villages?**
> _____
> _____
> _____

Guided Reading Workbook

A different culture developed in the woodlands along the Mississippi and Ohio rivers. The two rivers provided large amounts of fish to eat and fertile land to use. People also had access to transportation routes. Societies in this region were known for building huge earthen mounds. Historians call them the mound-building cultures. The Hopewell built their mounds as burial sites. Later, a more advanced culture named the Mississippians built mounds for religious ceremonies.

> **How were the mounds built by the Mississippians different from the mounds built by the Hopewell?**
>
> _____
> _____
> _____
> _____
> _____

LATER CULTURES

By the 1500s, there were thousands of Native American groups in North America. The environment in each region affected how people lived and culture developed. Many Northwestern cultures depended on fish like salmon for food. In these communities, **potlatches** were social events that encouraged trade and good relations. Objects like totem poles were important religious symbols.

Cultures that lived on the Great Plains were nomadic peoples. The region had few trees, so hunters used bows and arrows to provide buffalo hides for shelter and meat for food.

> **Why did Great Plains hunters provide buffalo hides for shelter?**
>
> _____
> _____

Southeastern groups like the Cherokee and the Seminole used **wampum** as currency. People in this region farmed, hunted, gathered plants, and fished. Villages were governed by councils.

In the Northeast, family and social life was based on the clan. Clans were responsible for the well-being of their members. Five Native American peoples formed the **Iroquois Confederacy**. This strong alliance waged war or made peace with peoples who were not part of the group.

> **What were the clans responsible for in Northeastern groups?**
>
> _____
> _____

CHALLENGE ACTIVITY

Critical Thinking: Compare and Contrast Use print or digital resources to research the Iroquois Confederacy and a modern-day alliance like NATO. Write a short summary that gives examples of how the organizations are the same and different from each other.

DIRECTIONS Look at each set of four terms. On the line provided, write the letter of the term that does not relate to the others.

_____ 1. a. strings of beads
   b. the Anasazi
   c. Cherokee and Seminole
   d. currency

_____ 2. a. clay
   b. pueblo
   c. form of architecture
   d. village council

_____ 3. a. feast
   b. increase trade
   c. clan
   d. social event

_____ 4. a. Great Plains
   b. powerful alliance
   c. Mohawk and Seneca
   d. war and peace

The Middle Ages

MAIN IDEAS
1. Geography has shaped life in Europe, including where and how people live.
2. Christianity spread to northern Europe through the work of missionaries and monks.
3. The Franks, led by Charlemagne, created a huge Christian empire and brought together scholars from around Europe.
4. Invaders threatened much of Europe in the 700s and 800s.

Key Terms and People

Eurasia the large landmass that includes Europe and Asia

Middle Ages the period lasting from about 500 to about 1500

medieval another name for the Middle Ages

Patrick Christian missionary credited with converting Ireland to Christianity

monks religious men who lived apart from society in isolated communities

monasteries communities of monks

Benedict monk responsible for creating the Benedictine Rule, a set of rules for monks

Charlemagne warrior and king who led the Franks in building a huge empire

Lesson Summary

GEOGRAPHY SHAPES LIFE IN EUROPE

Europe is a small but diverse continent with different landforms, water features, and climates. We call Europe a continent, but it is part of **Eurasia**, a large landmass that includes both Europe and Asia. The climates and vegetation vary widely from region to region. Its geography influenced where and how people lived. In southern Europe, most people lived on coastal plains or river valleys and farmed. Those near the sea became traders and seafarers. In northern Europe, the rivers provided transportation and towns grew along them. Farmers grew all sorts of crops on the excellent farmland near the cities. The flat land, however, made it easy for invaders to enter. These invasions changed Europe.

> Why is Europe considered to be part of Eurasia?
>
> _____
> _____
> _____

Guided Reading Workbook

CHRISTIANITY SPREADS TO NORTHERN EUROPE

As the Roman Empire fell, various groups from the north and east moved into former Roman lands, creating their own states and making their own kings. These kings often fought among themselves, dividing Europe into many small kingdoms. This marked the beginning of the **Middle Ages**, or **medieval** period.

In the early Middle Ages, most kingdoms of northern Europe were not Christian. The pope sent missionaries and converted much of Britain, then Germany, and France. One early missionary, **Patrick**, was an English Christian who took it upon himself to convert Ireland. Unlike missionaries, **monks** lived apart from society in isolated communities, where they prayed, worked, and meditated. Communities of monks, or **monasteries**, were built all over Europe in the Middle Ages. Most monks followed a strict set of rules created in the early 500s by **Benedict**.

> How was Europe ruled at the beginning of the Middle Ages?
>
> _____
> _____
> _____

> Why did Patrick go to Ireland?
>
> _____
> _____
> _____

THE FRANKS BUILD AN EMPIRE

In the 500s, a powerful Germanic tribe called the Franks conquered Gaul, the region we now call France. The Franks became Christian and created one of the strongest kingdoms in Europe. The Franks reached their greatest power during the 700s under **Charlemagne** (SHARH-luh-mayn). Religious scholarship flourished in Charlemagne's time.

> Underline the name of the most powerful leader of the Franks.

INVADERS THREATEN EUROPE

While Charlemagne was building his empire, Europe was being attacked on all sides by invaders. The most fearsome invaders were the Vikings from Scandinavia.

> Who were the most fearsome invaders during Charlemagne's reign?
>
> _____
> _____

CHALLENGE ACTIVITY

Critical Thinking: Make Inferences The life of a
monk was strict. Write a letter from the point of
view of someone who wishes to join a monastery.
Explain why you want to live the life of a monk.

DIRECTIONS Read each sentence and fill in the blank with the word
in the word pair that best completes the sentence.

1. The large landmass that includes both Europe and Asia is called
_____. **(Eurasia/Northern Europe)**

2. _____ were religious men who lived apart from society
in isolated communities. **(Charlemagne/Monks)**

3. The _____ fall between ancient times and modern
times. **(medieval/Middle Ages)**

5. One of the first missionaries to travel to northern Europe was
_____, who took it upon himself to teach people about
Christianity. **(Benedict/ Patrick)**

6. _____ was a brilliant warrior and a strong king who
led the Franks in building a huge empire. **(Patrick/Charlemagne)**

7. Monks live in communities called _____. **(monasteries/
medieval)**

8. An Italian monk by the name of _____ created a set of
rules that most European monasteries followed. **(Patrick/Benedict)**

9. Another name for the Middle Ages is the _____
period. **(monasteries/medieval)**

The Middle Ages

MAIN IDEAS
1. Feudalism governed how knights and nobles dealt with each other.
2. Feudalism spread through much of Europe.
3. The manor system dominated Europe's economy.
4. Towns and trade grew and helped end the feudal system.

Key Terms and People

knights warriors who fought on horseback

vassal a knight who promised to support a lord in exchange for land

feudalism the system that governs the relationship between lords and vassals

William the Conqueror French noble who conquered England and spread feudalism

manor large estate owned by a knight or lord

serfs workers who were tied to the land on which they lived

Eleanor of Aquitaine powerful French noblewoman who became queen of France and England

Lesson Summary
FEUDALISM GOVERNS KNIGHTS AND NOBLES

When the Vikings, Magyars, and Muslims began their raids in the 800s, the Frankish kings were unable to defend their empire. Nobles had to defend their own lands. Many nobles began to rule their lands as independent territories. These nobles needed soldiers. They gave **knights**, warriors who fought on horseback, land in exchange for military service. A noble who gave land to a knight was called a lord, while the knight was called a **vassal**. The system that governed the promises between lords and vassals is called **feudalism**.

Lords and vassals had responsibilities to each other. A lord had to send help if an enemy attacked a vassal. A lord had to be fair or vassals could break all ties with him. Vassals had to fight at a lord's command. They also had to house and feed a lord if he visited and sometimes pay him money.

> **Why did many nobles become rulers of their own lands?**
> _____
> _____
> _____

> **List two responsibilities of a vassal toward a lord.**
> _____
> _____
> _____
> _____
> _____

Lesson 2, *continued*

FEUDALISM SPREADS

Frankish knights introduced feudalism into northern Italy, Spain, and Germany. From Germany, knights carried feudalism into eastern Europe. Feudalism reached Britain when **William the Conqueror** invaded and made himself king of England.

> **Who brought feudalism to Britain?**
> _____
> _____

THE MANOR SYSTEM

An estate owned by a knight or lord was called a **manor**. As fighters, knights had no time to work in the fields. Most peasants, or small farmers, owned no land but needed to grow food to live. Knights let them live and farm land on their estates. In return, the peasants gave them food or other payment. **Serfs**, workers who were tied to the land on which they lived, were not allowed to leave without their lord's permission. Skilled workers also lived and worked on the manor. They traded goods and services to the peasants in exchange for food.

Women in the Middle Ages had fewer rights than men, but they still played important roles in society. Some women, like the French woman **Eleanor of Aquitaine**, even became politically powerful.

> **What did knights and peasants provide each other under feudalism?**
> _____
> _____
> _____

TOWNS AND TRADE GROW

Most people lived on manors or small farms during the Middle Ages. However, as Europe's population grew, more people began living in towns and cities. The invention of a horse collar and a heavier plow made more food available. Increased trade eventually led to the decline of feudalism because people could make a living by making or selling particular types of goods.

> **What changes helped lead to a decline in feudalism?**
> _____
> _____
> _____
> _____
> _____
> _____

CHALLENGE ACTIVITY

Critical Thinking: Summarize During the Middle Ages, the ability for people to improve their lives depended upon where they started out in life. Research the options for advancement for one of the following people: the lord of a manor, lady of a manor, a vassal, or a peasant. Then write a short summary describing any options this person had.

DIRECTIONS On the line provided before each statement, write **T** if a statement is true and **F** if a statement is false. If the statement is false, write the correct term on the line after each sentence that makes the sentence a true statement.

_____ 1. <u>William the Conqueror</u> declared himself king of England after defeating the English king near the town of Hastings.

_____

_____ 2. <u>Eleanor of Aquitaine</u> was a French woman who had great political power.

_____

_____ 3. A knight who promised to support a lord in exchange for money was called a <u>serf</u>.

_____

_____ 4. <u>Vassals</u> were tied to the land on which they lived and could not leave their land without permission from the lord.

_____

_____ 5. The best soldiers were <u>manors</u>, or warriors who fought on horseback.

_____

_____ 6. The large estate owned by a knight or a lord was called a <u>manor.</u>

_____

_____ 7. <u>Fiefs</u> were parcels of land that nobles gave knights for their military service.

_____

The Middle Ages

MAIN IDEAS
1. Popes and kings ruled Europe as spiritual and political leaders.
2. Popes fought for power, leading to a permanent split within the church.
3. Kings and popes clashed over some issues.

Key Terms and People

excommunicate casting an offender out of the church

Pope Gregory VII pope who excommunicated Emperor Henry IV

Emperor Henry IV Holy Roman ruler who challenged Pope Gregory VII

Lesson Summary

POPES AND KINGS RULE EUROPE

In the early Middle Ages, great nobles and their knights held most of the political power. As time passed this power began to shift to two types of leaders, popes and kings. Popes had great spiritual power. The kings had political power. Together, popes and kings controlled most of European society.

The pope was the head of the Christian Church in Western Europe. Since nearly everyone in the Middle Ages belonged to this church, the pope had great power. Christians believed that the pope was God's representative on Earth. Because the pope was seen as God's representative, it was his duty to decide what the church would teach. From time to time, a pope would write a letter called a bull to explain a religious teaching or outline a church policy.

It was also the pope's duty to decide when someone was acting against the church. For the most serious offenses, the pope could choose to **excommunicate**, or cast out, an offender from the church. The offender, upon death, would not get into heaven. This much power often put the pope in direct conflict with the kings.

> **Name two of the pope's responsibilities as leader of the Christian Church.**
> _____
> _____
> _____
> _____
> _____

> **Why do you think people feared the pope's ability to excommunicate them?**
> _____
> _____
> _____

Guided Reading Workbook

In 1000 Europe was divided into many small
states that were ruled by kings. Many of the kings
did not have much power. But the kings of
England, France, and the Holy Roman Empire
held a lot of power. In France and England, kings
inherited the throne through their fathers. The Holy
Roman Empire got its name because the empire
existed with the pope's approval. In the Holy
Roman Empire, the nobles elected the emperor.
The pope settled any disagreements among the
nobles.

> Underline how kings were
> selected in France and
> England. Then, circle how
> an emperor was selected in
> the Holy Roman Empire.

POPES FIGHT FOR POWER

The bishops of eastern Europe, unlike those
in western Europe, did not consider the pope
the head of the church. Pope Leo IX
excommunicated the bishop of Constantinople
when the bishop would not recognize the pope's
authority. This caused a permanent split, called a
schism, in the church. The bishop's supporters
formed the Orthodox Church. The pope headed
the Roman Catholic Church from Rome.

> What event caused a
> permanent split in the
> church?
>
> _____
> _____
> _____
> _____
> _____

KINGS AND POPES CLASH

Popes also argued with kings, particularly over
the king's right to select bishops. A dispute arose
when **Pope Gregory VII** did not like a bishop
chosen by the Holy Roman **Emperor Henry IV**.
Henry tried to remove the pope from office. The
pope excommunicated Henry. Henry had to beg
for the pope's forgiveness to remain in power.
After their deaths, a compromise was reached.
From then on, the pope would select religious
officials, but religious officials would have to
obey the emperor.

> How did Pope Gregory
> respond to Henry IV's
> attempt to remove him
> from power?
>
> _____
> _____
> _____

CHALLENGE ACTIVITY

Critical Thinking: Contrast Popes and kings both had power during the Middle Ages. Write two paragraphs to show how their powers were different using examples from the text.

DIRECTIONS Match the terms in the first column with the correct definition from the second column by placing the letter of the correct definition in the space provided before each term.

_____ 1. excommunicate

_____ 2. Pope Gregory VII

_____ 3. Henry IV

_____ 4. Roman Catholic Church

_____ 5. kings

_____ 6. Holy Roman Empire

_____ 7. popes

a. Holy Roman Emperor in 1073

b. their power was inherited from their fathers

c. excommunicated Emperor Henry IV

d. powerful spiritual leaders

e. to cast out from the church

f. state that existed with the pope's approval

g. led by a pope

DIRECTIONS Read each sentence and circle the term in the word pair that best completes each sentence.

8. After a disagreement over who could select bishops, _____ was excommunicated from the church. **(Henry IV/ Pope Gregory VII)**

9. People feared being _____ because they would not go to heaven when they died. **(evicted/excommunicated)**

10. Because the _____ was seen as God's representative, it was his duty to decide what the church would teach. **(pope/king)**

11. The _____, ruled by an emperor, got its name because the pope approved of it. **(Roman Catholic Church/Holy Roman Empire)**

The Middle Ages

MAIN IDEAS
1. The pope called on Crusaders to invade the Holy Land.
2. Despite some initial success, the later Crusades failed.
3. The Crusades changed Europe forever.

Key Terms and People

Crusades a long series of wars fought between Christians and Muslims over control of Palestine

Holy Land the European name for Palestine, the region where Jesus had lived, preached, and died

Pope Urban II head of the Roman Catholic Church who started the Crusades

King Richard I English king who led the third, ill-fated Crusade to seize Palestine

Saladin Turkish leader of the Muslim forces that prevented England from taking Palestine

Lesson Summary
CRUSADERS INVADE THE HOLY LAND

The **Crusades** were a long series of wars between Christians and Muslims in Southwest Asia. The Europeans fought the Muslims to retake Palestine. Christians call the region the **Holy Land** because it was where Jesus had lived, preached, and died.

For many years, Palestine had been ruled by Muslims. In general, the Muslims did not bother Christians who visited the region. In the late 1000s, however, a new group of Turkish Muslims captured the city of Jerusalem. Pilgrims returning to Europe said that these Turks had attacked them.

Before long the Turks began to raid the Byzantine Empire. The Byzantine emperor asked **Pope Urban II** of the Roman Catholic Church for help. Although the Byzantines were Eastern Orthodox Christians and not Roman Catholic, the pope agreed to help.

> Why did Christians call Palestine the "Holy Land"?
> _____
> _____

> Underline the name of the person who made the call to arms that led to the Crusades.

Pope Urban called on Christians to retake the Holy Land from the Muslim Turks. Crusaders from all over Europe flocked to France to prepare to fight. About 5,000 Crusaders left Europe for the Holy Land in 1096. Many were peasants, not soldiers. On their way to the Holy Land, the peasant Crusaders attacked Jews in Germany. They blamed the Jews for Jesus's death. Turkish troops killed most of these untrained peasants before they even reached the Holy Land. However, the nobles and knights, in 1099, were able take Jerusalem and set up four kingdoms there.

> **What happened to the peasant Crusaders?**
>
> _____
>
> _____
>
> _____
>
> _____

LATER CRUSADES FAIL

Within 50 years the Muslims had started taking land back from the Christians. The Europeans launched more Crusades, but these invasions ended in defeat for the Christians. The Third Crusade started as a group effort between the German, French, and English kings. But only **King Richard I** of England stayed on to fight. His opponent was the brilliant Muslim leader **Saladin**, known for his kindness toward fallen enemies. Eventually, King Richard left the Holy Land, which was still under Muslim control. By 1291, Muslim armies had taken back all of the Holy Land. The Crusades were over.

> **Underline the name of the English and Muslim leaders fighting in the Third Crusade.**

CRUSADES CHANGE EUROPE

The Crusades increased trade between Europe and Asia. In some cases, the Crusades increased the power of the European kings. But the main impact of the wars was divisive. The Crusades hurt the trust European Jews had developed with Christians. The Crusades also caused distrust between Muslims and Christians. Those tensions are still felt today.

> **How did the Crusades affect relations between Europe and Asia?**
>
> _____
>
> _____
>
> _____
>
> _____
>
> _____
>
> _____

Guided Reading Workbook

CHALLENGE ACTIVITY

Critical Thinking: Make Judgments Using what
you know, write a brief paper describing how the
Crusades continue to have an impact on our
society today.

Crusades	Holy Land	King Richard I	Muslims
Palestine	Pope Urban II	Saladin	

DIRECTIONS Read each sentence and fill in the blank with the word
from the word bank that best completes the sentence.

1. _____ agreed to help the Byzantines who were attacked
   by Muslim Turks in the Holy Land.

2. The leader of the Muslim forces who was respected for his kindness toward
   fallen enemies was _____.

3. The _____ were a long series of wars between
   Christians and Muslims in Southwest Asia.

4. Though the rulers of England, France, and the Holy Roman Empire led
   armies during the Third Crusade, only _____ of
   England stayed in the Holy Land to fight.

5. Palestine is called the _____ because it was the region
   where Jesus had lived, preached, and died.

6. The goal of the Crusades was to take the control of
   _____ away from the Muslim Turks.

7. The English leader _____ returned home with
   Jerusalem still in Muslim hands.

8. Following the Crusades, tension between Christians and Jews and
   _____ grew.

The Middle Ages

MAIN IDEAS
1. The Christian Church shaped both society and politics in medieval Europe.
2. Orders of monks and friars did not like the church's political nature.
3. Church leaders helped build the first universities in Europe.
4. The church influenced the arts in medieval Europe.

Key Terms and People

clergy church officials

religious order group of people who dedicate their lives to religion and follow common rules

Francis of Assisi founder of the Franciscan order

friars members of religious orders who lived and worked among the general public

Thomas Aquinas philosopher who showed how religious faith and reason could coexist

natural law Thomas Aquinas's concept that God created a law that governed how the world operated

Lesson Summary

THE CHURCH SHAPES SOCIETY AND POLITICS

The **clergy**, church officials, were very influential in medieval European culture and politics. For many people in the European Middle Ages, life revolved around the local church. Markets, festivals, and religious ceremonies all took place there. Some people made pilgrimages, or journeys to religious locations.

The church owned a lot of land in Europe because many people left their property to the church when they died. In this way the church became a major feudal lord. Of all the clergy, bishops and abbots were most involved in political matters. They often advised local rulers.

> **How did the church become a feudal lord during the Middle Ages?**
>
> _____
>
> _____
>
> _____

Lesson 5, *continued*

MONKS AND FRIARS

Some people thought that the church was becoming too involved with politics. The French monks of Cluny established a new **religious order**. They dedicated their lives to religion and followed a strict schedule of worship. Other new orders followed. Women created religious communities in convents. Most monks lived apart from society, but two new religious orders developed for those who wanted to live, work, and teach among people. These were the Dominicans, started by Dominic de Guzmán, and the Franciscans, started by **Francis of Assisi**. The members of these orders were called **friars**.

> **Underline the sentence that explains why the monks of Cluny established a new religious order.**

> **How were the Dominicans and Franciscans different from the orders who lived in monasteries?**
> _____
> _____
> _____

UNIVERSITIES ARE BUILT

Europe's first universities were built by the church. Religion, law, medicine, and philosophy were taught. Scholars wanted to establish a connection between religious faith and human reason. The Dominican friar **Thomas Aquinas** wrote a reasoned argument for the existence of God. He also developed a philosophical system called **natural law** to show how God had ordered the world.

> **Why did Thomas Aquinas write about the existence of God?**
> _____
> _____
> _____
> _____

THE CHURCH AND THE ARTS

In the 1100s Europeans built great Gothic cathedrals that are beautiful architectural achievements. They were symbols of people's faith. Everything, including the high ceilings and stained glass windows, were designed to show respect for God. Everything inside the church, from the clergy's robes to the books used, were works of art.

> **Why do you think so much medieval European art was made for the church?**
> _____
> _____
> _____
> _____
> _____

CHALLENGE ACTIVITY

Critical Thinking: Draw Conclusions Which medieval religious people do you agree with the most—those involved in politics, the monks who left society, or the friars who believed in working among the people? Write a one-page paper defending your views.

DIRECTIONS Read each sentence and fill in the blank with the word in the word pair that best completes the sentence.

1. As a young man, _____ gave all of his possessions away and began preaching and tending to people who were poor or ill. **(Francis of Assisi/Thomas Aquinas)**

2. _____, according to Thomas Aquinas, is created by God and governs how the world operates. **(Natural law/Religious order)**

3. Journeys to religious locations are also referred to as _____. **(friars/pilgrimages)**

4. Dominican philosopher _____ believed reason and faith could work together. **(Francis of Assisi/Thomas Aquinas)**

5. The _____, or church officials, and their teachings were very influential in European culture and politics. **(friars/clergy)**

6. A group of people who dedicate their lives to religion and follow common rules is a _____. **(clergy/religious order)**

7. _____ were people who belonged to religious orders but lived and worked among the general public. **(Friars/Clergy)**

The Middle Ages

Lesson 6

MAIN IDEAS
1. Magna Carta caused changes in England's government and legal system.
2. The Hundred Years' War led to political changes in England and France.
3. The Black Death led to social changes.
4. The church reacted to challengers by punishing people who opposed its teachings.
5. Christians fought Moors in Spain and Portugal in an effort to drive all Muslims out of Europe.
6. Jews faced discrimination across Europe in the Middle Ages.

Key Terms and People

Magna Carta document written by English nobles and signed by King John listing rights the king could not ignore

Parliament lawmaking body that governs England

Hundred Years' War long conflict between England and France during the 1300s and 1400s

Joan of Arc teenage peasant girl who rallied the French troops during the Hundred Years' War

Black Death deadly plague that killed millions of Europeans from 1347 and 1351

heresy religious ideas that oppose accepted church teachings

Reconquista Christian efforts to retake Spain from the Muslim Moors

King Ferdinand Aragon prince who married Isabella of Castile to rule a united Spain

Queen Isabella Castilian princess who ruled Spain with her husband, Ferdinand of Aragon

Spanish Inquisition organization of priests charged with seeking out and punishing non-Christians

Lesson Summary
MAGNA CARTA CAUSES CHANGE IN ENGLAND

In 1215, a group of English nobles decided to force the king to respect their rights. They made King John approve a document listing 63 rights the king had to follow. This document was called **Magna Carta**, or "Great Charter." This charter became a key principle of English government

What was Magna Carta?
_____
_____
_____
_____

and an important step in the development of democracy.

The kings soon turned to a council of nobles for advice and money. This council developed into **Parliament**, the lawmaking body that still governs England today.

Who made up the original British Parliament?
_____
_____

THE HUNDRED YEARS' WAR

In Europe, kings were not giving up their power, but other events forced changes. The **Hundred Years' War**, a long conflict between England and France, started when the English king invaded France. Nearly 100 years later **Joan of Arc**, a teenage peasant girl, rallied the French troops. The English killed Joan, but the French won the war.

Why was Joan of Arc's feat truly remarkable?
_____
_____
_____
_____
_____

THE BLACK DEATH

During the Hundred Years' War an even greater crisis arose. This crisis was the **Black Death**, a deadly plague that swept through Europe between 1347 and 1351. The plague originally came from infected rats from central and eastern Asia.

Some historians think the Black Death killed a third of Europe's population—perhaps 25 million people. This caused sweeping changes all over Europe. The old manor system, already weakened by the growth of cities, fell apart. Plague survivors found their skills in high demand. They could demand wages for their labor. Many fled their manors, moving to Europe's growing cities. The power of the church also began to decline.

Underline the estimated number of victims of the Black Death.

How did the Black Death change Europe?
_____
_____
_____
_____
_____

Lesson 6, *continued*

THE CHURCH REACTS TO CHALLENGERS

Around 1100, some Christians felt that the clergy were more concerned with money and land than with God. Others did not agree with the church's ideas and preached their own ideas about religion. Religious ideas that oppose church teachings are called **heresy**. Church officials sent priests and friars throughout Europe to find heretics.

In the early 1200s, Pope Innocent III called for a crusade against heretics in southern France. The result was a bloody struggle that lasted about 20 years, destroying towns and cities and costing thousands of lives.

> **What two things did some Christians feel that the clergy was more concerned with than God?**
>
> _____
>
> _____

CHRISTIANS FIGHT THE MOORS

In Spain, the reign of the Muslim Moors collapsed in the 1000s. Christian kingdoms in Spain started a war to drive them out. They called their war **Reconquista** (reh-kahn-KEES-tuh), or reconquest. The kingdom of Castile freed itself of Muslim rule. Portugal and Aragon soon followed. Castile and Aragon became united by the marriage of two royals, **King Ferdinand** of Aragon and **Queen Isabella** of Castile. Spain became a nation-state. In addition to banning Islam, the royals required all Jews to convert to Christianity or leave.

> **What was the Reconquista?**
>
> _____
>
> _____

Ferdinand and Isabella created the **Spanish Inquisition**, an organization of priests that found and punished non-Christians. The inquisition executed about 2,000 people in Spain and almost 1,400 more in Portugal.

> **How many people in both Portugal and Spain died at the hands of the Spanish Inquisition?**
>
> _____
>
> _____

JEWS FACE DISCRIMINATION

Jews were persecuted all over Europe. Many Christians blamed all Jews for the persecution and death of Jesus. Some people even blamed the Jews for the Black Death. In many kingdoms, Jews were driven out by angry mobs, and sometimes by the kings themselves. They had to flee from their homes or die.

> **Name two things that some medieval Europeans blamed on the Jews.**
>
> _____
>
> _____

Guided Reading Workbook

CHALLENGE ACTIVITY

Critical Thinking: Make Inferences Write a one-page paper explaining how our lives might be different if the Magna Carta had *not* been created.

DIRECTIONS Match the terms in the first column with their correct definition from the second column by placing the letter of the correct definition in the space provided before each term.

_____ 1. Magna Carta

_____ 2. Parliament

_____ 3. Hundred Years' War

_____ 4. Joan of Arc

_____ 5. Black Death

a. teenage peasant girl that rallied the French troops

b. long conflict between England and France

c. a document listing rights that the king could not ignore

d. a deadly plague that swept through Europe between 1347 and 1351

e. the lawmaking body that governs England today

DIRECTIONS Read each sentence and fill in the blank with the word in the word pair that best completes the sentence.

6. King _____ was a prince from Aragon, one of the largest Spanish kingdoms. **(John/ Ferdinand)**

7. The _____ was the effort to retake Spain from the Moors. **(Reconquista/Hundred Years War)**

8. The _____ was an organization of priests that looked for and punished non-Christians in Spain. **(Reconquista/Spanish Inquisition)**

9. _____ was married to King Ferdinand and together they ruled all of Spain. **(Queen Isabella/Joan of Arc)**

10. Religious ideas that disagree with church teachings are called _____. **(Black Death/heresy)**

Guided Reading Workbook

The Renaissance

Lesson 1

MAIN IDEAS
1. European trade with Asia increased in the 1300s.
2. Trade cities in Italy grew wealthy and competed against each other.
3. As Florence became a center for arts and learning, the Renaissance began.

Key Terms and People

Marco Polo European explorer who traveled through Asia in the 1200s

interest a fee that borrowers pay for the use of someone else's money

Cosimo de' Medici wealthy banker who turned Florence into a center of arts, culture, and education

Renaissance period following the Middle Ages, characterized by renewed interest in Greek and Roman culture and an emphasis on people as individuals

Lesson Summary
TRADE WITH ASIA

Despite the Black Death's terrible death toll, the disease did not harm farmland, buildings, ships, machines, or gold. Survivors used these things to raise more food or make new products. Europe's economy began to grow. Some new products from the east appeared in markets. Traders brought these new goods across the Silk Road, a caravan route from Europe to China that had fallen into disuse. In the 1200s, the Mongols reopened the Silk Road.

A traveler named **Marco Polo** journeyed along the Silk Road. When he and his family arrived in China, they met the Mongol emperor Kublai Khan. He made Marco Polo a government official.

Marco Polo visited India and Southeast Asia as a messenger for the emperor. He spent 20 years in Asia. When he returned to Venice, a writer helped him record his journey. His descriptions made Europeans curious about Asia. People began to demand goods from Asia. Trade between Europe and Asia increased.

> **List two consequences of the Black Death.**
> _____
> _____
> _____
> _____
> _____
> _____
> _____
> _____

> **Who recorded information about his journey that made Europeans curious about Asia?**
> _____

Guided Reading Workbook

TRADE CITIES IN ITALY

By the 1300s, Florence, Genoa, Milan, and Venice had become major trading centers in Italy. Venice and Genoa were port cities. Huge ships brought goods from Asia into their harbors. From there, merchants shipped the goods across Europe. However, more than goods were exchanged in these cities. People from many cultures interacted. Ideas began to spread throughout Europe and other places.

Italian cities also were manufacturing centers. They made many specialized products. Venice produced glass. Milan was known for weapons and silk. Florence was a center for weaving wool into cloth. Economic activity made Italy's merchant families wealthy.

> Underline the names of the major trading cities in Italy during the 1300s.

> How did ideas begin to spread throughout Europe?
> _____
> _____
> _____

FLORENCE

Florence developed a banking system used all over Europe. Bankers made money by charging **interest**, which is a fee that borrowers pay for the use of someone else's money. The greatest bankers were the Medici family, who were also the richest family in Florence. In Italian cities, rich families controlled the government. By 1434, **Cosimo de' Medici** ruled Florence. He wanted to make Florence the most beautiful city in the world. He hired artists to decorate his palace and architects to redesign many buildings. He valued education and Florence became a center of art, literature, and culture. This love of art and education was key to the **Renaissance**, which means "rebirth." It followed the Middle Ages, but its ideas were different from that period. It saw an interest in Greek and Roman writings and emphasized people as individuals.

> Who usually controlled the Italian cities during this time period?
> _____

> How did the Renaissance come about?
> _____
> _____
> _____
> _____
> _____

CHALLENGE ACTIVITY

Critical Thinking: Make Inferences Why do you think beauty and education were so important to the Medici family of Florence? Write a short paper explaining your answer.

Cosimo de' Medici	interest
Marco Polo	Renaissance

DIRECTIONS Read each sentence and fill in the blank with a word from the word bank that best completes the sentence.

1. A fee that borrowers pay for the use of someone else's money is called

   _____.

2. The period that followed the Middle Ages during which interest in Greek and Roman writings was revived was the _____.

3. The European explorer from Venice who spent 20 years traveling in Asia and then wrote about his journey was _____.

4. A wealthy banker who turned Florence into a center of arts, culture, and education was _____.

The Renaissance

MAIN IDEAS
1. During the Italian Renaissance, people found new ways to see the world.
2. Italian writers contributed great works of literature.
3. Italian art and artists were among the finest in the world.
4. Science and education made advances during this time.

Key Terms and People

humanism emphasis on human value and achievement

Dante Alighieri Italian poet who wrote *The Divine Comedy*

Niccolo Machiavelli political writer who wrote *The Prince*

Petrarch Renaissance poet and scholar who helped change education

perspective technique in art to represent a three-dimensional scene on a flat space so that it looks real

Michelangelo master artist who painted the ceiling of the Vatican's Sistine Chapel

Leonardo da Vinci master inventor, engineer, and artist who painted the *Mona Lisa*

Lesson Summary
NEW WAYS TO SEE THE WORLD

During the Middle Ages, most people in Europe were devoted to Christianity. The same was true during the Renaissance. However, Renaissance people were interested in ideas and in the positive qualities that make us human. This new emphasis on human value and achievement was called **humanism**. There was a revived interest in history, ancient Greek and Roman writings, and the humanities. Artists and architects were inspired by these writings, Roman ruins, and classical statues.

> How were the humanists of the Renaissance different from the people of the Middle Ages?
>
> _____
> _____
> _____

ITALIAN WRITERS

The poet **Dante Alighieri** wrote in Italian, the language of the common people, rather than in Latin. His major work was *The Divine Comedy*. A later politician and writer, **Niccolo Machiavelli,**

Guided Reading Workbook

Lesson 2, continued

advised leaders on how they should rule in his book *The Prince*. A poet and scholar, **Petrarch**, explored classical thought and Christian teachings. Some historians believe that humanism would not have developed without Petrarch's ideas.

> How might Machiavelli's experience as a politician have helped him write *The Prince*?
> _____
> _____
> _____
> _____

ITALIAN ART AND MUSIC

Italian artists used new techniques such as perspective. **Perspective** shows a three-dimensional scene on a flat surface so that it looks real. Italian artists showed people as individuals by giving them clear personalities.

> Underline the sentence that explains how perspective helped Renaissance artists draw more realistically.

A Renaissance person is someone who does everything well. Two men best fit this name. **Michelangelo** had many talents. He designed buildings, wrote poetry, made sculptures, and was a master painter. One of his most famous works is the painting on the ceiling of the Sistine Chapel in the Vatican. Another master in the arts was **Leonardo da Vinci**. Some say he was the greatest genius who ever lived. He was a sculptor, painter, architect, inventor, engineer, and map maker. He also studied anatomy. Like Michelangelo's works, many of his works had religious themes, but not all. Two of his famous works are *The Last Supper* and the *Mona Lisa*.

> Why was Leonardo da Vinci considered a Renaissance man?
> _____
> _____
> _____
> _____
> _____

SCIENCE AND EDUCATION

Scholars in Italy and other parts of Europe read Greek and Roman texts on scientific subjects and then made their own scientific advances. Engineers and architects used new mathematical formulas to strengthen buildings. Renaissance scientists studied astronomy. Some wrote almanacs based on the idea that Earth was round. Other scholars made more accurate maps. The changes that occurred in the arts and sciences spread beyond Italy, which led to changes in education. Petrarch wrote about the importance of knowing history. His ideas would affect education for many years.

> Why might Petrarch have thought it was important to know history?
> _____
> _____
> _____
> _____
> _____

Guided Reading Workbook

CHALLENGE ACTIVITY

Critical Thinking: Elaborate Now is the time to stop and think big, like the Renaissance humanists did. Write for five minutes, listing every great thing you ever might want to do in your life.

DIRECTIONS On the line provided before each statement, write **T** if a statement is true and **F** if a statement is false. If the statement is false, write the correct term on the line after each sentence that makes the sentence a true statement.

_____ 1. <u>Michelangelo</u>, whose work included the famous portrait *Mona Lisa*, was an expert painter.

_____

_____ 2. A technique in art that was used to make a three-dimensional scene on a flat space appear real was known as <u>humanism</u>.

_____

_____ 3. An Italian writer who contributed great works of literature to the Renaissance and wrote in Italian instead of Latin was <u>Dante Alighieri</u>.

_____

_____ 4. The painting that covers the ceiling of the Sistine Chapel in the Vatican was painted by <u>Leonardo da Vinci</u>.

_____

_____ 5. <u>Renaissance</u> is way of thinking and learning that stresses the importance of human abilities and actions.

_____

_____ 6. *The Prince*, written by an Italian writer and politician <u>Niccolo Machiavelli</u>, gave leaders advice on how they should rule.

_____

_____ 7. The Renaissance poet and scholar who had strong ideas about humanism and wrote about the importance of history was <u>Petrarch</u>.

_____

Name _____ Class _____ Date _____

The Renaissance

 MAIN IDEAS
1. Paper, printing, and new inventions led to the spread of new ideas.
2. The ideas of the Northern Renaissance differed from those of the Italian Renaissance.
3. Literature beyond Italy also thrived in the Renaissance.

Key Terms and People

Johann Gutenberg German inventor of a printing press with movable type

Christian humanism combination of humanism and Christianity

Desiderius Erasmus priest and Christian humanist who critiqued corrupt clergy

Albrecht Dürer German painter who is also known for his block printing

Miguel de Cervantes Spanish writer of *Don Quixote*, a novel that mocked medieval habits and customs

William Shakespeare English dramatist and poet inspired by the Renaissance

Lesson Summary
SPREAD OF NEW IDEAS

Travelers and artists helped spread Renaissance ideas throughout Europe. The development of printing, however, was a major step in spreading ideas. For the first time, thousands of people could read books and share ideas about them.

Papermaking came from China to the Middle East and from there to Europe. European factories were making paper by the 1300s. Then in the mid-1400s, a German named **Johann Gutenberg** developed a printing press that used movable type. Using this method, an entire page could be printed at once. The first printed book was a Bible printed in Latin. Soon it was translated into common languages and printed. People wanted to learn to read, which made them want more education.

Scholars from around Europe came to Italy to study. Universities opened throughout Europe and most teachers were humanists. Only men

> What development contributed to the spread of ideas?
>
> _____
> _____

> The Bible was the first book printed using Gutenberg's movable type. Why do you think that is?
>
> _____
> _____

Guided Reading Workbook

could attend universities, but women helped spread Renaissance ideas. They were educated at home, and some became powerful political figures when they married European nobles. They encouraged the spread of ideas in their husbands' lands.

THE NORTHERN RENAISSANCE

Northern European scholars changed some Renaissance concepts because they related humanism to religious topics. This combination of humanism with religion is called **Christian humanism.** These scholars believed the church was corrupt and called for church reform. A Dutch priest, **Desiderius Erasmus**, was one of these scholars. He believed in the idea that humans had free will. He criticized corrupt clergy and wanted to get rid of some church rituals.

> How did northern European scholars change some Renaissance concepts?
>
> _____
>
> _____
>
> _____
>
> _____

Northern Europeans also changed some Renaissance ideas about art. Northern artists created paintings that were realistic, showing humans' physical flaws. German artist **Albrecht Dürer** painted objects in great detail. He is known for his prints.

> Underline the name of a famous northern Renaissance painter who drew in a realistic style.

LITERATURE BEYOND ITALY

Writers from countries other than Italy also included Renaissance ideas in their works. Many were inspired by how different life had become since the Middle Ages. In Spain, **Miguel de Cervantes** wrote *Don Quixote*. Cervantes poked fun at the romantic tales of the Middle Ages. The Renaissance also inspired the great English playwright and poet **William Shakespeare**. He wrote more than 30 comedies, tragedies, and histories. London audiences of the late 1500s and 1600s packed the theatre to see Shakespeare's plays.

> In what book did Cervantes make fun of the Middle Ages?
>
> _____

CHALLENGE ACTIVITY

Critical Thinking: Explain How did the northern Europeans build upon Renaissance ideas? Write a paragraph using specific examples.

DIRECTIONS Read each sentence and fill in the blank with the word in the word pair that best completes the sentence.

1. _____ is a blend of humanist and religious ideas. **(Miguel de Cervantes /Christian humanism)**

2. A printing press that used movable type was developed in the 1400s by the German _____. **(Albrecht Dürer/Johann Gutenberg)**

3. The English dramatist and poet who wrote more than 30 comedies, tragedies, and histories was _____. **(William Shakespeare/Miguel de Cervantes)**

4. _____, a Dutch priest, criticized corrupt clergy and wanted to get rid of some church rituals that he considered meaningless. **(Albrecht Dürer/Desiderius Erasmus)**

5. _____ wrote *Don Quixote*, which poked fun at the romantic tales of the Middle Ages. **(William Shakespeare/Miguel de Cervantes)**

6. One of the most famous artists of the northern Renaissance was a German, _____. **(Albrecht Dürer/Johann Gutenberg)**

Name _____ Class _____ Date _____

The Reformation

MAIN IDEAS
1. The Catholic Church faced challengers who were upset with the behavior of Catholic clergy and with church practices.
2. Martin Luther urged reform in the Catholic Church, but he eventually broke away from the church.
3. Other reformers built on the ideas of early reformers to create their own churches.

Key Terms and People

Reformation reform movement of Western Christianity

indulgence a relaxation of penalties for sins people had committed sold by the church

purgatory in Catholic theology, a place where souls went before they went to heaven

Martin Luther priest who criticized the church abuses and started the Reformation

Protestants those who protested against the Catholic Church

John Calvin reformer who believed in the idea of predestination

King Henry VIII English king who started the Church of England

Lesson Summary
THE CATHOLIC CHURCH FACES CHALLENGERS

By the late Renaissance people began complaining about the Catholic Church. They wanted church leaders to rid the church of corruption and focus on religion. Their calls led to a reform movement of Western Christianity called the **Reformation**.

Some reformers thought that the clergy were not very religious anymore. Others thought that the pope was too involved in politics. Others thought the church had grown too rich. The sale of indulgences was a serious problem. An **indulgence** was a relaxation of penalties for sins people had committed. The church claimed it reduced the punishment that a person would

> List four reasons for the Reformation.
>
> _____
> _____
> _____
> _____
> _____

receive in purgatory for sins they had committed while they were alive. **Purgatory** was the place where souls went before going to heaven. Many Christians thought the church was letting people buy their way into heaven. The church's unpopular practices weakened its influence.

MARTIN LUTHER URGES REFORM

In 1517, a priest named **Martin Luther** called for reform. He nailed a list of complaints to a church door in Germany. Luther criticized the church's practices. He outlined many of his own beliefs. They included that people could have a direct relationship with God and that as long as people believed in God and lived by the Bible, their souls would be saved. Luther was excommunicated and ordered to leave the empire. His ideas led to a split in the church. Those who protested against the Catholic Church were known as **Protestants**. Some of his followers became known as Lutherans. Many German nobles liked Luther's ideas. This led to Lutheranism becoming the dominant church in northern Germany.

> Which man's ideas led to a split in the Catholic Church?
>
> _____

> Underline the name of the group who protested against the Catholic Church.

OTHER REFORMERS

Another influential reformer was **John Calvin**. His teachings included predestination—the idea that God knew who would be saved even before they were born. **King Henry VIII** was a major figure in the Reformation in England. After the pope refused to officially end Henry's marriage, Henry made himself the head of a new church, the Church of England. He broke from the Catholic Church for personal reasons and did not change many church practices. However, his break from the church opened the door for other Protestant beliefs to take hold in England.

> What role did King Henry VIII play in the Reformation?
>
> _____
>
> _____
>
> _____
>
> _____
>
> _____
>
> _____

CHALLENGE ACTIVITY

Critical Thinking: Describe Imagine how you might feel if you were Martin Luther, pinning his complaints to the church door. Think of something you personally care about and write a list of things that need to change. Your list should have at least 10 items.

DIRECTIONS Write two descriptive phrases that describe the term.

1. Reformation _____

    _____

2. Protestants _____

    _____

3. indulgence _____

    _____

DIRECTIONS On the line provided before each statement, write **T** if a statement is true and **F** if a statement is false. If the statement is false, write the correct term on the line after each sentence that makes the sentence a true statement.

_____ 4. Martin Luther was an influential reformer who mainly taught predestination, or the idea that God knew who would be saved even before they were born.

    _____

_____ 5. Henry VIII was the English king who started the Church of England.

    _____

_____ 6. John Calvin was a priest who criticized the Catholic Church and started the Reformation.

    _____

_____ 7. Indulgences, a part of Catholic theology, was a place where souls went before going to heaven.

    _____

The Reformation

MAIN IDEAS
1. The influence of the church created a Catholic culture in Spain.
2. Catholic reforms emerged in response to the Reformation.
3. Missionaries worked to spread Catholic teachings.

Key Terms and People

Catholic Reformation the effort to reform the Catholic Church from within

Ignatius of Loyola man responsible for founding the Jesuit order

Jesuits religious order founded to serve the pope and spread Catholic teachings

Francis Xavier Jesuit missionary who went to Asia and brought Catholicism to parts of India and Japan

Lesson Summary
CATHOLIC CULTURE IN SPAIN

The effort to reform the Catholic Church from within is called the **Catholic Reformation**. Throughout the late 1500s and 1600s, Catholic leaders worked to strengthen the church and stop the spread of Protestantism. Many leaders came from southern Europe, especially Spain.

For centuries, what is now Spain had three religions. Muslims, Christians, and Jews lived and worked together. Eventually, the Catholic rulers decided to force Muslims and Jews out of Spain. To enforce their decision, Spanish monarchs ordered the Spanish Inquisition to find and punish any Muslims or Jews left in Spain. The Inquisition hunted down and punished converted Muslims and Jews who were suspected of keeping their old beliefs. Then the Inquisition also started seeking out Protestants. By the late 1400s and 1500s, the Spanish church had no opposition.

> Underline the name for efforts to reform the Catholic Church from within.

> The followers of which three religious groups were found in Spain?
> _____
> _____

CATHOLIC REFORMS

In an attempt to win back support for the church, Catholic reformers created many new religious orders in southern Europe in the 1500s. **Ignatius Loyola** founded the Society of Jesus, or the Jesuits. The **Jesuits** were a religious order created to serve the pope and the church. One of the Jesuits' goals was to teach people about Catholic ideas. They hoped that a strong Catholic education would turn people away from Protestant ideas.

> How did the Jesuits hope to bring people to the Catholic Church?
>
> _____
> _____
> _____
> _____
> _____

Many Catholic leaders thought greater change was needed. They assembled at the Council of Trent to discuss church reforms. This council met three times between 1545 and 1563. The council restated the importance of the clergy in interpreting the Bible, but created new rules for the clergy. The council endorsed Catholic teachings and instituted reforms. Now there was a clear distinction between Catholic and Protestant beliefs and practices. The pope created religious courts to punish any Protestants found in Italy. He also threatened excommunication for those who read Protestant books.

> Underline the name of the group assembled to discuss church reforms.

MISSIONARIES SPREAD CATHOLIC TEACHINGS

Rather than change the church, many Catholics decided to help it grow by becoming missionaries. Their goal was to take Catholic teachings to people around the world. Many missionaries were Jesuits, including the most important, the priest **Francis Xavier**. He traveled throughout Asia in the mid-1500s, bringing Catholicism to parts of India and Japan. As a result of his efforts, many people in those regions became Catholics. Catholic missionaries baptized millions of people around the world. Through their efforts the effects of the Catholic Reformation reached far beyond Europe.

> What was the goal of missionaries?
>
> _____
> _____
> _____
> _____
> _____

> Where did Francis Xavier go to convert people to Catholicism?
>
> _____
> _____

CHALLENGE ACTIVITY

Critical Thinking: Make Judgments Think about what happened during the Catholic Reformation. Write a paragraph on your view of the Catholic Reformation. Include whether you think the reforms were effective and why.

DIRECTIONS Read each sentence and fill in the blank with the word in the word pair that best completes the sentence.

1. The Jesuit missionary who went to Asia and brought Catholicism to parts of Japan and India was _____. **(Francis Xavier/Ignatius of Loyola)**

2. The _____ was the effort made by the Catholic Church to reform its practices. **(Jesuits/Catholic Reformation)**

3. The _____ were a religious order founded to serve the pope and spread Catholic teachings. **(Spanish Inquisition/Jesuits)**

4. The man who founded the Jesuit order was _____. **(Ignatius of Loyola/Francis Xavier)**

5. The _____ endorsed Catholic teachings and instituted reforms. **(Catholic Reformation/Council of Trent)**

6. The purpose of the _____ was to find and punish any Muslims or Jews left in Spain during the late 1400s and 1500s. **(Spanish Inquisition/Council of Trent)**

The Reformation

MAIN IDEAS
1. Religious division occurred within Europe and the Americas.
2. Religious wars broke out between Protestants and Catholics.
3. Social changes were a result of the Reformation.

Key Terms and People

Huguenots French Protestants

Edict of Nantes law granting religious freedom in most of France

Thirty Years' War long series of wars between Catholics and Protestants involving much of Europe

congregation church assembly

federalism sharing of power between national and local governments

Lesson Summary
RELIGIOUS DIVISION

At the beginning of the 1500s, nearly all of Europe was Catholic. But the situation had changed dramatically 100 years later. In many southern European countries, such as Spain, most people remained Catholic. However, in the northern countries such as England, Scotland, and the Scandinavian countries, most people were Protestant. The emperor of the Holy Roman Empire allowed each prince to choose the religion for his territory. As a result, the empire became a patchwork of small kingdoms, some Catholic and some Protestant. Keeping peace was often difficult.

The explorers and missionaries who went to other parts of the world took their religions with them. This influenced the distribution of religions around the world. For example, parts of Canada and most of Mexico, Central America, and South were settled by people from Catholic countries.

> Which part of Europe became mainly Protestant in the span of only 100 years?
> _____

> Underline the regions settled by people from Catholic countries.

The 13 colonies that became the United States were settled by Protestants from England and so became mostly Protestant.

| Circle the region settled by Protestants. |

RELIGIOUS WARS

Disagreements about religion and violence often went hand and hand. Although most people in France stayed Catholic, some became Protestants. French Protestants were called **Huguenots**. But the king of France outlawed the Huguenots. So a series of conflicts between Catholics and Huguenots began that led to years of bloody war. The worst incident was the St. Bartholomew's Day Massacre in 1572. In one night, Catholic rioters killed about 3,000 Protestants in Paris. The war in France ended in 1598 with the **Edict of Nantes**. It granted religious freedom to most of France.

| Why do you think the Huguenots chose to fight? |

The Holy Roman Empire also had wars. Starting in Prague with Protestants overthrowing their Catholic leader, the revolt evolved into the **Thirty Years' War**. This was a long series of wars that involved many European countries. After 30 years of fighting, peace was reached. Rulers then determined the religion for their countries, but the Holy Roman Empire ceased to exist.

| Underline the place where the Thirty Years' War started. |

SOCIAL CHANGES

Before the Reformation, most Europeans had no voice in governing the Catholic Church. But most Protestant churches did not have clergy. Instead, each **congregation**, or church assembly, made its own rules. People began to think that their own ideas were important. This led to demands for more political power, which led to **federalism**, the sharing of power between national and local governments. People became willing to question authority and figure out things on their own. This desire people had to investigate led them to turn increasingly to science.

| Underline the sentence that explains how religious reform led to political reform. |

CHALLENGE ACTIVITY

Critical Thinking: Explain You have been reading a lot about the Reformation period. What is the most important thing that has come out of the Reformation that still impacts society today? Write a one-page essay explaining you answer.

DIRECTIONS Match the terms in the first column with their correct definition from the second column by placing the letter of the correct definition in the space provided before each term.

_____ 1. Edict of Nantes

_____ 2. congregation

_____ 3. Huguenots

_____ 4. federalism

_____ 5. Thirty Years' War

a. church assembly

b. law granting religious freedom in most of France

c. sharing of power between national and local governments

d. long series of wars between Catholics and Protestants involving much of Europe

e. French Protestants

The Scientific Revolution

MAIN IDEAS
1. The Scientific Revolution marked the birth of modern science.
2. The roots of the Scientific Revolution can be traced to ancient Greece, the Muslim world, and Europe.

Key Terms and People

Scientific Revolution series of events that led to the birth of modern science

science a particular way of gaining knowledge about the world

theories explanations developed by scientists to explain observable facts

Ptolemy Greek astronomer whose work was based on observation and logic

rationalists people who looked at the world in a rational, reasonable, and logical way

alchemy the study of different natural substances, such as metals

Lesson Summary

THE BIRTH OF MODERN SCIENCE

The series of events that led to the birth of modern science is called the **Scientific Revolution**. It occurred between 1540 and 1700. Science was a radical new idea as it was a completely different way of looking at the world. Before this time, educated people relied on authorities—the ancient Greek writers or Catholic Church officials—for explanations about the world. Afterward, people gained knowledge by observing the world around them and forming logical conclusions.

Science is a particular way of gaining knowledge. Scientists identify facts by observation and then develop **theories,** which are explanations based on the facts. Theories must be tested to see if they are true. Before the Scientific Revolution, this way of learning about the world did not exist.

> What was so revolutionary about the Scientific Revolution?
>
> _____
> _____
> _____
> _____

Guided Reading Workbook

ROOTS OF THE REVOLUTION

Some of the basic ideas of science are ancient. The Greek philosopher Aristotle's greatest contribution to science was the idea that people should observe the world carefully and draw logical conclusions about what they see. The Greek thinker **Ptolemy** studied and wrote about astronomy, logic, and geography. Aristotle, Ptolemy and other Greek thinkers were **rationalists**, people who looked at the world in a rational, or reasonable and logical, way. Europeans studied their works and began to view the world in a rational way. They began to think like scientists.

Europeans could study ancient Greek writings because Muslim scholars had translated them into Arabic. Later, Arabic versions were translated into Latin, which was read in Europe. This work preserved ancient knowledge and spread interest in science to Europe.

Religious scholars also played a role in preserving Greek ideas. The Jewish scholar Maimonides wrote to unite Aristotle's work with Jewish ideas. The scholar Thomas Aquinas did the same with Christian ideas. The Catholic Church helped pay for scientific research and sent priests to universities. The Church supported the teaching of math and science.

Other developments in Europe helped bring about the Scientific Revolution. Humanist artists and writers spent their time studying the natural world. Another development was a growing interest in **alchemy** (AL-kuh-mee), a forerunner of chemistry. Alchemists are best known for trying, and failing, to change other metals into gold. They experimented with natural substances to learn more about nature.

> **What roots did science have in ancient Greece?**
> _____
> _____
> _____
> _____
> _____

> **Name two scholars who united Greek ideas with religion.**
> _____
> _____
> _____

Guided Reading Workbook

CHALLENGE ACTIVITY

Critical Thinking: Make Inferences Write a
one-page creative essay describing a world
without any rationalist ideas. How would people
understand their world without reason and logic?

DIRECTIONS On the line provided before each statement, write **T** if
a statement is true and **F** if a statement is false. If the statement is
false, write the correct term on the line after each sentence that
makes the sentence a true statement.

_____ 1. The <u>Renaissance</u> looked at the world in a reasonable and logical way.

_____

_____ 2. The series of events that led to the birth of modern science is called the
<u>rationalists</u>.

_____

_____ 3. <u>Theories</u> are explanations scientists develop to explain observed facts.

_____

_____ 4. <u>Ptolemy</u> wrote about astronomy, geography, and logic.

_____

DIRECTIONS Write three adjectives or a descriptive phrase that describes
the term or person given.

5. Aristotle _____

_____

6. science _____

_____

7. rationalists _____

_____

8. theories _____

_____

9. alchemy _____

_____

The Scientific Revolution

MAIN IDEAS
1. The discovery of the Americas led scholars to doubt ancient Greek ideas.
2. Advances in astronomy were key events of the Scientific Revolution.
3. Sir Isaac Newton developed laws that explained much of the natural world.
4. New inventions helped scientists study the natural world.

Key Terms and People

Nicolaus Copernicus Polish astronomer who theorized that the planets orbit the sun

Tycho Brahe Danish astronomer who made detailed charts of the stars' movements

Johannes Kepler German astronomer who proved that planets' orbits are elliptical

Galileo Galilei Italian scientist and astronomer who tested his theories in experiments

Sir Isaac Newton English scientist who discovered laws of motion and of gravity

barometer scientific instrument that measures air pressure

Lesson Summary
DISCOVERY LEADS TO DOUBT

In 1492, Columbus found a new continent. The world map of the ancient Greek scholar, Ptolemy, did not show this entire continent. Scholars began to question the accuracy of all of the ancient authorities for the first time. More and more, observations the Europeans made did not fit with what the authorities had described. Such observations helped lead to the Scientific Revolution.

Why do you think Columbus's discovery of a continent cast doubt on the writings of ancient authorities?

_____

_____

_____

_____

_____

ADVANCES IN ASTRONOMY

Ptolemy thought that the planets moved around the earth. For 1,400 years, people accepted this belief as fact. Polish astronomer **Nicolaus Copernicus** disagreed with him. Copernicus thought

Underline the name of the astronomer that Copernicus proved wrong.

Guided Reading Workbook

the planets orbited the sun. His 1543 book, *On the Revolution of Celestial Spheres*, explained his theory based on what he observed in the sky.

An important Danish astronomer was **Tycho Brahe** (TYOO-koh BRAH-huh). He spent most of his life observing the stars. In the late 1500s, Brahe charted the positions of more than 750 stars through careful observation and detailed accurate records. Careful recording of information allows other scientists to use what has been previously learned.

The German astronomer **Johannes Kepler** proved that the planets orbit the sun in oval-shaped orbits. **Galileo Galilei** was the first person to study the sky with a telescope. He was also interested in mechanics—the study of objects and motion. He was the first to use experiments to test his theories.

> **Name two astronomers who studied after Copernicus.**
>
> _____
>
> _____

SIR ISAAC NEWTON

With his book *Principia Mathematica* published in 1687, **Sir Isaac Newton** became one of the most important scientists of all time. He reviewed and evaluated all previous scientific work, coupled it with his own observations, and developed four theories about how the natural world worked. He also developed mathematical calculus.

> **What book established Issac Newton as an important scientist?**
>
> _____

NEW INVENTIONS

Scientists invented new and better tools to study the natural world. The **barometer**, invented in 1643, is an instrument that measures air pressure. It is used to help forecast the weather. Other inventions included the microscope, telescope, and the thermometer. They all allowed scientists to make more accurate observations of the world and to conduct experiments.

> **List three inventions that helped the development of science.**
>
> _____
>
> _____
>
> _____

CHALLENGE ACTIVITY

Critical Thinking: Make Judgments Consider the accomplishments of the scientists who lived during the Scientific Revolution. Which scientist do you think made the largest contributions to science? Write a one-page essay that explains your choice.

DIRECTIONS On the line provided before each statement, write **T** if a statement is true and **F** if a statement is false. If the statement is false, write the correct term on the line after each sentence that makes the sentence a true statement.

_____ 1. The series of events that led to the birth of modern science is called the <u>Scientific Revolution</u>.

_____

_____ 2. The Italian scientist <u>Tycho Brahe</u> regularly used experiments to test his theories.

_____

_____ 3. <u>Tycho Brahe</u> was a Danish astronomer who kept detailed records of his observations of the stars.

_____

_____ 4. English scientist <u>Galileo Galilei</u> made observations about gravity and the behavior of objects in motion.

_____

_____ 5. The <u>thermometer</u> is a scientific instrument that measures air pressure.

_____

_____ 6. <u>Nicolaus Copernicus</u> was a German astronomer who tried to map the orbits of the planets.

_____

_____ 7. <u>Nicolaus Copernicus</u> was a Polish astronomer who wrote *On the Revolution of the Celestial Spheres.*

_____

_____ 8. <u>Sir Isaac Newton</u> invented calculus, an advanced form of mathematics that scientists use to solve complex problems.

_____

Guided Reading Workbook

The Scientific Revolution

MAIN IDEAS
1. The ideas of Francis Bacon and René Descartes helped clarify the scientific method.
2. Science influenced new ideas about government.
3. Medical treatments changed as scientists better understood the human body.
4. Science and religion developed a sometimes uneasy relationship.

Key Terms and People

Francis Bacon English philosopher who argued for systematic scientific research

René Descartes French philosopher who argued for clear thinking and reason to establish proof

scientific method step-by-step procedure for performing experiments or research

hypothesis a solution that the scientist proposes to solve a problem

Lesson Summary
BACON, DESCARTES, AND THE SCIENTIFIC METHOD

The Scientific Revolution led to a dramatic change in the way people learned about the world. The new, scientific way of gaining knowledge had far-reaching effects. Science became the most effective way to learn about the natural world.

> Underline the sentence that explains how science changed people during the Scientific Revolution.

Two important philosophers played a leading role in supporting science. **Francis Bacon** from England and **René Descartes** (ruh-NAY day-CART) from France encouraged the use of orderly experiments and clear reasoning. Descartes believed that nothing should be accepted as true if it could not be proven to be true. Their ideas led to the development of the **scientific method**, a step-by-step procedure for doing scientific research through observation and experimentation. These are the main principles of modern science. There are six basic steps in

> What are the main principles of modern science?
> _____
> _____
> _____
> _____

the scientific method, starting with stating the
problem and gathering information. The third
step is forming a hypothesis. A **hypothesis** is a
solution that the scientist proposes to solve the
problem. Fourth is testing the hypothesis by
performing experiments. The fifth step is
recording and analyzing the data gathered from
the experiments. The final step is drawing
conclusions from the data.

SCIENCE AND GOVERNMENT

Science had a great impact on society and politics.
Human reason, or logical thought, was a
powerful tool. Philosophers thought they could
use reason to improve society. If laws governed
nature, laws could govern human behavior as well.
Scientists' use of reason and logic helped pave the
way for new democratic ideas in Europe, such as
personal freedom, individual rights, and equality.

> **Underline three democratic ideas new to Europe.**

ADVANCES IN MEDICINE

The field of medicine changed thanks to the
scientific methods. Doctors' observations and
experiments led to changes in the way they
treated sick patients. The invention of the
microscope allowed scientists to see things not
visible to the human eye.

> **What was one effect of the Scientific Revolution in the field of medicine?**
> _____
> _____
> _____

SCIENCE AND RELIGION

The advances of science also brought conflict.
The Roman Catholic Church leaders tried to
force scientists to reject findings that opposed the
Church's teachings. Galileo was put on trial for
saying that the planets orbit the sun. The Church
taught that the earth was the center of the
universe and did not move. Galileo was
threatened with torture unless he agreed with
the church.

> **Why was Galileo put on trial?**
> _____
> _____
> _____
> _____
> _____
> _____

Interestingly, Galileo and other scientists did not think science went against religion. They believed it helped people understand that these natural laws were God's creation.

CHALLENGE ACTIVITY

Critical Thinking: Summarize Write an essay describing the significance of the scientific method in modern science.

DIRECTIONS Match the terms in the first column with their correct definition from the second column by placing the letter of the correct definition in the space provided before each term.

_____ 1. scientific method

_____ 2. Galileo Galilei

_____ 3. microscope

_____ 4. René Descartes

_____ 5. Scientific Revolution

_____ 6. hypothesis

a. a solution that the scientist proposes to solve a problem

b. French philosopher who believed that nothing should be accepted as true if it could not be proven to be true

c. step-by-step process for performing experiments and other scientific research

d. invention that helped doctors see things too small for the human eye alone

e. Italian scientist put on trial by the Roman Catholic Church for publicly saying that the planets orbit the sun and not the earth

f. time when people began to question the accepted wisdom about medicine and the human body

The Age of Exploration

MAIN IDEAS
1. Europeans had a desire and opportunity to explore.
2. Portuguese and Spanish explorations led to discoveries of new trade routes, lands, and people.
3. English and French explorers found land in North America.
4. A new European worldview developed because of the discoveries.

Key Terms and People

Henry the Navigator Portuguese prince who started a sailing school and funded many expeditions

Vasco da Gama first explorer to sail safely around Africa to India

Christopher Columbus Italian explorer who accidentally discovered the Americas

Ferdinand Magellan Portuguese navigator who first circumnavigated the globe

circumnavigate to go all the way around

Francis Drake famous English pirate who robbed Spanish ships in the Americas

Spanish Armada huge fleet of Spanish ships defeated during an attack on England in 1588

Lesson Summary
DESIRE AND OPPORTUNITY TO EXPLORE

During the 1400s, technology like the astrolabe and the sextant helped European sailors reach faraway places and return home safely. More accurate maps and ships called caravels encouraged explorers to set off to search for new trade routes to Asia and find rare spices. They also wanted to spread Christianity and discover new lands and people.

> Underline four motivations that encouraged European explorers during the 1400s.

PORTUGUESE AND SPANISH EXPLORATIONS

Henry the Navigator built an observatory and started a sailing school. Sailors often paid attention to the earlier voyages of others. **Vasco da Gama** used information that another sailor had learned to help him became the first person to sail safely around Africa to India.

> What did Vasco da Gama and other sailors do to help them sail?
>
> _____
> _____
> _____
> _____
> _____

Christopher Columbus was an Italian who worked for Spain. Knowing the world was round, he headed west to reach Asia but accidentally discovered the Americas instead. It was **Ferdinand Magellan**, a Portuguese navigator sailing for Spain, who first **circumnavigated** the globe. Unfortunately, he was killed before the end of the journey. Following Columbus's path, the Spanish conquistadors sailed to the Americas in the early 1500s and conquered the Inca and Aztec civilizations.

> **What happened to Ferdinand Magellan when he circumnavigated the globe?**
>
> _____
>
> _____

EUROPEANS IN AMERICA

Portugal and Spain controlled southern trade routes, so French and English explorers went north. These early journeys again confused North America with Asia, but France and England claimed the land. The famous pirate **Francis Drake**, who worked for England, raided Spanish ships for their treasures. Spain responded by sending the **Spanish Armada** to attack England in 1588. The English navy defeated the Armada with the help of a great storm at sea. Spanish sea power never recovered.

> **What happened to Spanish sea power after the English navy defeated the Spanish Armada?**
>
> _____
>
> _____

A NEW EUROPEAN WORLDVIEW

After the voyages of the 1400s and 1500s, Europeans learned that some of their geographic knowledge had been wrong. They created new maps that helped spread European influence around the world.

> **What did Europeans learn after the voyages of the 1400s and 1500s?**
>
> _____
>
> _____
>
> _____

CHALLENGE ACTIVITY

Critical Thinking: Elaborate Assume that you are an explorer living in Spain, Portugal, France, or England during the 1400s. You need to persuade a rich patron to pay for a sailing expedition. Write a proposal in which you explain the purpose for your trip and list several reasons for taking it.

Guided Reading Workbook

DIRECTIONS Write a word or descriptive phrase to describe
each term.

1. Christopher Columbus _____

_____

2. circumnavigate _____

_____

3. Ferdinand Magellan _____

_____

4. Henry the Navigator _____

_____

5. Sir Frances Drake _____

_____

6. Spanish Armada _____

_____

7. Vasco da Gama _____

_____

The Age of Exploration

MAIN IDEAS
1. Plants and animals were exchanged among Europe, Asia, Africa, and the Americas.
2. Culture and technology changed as ideas were exchanged between Europe and the Americas.
3. Society and the economy changed in Europe and the Americas.

Key Terms and People

Columbian Exchange exchange of plants, animals and ideas between the New World (the Americas) and the Old World (Europe)

plantations large farms

Bartolomé de las Casas Spanish priest who opposed harsh treatment of the Indians and wanted to bring slaves from Africa to work the plantations

racism belief that some people are better than others because of racial traits

Lesson Summary
PLANTS AND ANIMALS

One primary effect of European sea explorations was the exchange of plants, animals, and ideas between the New World (the Americas) and the Old World (Europe). This is called the **Columbian Exchange**.

Europeans brought crops such as bananas and sugarcane from Asia to Central and South America. They also planted oranges, onions, and lettuce. Cows, goats, sheep, horses, pigs, and chickens were also brought to the New World. Europeans took home tomatoes, potatoes, beans, squash, avocados, pineapples, tobacco, and chili peppers. This exchange changed the eating habits of the entire world, not just Europe and the Americas. Sweet potatoes and peanuts became popular in Africa. In China, peanuts and maize became major crops.

> Which two places were connected by the Columbian Exchange?
>
> _____
> _____
> _____

> Underline the crops that the Europeans brought to the New World. Circle the crops that they took home to Europe.

Lesson 2, *continued*

CULTURE AND TECHNOLOGY

Besides food and animals, religion and language were probably the biggest changes Europeans brought to the New World. Both Protestant and Catholic missionaries traveled to the Americas. They set up schools to convert people to Christianity and teach them European languages. In some places, Christianity blended with local customs to create new religious practices.

The Europeans also introduced technologies and animals that made life and work easier to do. Horses were used for transportation and oxen and the plough for farming. Guns, steel, and the wheel also came to the New World. **Plantations** and mining developed from these innovations. These new industries were mostly run by the Europeans.

> **Why did missionaries set up schools in the New World?**
>
> _____
> _____
> _____

> **What two factors allowed plantations and mining to begin in the Americas?**
>
> _____
> _____

SOCIETY AND THE ECONOMY

Sugarcane plantations and mines made a lot of money for Spain and Portugal. But American Indians were forced into slave labor to work in these industries. Many Native Americans died as a result of harsh treatment and new diseases.

Spanish priest **Bartolomé de las Casas** did not like the way the Indians were treated on the plantations. Unfortunately, his solution to the problem was to use Africans as slaves instead of American Indians. This created a new society based on **racism**. The white Europeans thought they were superior to the darker-skinned Indians and Africans, as well as those of mixed blood.

> **Why did Bartolomé de las Casas suggest to use Africans as slaves?**
>
> _____
> _____
> _____

CHALLENGE ACTIVITY

Critical Thinking: Analyze Effects Write a short paragraph that identifies and explains the effects of the plantation system on the Americas.

Lesson 2, *continued*

Bartolomé de las Casas	Columbian Exchange	oxen
plantations	Protestant	racism
Spain		

DIRECTIONS Read each sentence and fill in the blank with a word
from the word bank that best completes the sentence.

1. Due to _____, white Europeans thought they were
   superior to darker-skinned Indians and Africans, and those of mixed blood.

2. Catholic and _____ missionaries from Europe brought
   religion and language to the New World.

3. Animals and technologies like _____ and the plough
   made farming easier to do.

4. Through the _____, crops, animals, and ideas went back
   and forth between Europe and the Americas.

5. The sugarcane crop made a lot of money for _____ and
   Portugal.

6. Large farms called _____ were mostly run by the
   Europeans.

7. _____ was the name of the Spanish priest who wanted to
   use Africans as slaves instead of American Indians.

The Age of Exploration

 MAIN IDEAS
1. A new economic system called mercantilism emerged.
2. New trading patterns developed in the 1600s and 1700s.
3. Power in Europe shifted as a result of new trade routes, banking, and increased manufacturing.
4. Market economies changed business in Europe.

Key Terms and People

mercantilism trading system in which the government controls all economic activity

balance of trade relationship between imported goods and exported goods

cottage industry home-based manufacturing businesses run by families

atlas collection of maps

capitalism system in which individuals and private businesses run most industries

market economy system in which individuals decide what goods and services to buy

Lesson Summary
A NEW ECONOMY

Mercantilism was the main economic policy in Europe between 1500 and 1800. In this system, the government controls all economic activity in a country and its colonies. The government becomes stronger and richer.

To stay rich, countries tried to maintain a **balance of trade**. They exported more goods than they imported. Each colony only traded with its home country. Colonies were places to acquire raw materials like wood, cotton, and dyes. When the time came to sell finished manufactured products, they were sold in the colonies. These products were made by an increasing number of European families who ran businesses called **cottage industries**.

> What effect does mercantilism have on government?
>
> _____
>
> _____
>
> _____

> Where was the only place where a colony could trade raw materials and manufactured products?
>
> _____
>
> _____

NEW TRADING PATTERNS

The triangular trade network sent raw materials, manufactured products, and slaves back and forth to Europe, Africa, and the Americas. Portuguese, English, and Dutch traders increased the new Atlantic slave trade by cramming Africans into ships without food or water. People got sick, and many died.

> Underline the three things that were sent back and forth in the triangular trade network. Circle the three places that were part of the triangular trade network.

POWER SHIFTS IN EUROPE

Mercantilism was most successful in Portugal and Spain, but the English and French discovered new northern trade routes. They also established a banking system that helped shift economic power in their favor. A new book of much better maps, called an **atlas**, helped improve northern trading expeditions. The Dutch were the first to form a company to deal directly with trade from Africa and Asia. This helped Dutch merchants control many trading posts in these regions and in India and Japan.

> How were Dutch merchants able to control trading posts in Asia and Africa?
> _____
> _____
> _____
> _____

MARKET ECONOMIES

Increased wealth in Europe led to an increased demand for manufactured goods. People came up with ways to increase the supply to meet the demand for goods. This created the basis of **capitalism**. Capitalism encourages competition among manufacturers and creates a **market economy**. Individuals decide what goods and services they want to buy.

> What does capitalism encourage among manufacturers?
> _____

CHALLENGE ACTIVITY

Critical Thinking: Develop You are a shoemaker in England during the 1700s. You hear that the American colonies are in desperate need of shoes. A trader asks you if you can fill an order for 5,000 pairs of shoes—by next week! You say yes. Develop a plan to fill the order.

DIRECTIONS On the line before each statement, write **T** if the statement is true and **F** if the statement is false. If the statement is false, change the underlined term to make the sentence true. Then write the correct term on the line after the sentence.

_____ 1. An <u>atlas</u> is a collection of maps that helped improve northern trading expeditions.

_____

_____ 2. In a <u>cottage industry</u>, individuals decide what goods and services they want to buy.

_____

_____ 3. The government controls all economic activity in the trading system called <u>capitalism</u>.

_____

_____ 4. Countries tried to maintain a <u>balance of trade</u> so they could stay rich.

_____

_____ 5. Private businesses and individuals run most industries in the system of <u>mercantilism</u>.

_____

_____ 6. A home based manufacturing business run by families is a <u>market economy</u>.

_____

Enlightenment and Revolution

Lesson 1

> **MAIN IDEAS**
> 1. The Enlightenment was also called the Age of Reason.
> 2. The Enlightenment's roots can be traced back to earlier ideas.
> 3. New ideas came mainly from French and British thinkers.

Key Terms and People

Enlightenment period in which people valued the use of reason as a guide to improving society

Voltaire French philosopher and writer who mocked government and religion

salon social gathering in which people discuss ideas

Mary Wollstonecraft British writer who believed women should have the same rights as men

Lesson Summary

THE AGE OF REASON

Discoveries made during the Scientific Revolution and explorers led to changes in Europe. Many scholars challenged long-held beliefs about science, religion, and government. They relied on reason, or logical thought, to explain how the world worked. They believed human reason could be used to reach three great goals—knowledge, freedom, and happiness. This time period is called the **Enlightenment**. It is also known as the Age of Reason.

> Underline the three goals that scholars believed humans could achieve through the use of reason.

THE ENLIGHTENMENT'S ROOTS

The main ideas of the Enlightenment came from earlier eras. Enlightenment thinkers looked to the Greeks, Romans and the history of Christianity. They also got ideas from the Renaissance, the Reformation, and the Scientific Revolution. For example, the ancient Greeks observed the order in the natural world, and Roman thinkers had the idea that natural law governed how the world worked. Enlightenment thinkers applied these beliefs of natural laws to the human world of

> Where did Enlightenment scholars get their ideas?
>
> _____
> _____
> _____
> _____

society and government. They questioned the Christian Church's religious beliefs and power. They learned from the Renaissance thinkers who believed that humans had value and the scientists from the Scientific Revolution who used the scientific method.

NEW IDEAS

Enlightenment thinkers expanded on ideas from history to think about the world in a new way. They believed the use of reason could improve society. To do so, they had to share their ideas with others.

French philosophers made many of the ideas of the Enlightenment popular. The philosopher **Voltaire** (vohl-TAYR) believed humans could improve their lives and poked fun at government and religion in his writings. When he was censored for his writings, Voltaire spoke out. He said, "I [may] disapprove of what you say, but I will defend to the death your right to say it." This is the Enlightenment goal of freedom of thought.

Enlightenment ideas spread. An important place for the exchange of ideas was the salon. The **salon** was a social gathering held to discuss ideas. Some British men and women also began to publish their ideas in books, pamphlets, and newspaper articles. The British writer **Mary Wollstonecraft** wrote that women should have the same rights as men. The British writer Adam Smith believed economics was governed by natural laws and should not be controlled by governments.

> **Why do you think Voltaire's writings were censored?**
> _____
> _____
> _____
> _____
> _____

> **What did Enlightenment thinkers do to spread their ideas?**
> _____
> _____
> _____

CHALLENGE ACTIVITY

Critical Thinking: Develop If you were to hold a salon today, what would the topics of discussion include? List three important topics you would discuss and your ideas on how to resolve these issues.

| Enlightenment | Mary Wollstonecraft | Voltaire | salon |

DIRECTIONS Use the vocabulary terms in the word bank to write a summary of how the thinkers of the Enlightenment developed their ideas.

_____

_____

_____

_____

_____

_____

_____

_____

_____

_____

_____

_____

_____

_____

_____

_____

_____

_____

_____

_____

_____

Enlightenment and Revolution

MAIN IDEAS
1. The Enlightenment influenced some monarchies.
2. Enlightenment thinkers helped the growth of democratic ideas.
3. In the Americas, the Enlightenment inspired a struggle for independence.

Key Terms and People

unlimited government where one person or group holds all the power

limited government state in which power is checked by laws and institutions

John Locke English philosopher who said government is a contract between the ruler and the people

natural rights Locke's idea that every person has the right to life, liberty, and property

majority rule system in which ideas and decisions supported by the most people are followed

Charles-Louis Montesquieu French philosopher who said government should be divided into separate branches, each branch limiting the power of the other branch

Jean-Jacques Rousseau French writer who proposed the idea of popular sovereignty

popular sovereignty government that expresses the will of the people

Lesson Summary
ENLIGHTENMENT INFLUENCE ON MONARCHIES

In the 1600s and 1700s, kings, queens, and emperors ruled Europe. People believed God had given them the right to rule as they chose. This is **unlimited government** in which one person or group holds all power. **Limited government** is one that is not all-powerful and is checked by laws and institutions that represent the will of the people. The spread of Enlightenment ideas pushed some monarchs to make life better for commoners. They made laws they thought would make people happier. Empress Catherine the Great of Russia increased the number of schools for the people.

> In Europe in the 1700s, what was the type of government in most countries?
>
> _____
> _____

Lesson 2, *continued*

DEMOCRATIC IDEAS

Enlightenment thinkers challenged rule by divine right. English philosopher **John Locke** wrote that government should be a contract between the ruler and the people that limits the ruler's power. Locke said that all people had **natural rights**, which included the rights to life, liberty, and property. He believed in **majority rule**, a system in which the ideas and decisions supported by the most people are followed. Government should be for the common good of the people. Frenchman **Charles-Louis Montesquieu** (mohn-te-SKYOO) said that government should be divided into separate branches to protect people's freedom. Each branch is limited by the others. French thinker **Jean-Jacques Rousseau** (roo-SOH) believed in **popular sovereignty**, the idea that governments should express the will of the people.

> **What is majority rule?**
> _____
> _____
> _____
> _____

THE ENLIGHTENMENT IN THE AMERICAS

The philosophers' ideas spread from Europe to the British colonists in North America. The British government created new taxes to raise funds to fight the French, who also controlled land in North America. The colonists thought the taxes were unfair. Two leaders, Benjamin Franklin and Thomas Jefferson, applied the ideas of the Enlightenment to the colonists' complaints. They wanted independence for the colonies. Jefferson supported the separation of religion and political power.

> **Why were the colonists upset with the British government?**
> _____
> _____
> _____

CHALLENGE ACTIVITY

Critical Thinking: Compare Imagine living today under a king who could rule as he pleased. Compare this to your life now in which you live with limited government. Write a one-page essay explaining what would be different and what would be the same.

Guided Reading Workbook

Charles-Louis Montesquieu	Jean-Jacques Rousseau	John Locke
limited government	majority rule	natural rights
popular sovereignty	unlimited government	

DIRECTIONS Read each sentence and fill in the blank with a word from the word bank that best completes the sentence.

1. French thinker _____ believed that governments should express the will of the people.

2. Frenchman _____ claimed that a government should be divided into separate branches to protect people's freedom.

3. John Locke wrote that all people had _____, which include the rights to life, liberty, and property.

4. _____ is a system where one person, or a small group, holds all of the power.

5. _____ is not all powerful and is checked by laws that were created by the will of the people.

6. The British philosopher and writer _____ wrote that government should be a contract between the ruler and the people that limits the ruler's power.

7. _____ is the principle that governments should express the will of the people.

Guided Reading Workbook

Enlightenment and Revolution

MAIN IDEAS
1. Revolution and reform changed the government of England.
2. Enlightenment ideas led to democracy in North America.
3. The French Revolution caused major changes in France's government.

Key Terms and People

English Bill of Rights document that listed the rights of the British people, passed in 1689

rule of law principal that everyone, including monarchs, is subject to the laws of the land

Declaration of Independence document declaring the American colonies' independence from British rule in 1776

Declaration of the Rights of Man and of the Citizen document issued during the French Revolution granting freedom of speech, the press, and religion for the French

Lesson Summary
REVOLUTION AND REFORM IN ENGLAND

In England, the uneasy relationship been Parliament and the monarchy exploded into a civil war in 1642. A series of rulers took power before Parliament invited William of Orange to invade and become king in 1688. William took power, but only after agreeing to sign an **English Bill of Rights** for Parliament and the English people in 1689. William became king, but shared power with Parliament. The monarchs had to follow the laws of the land like everyone else. This principle is known as the **rule of law**.

When was the English Bill of Rights signed?
_____
_____
_____

DEMOCRACY IN AMERICA

The English Bill of Rights did not apply to the American colonies. The colonies developed their own governing bodies, but were still subject to taxes and laws they considered to be unfair. When their protests were put down by British

Underline the phrase that shows the main American grievances against English rule.

Guided Reading Workbook

troops, the colonists organized militias, groups of armed men, to protect themselves. In 1776, the colonial leaders met and Thomas Jefferson drafted the **Declaration of Independence**, announcing the colonies' independence from British rule.

The Declaration clearly expresses Enlightenment ideals. When its army was defeated by the colonial army, Britain was forced to recognize the independence of the colonies. A new government plan for the United States, the U.S. Constitution, was developed by James Madison and others. It reflected Montesquieu's idea about separate branches.

> **Why did American colonists organize militias?**
> _____
> _____
> _____

> **Circle the name of the person who wrote the document announcing the colonies' independence from British rule.**

THE FRENCH REVOLUTION

The American Revolution inspired the French to rebel against their own king. Most commoners in France had no say in government at all, paid high taxes, and had very few rights. A National Assembly was formed to demand rights from King Louis XVI, but he refused to listen.

The French Revolution began in 1789. The revolution's leaders issued a document similar to the English Bill of Rights and the American Declaration of Independence, called the **Declaration of the Rights of Man and the Citizen**. During the revolution, King Louis XVI was tried and executed. It took the French several years to develop a stable new government, but they created a democracy.

> **Why were the commoners of France angry at the king?**
> _____
> _____
> _____

> **What happened to Louis XVI during the revolution?**
> _____
> _____

CHALLENGE ACTIVITY

Critical Thinking: Make Inferences You are a revolutionary agitator in England, in the British colonies in America, or in France. How would you inspire your neighbors and friends to join you in the fight? Develop a character and write a persuasive speech that is historically appropriate to the period.

Lesson 3, *continued*

DIRECTIONS Read each sentence and fill in the blank with the word in the word pair that best completes the sentence.

1. The _____ was signed by William of Orange before he became king. **(English Bill of Rights/ Declaration of the Rights of Man and of the Citizen)**

2. Before William became king he agreed to share power with Parliament and follow the principle of the _____. **(Declaration of Independence/rule of law)**

3. The _____, which came out of the French Revolution, was similar to the English Bill of Rights. **(Declaration of Independence/Declaration of the Rights of Man and of the Citizen)**

4. Thomas Jefferson wrote the _____, which declared the colonies' independence from British rule. **(Declaration of Independence/Declaration of the Rights of Man and of the Citizen)**

5. James Madison was a main author of the _____, which adopted Montesquieu's idea of dividing power among separate branches of government. **(U.S. Constitution/rule of law)**

Guided Reading Workbook

Name _____ Class _____ Date _____

Enlightenment and Revolution

MAIN IDEAS
1. During the Napoleonic Era, Napoleon conquered vast territories in Europe and spread reforms across the continent.
2. At the Congress of Vienna, European leaders tried to restore the old monarchies and ensure peace.
3. Inspired by revolutionary ideals in Europe, Latin American colonies began to win their independence.

Key Terms and People

Napoleon Bonaparte French general who became emperor

coup d'état forceful overthrow of a government

Klemens von Metternich Austrian prince who led the Congress of Vienna

conservatism movement to preserve the old social order and governments

liberalism movement for individual rights and liberties

Simon Bolívar a leader of South American independence movements

Lesson Summary
THE NAPOLEONIC ERA

Napoleon Bonaparte became a hero in France after the French Revolution. In 1799, he took power in a **coup d'état**, the forceful overthrow of the government. While he was emperor, France controlled much of Europe. He improved the education and banking systems. Napoleon issued a new set of laws, called the Napoleonic Code, that brought new freedoms to the French people. But he did not allow opposition to his rule, and he punished those who opposed him.

Napoleon's rule ended after the British defeated his navy and Russia defeated his armies. European nations worked together to remove him from power. They forced him to leave France. A year later, he returned and raised a new army. Napoleon was defeated by British and Russian forces at the Battle of Waterloo in Belgium in June 1815.

> Why do you think the new set of laws was known as the Napoleonic Code?
>
> _____
>
> _____

THE CONGRESS OF VIENNA

At the Congress of Vienna, European leaders met to write a peace settlement. Prince **Klemens von Metternich** (MEH-tuhr-nik) of Austria led the meetings. France was forced to give back territories conquered by Napoleon. The shapes of the countries near France were changed to balance power in Europe. These changes were to ensure that no one power could threaten the rest of Europe.

These leaders opposed the ideals of the French Revolution. They preferred **conservatism** and the way things had been. They wanted the old system and old rulers to continue. **Liberalism**, which was built on individual rights, gained strength in the next few decades. Conservatives remained in control, but things had begun to change.

> What was the goal of the Congress of Vienna?
> _____
> _____

> Why did European leaders oppose the ideals of the French Revolution?
> _____
> _____
> _____
> _____

LATIN AMERICAN INDEPENDENCE

The ideals of the French Revolution spread through the Caribbean and South America. Many colonies fought for their independence. In the French colony of Haiti, Toussaint L'Ouverture led a slave rebellion. The result was Haiti's independence. **Simon Bolívar** led the fight for independence across South America. By 1831, a dozen Latin American nations had won their freedom.

Bolívar tried to build peace on the continent. But the new nations fought over borders. There was also conflict between conservatives and liberals. Conservatives wanted the rich to control the new governments. Liberals wanted the people to vote for leaders. These conflicts caused many governments to be unstable. There were many changes of leaders as the governments rose and fell.

> List one reason that the new governments in Latin America became unstable.
> _____
> _____
> _____
> _____

CHALLENGE ACTIVITY

Critical Thinking: Explain Write a paragraph explaining why changes in government often occur as a result of conflict.

DIRECTIONS Look at each set of four vocabulary terms. On the line provided, write the letter of the term that does not relate to the others.

_____ 1. a. overthrow of government
   b. coup d'état
   c. conservatism
   d. Napoleon Bonaparte

_____ 2. a. Klemens von Metternich
   b. Simon Bolívar
   c. South America
   d. revolutionary

_____ 3. a. Klemens von Metternich
   b. prince of Austria
   c. conservatism
   d. liberalism

_____ 4. a. Latin America
   b. Napoleon Bonaparte
   c. South America
   d. Haiti

_____ 5. a. Enlightenment
   b. Simon Bolívar
   c. Klemens von Metternich
   d. liberalism